For Miyako

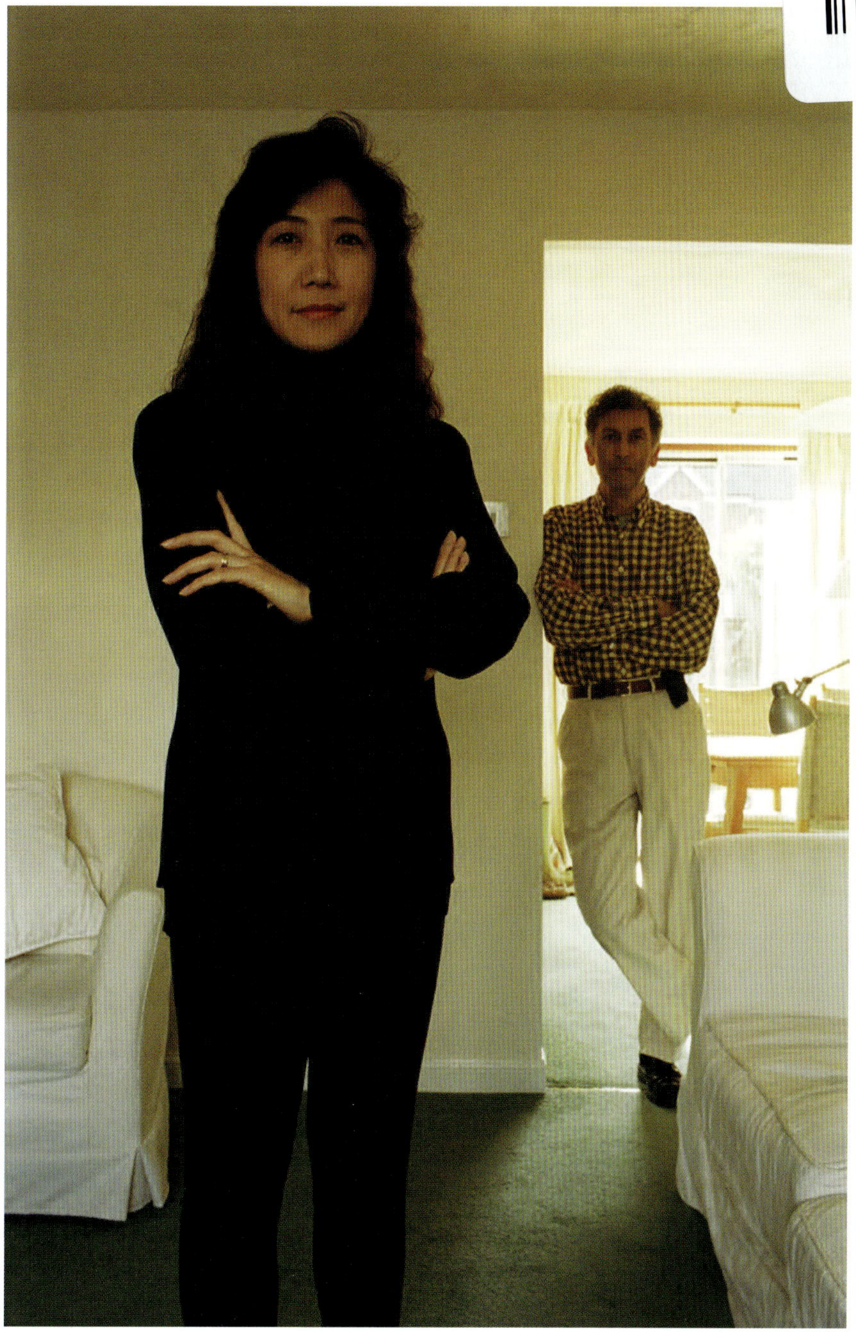

Miyako and myself at home in South London, 2001.

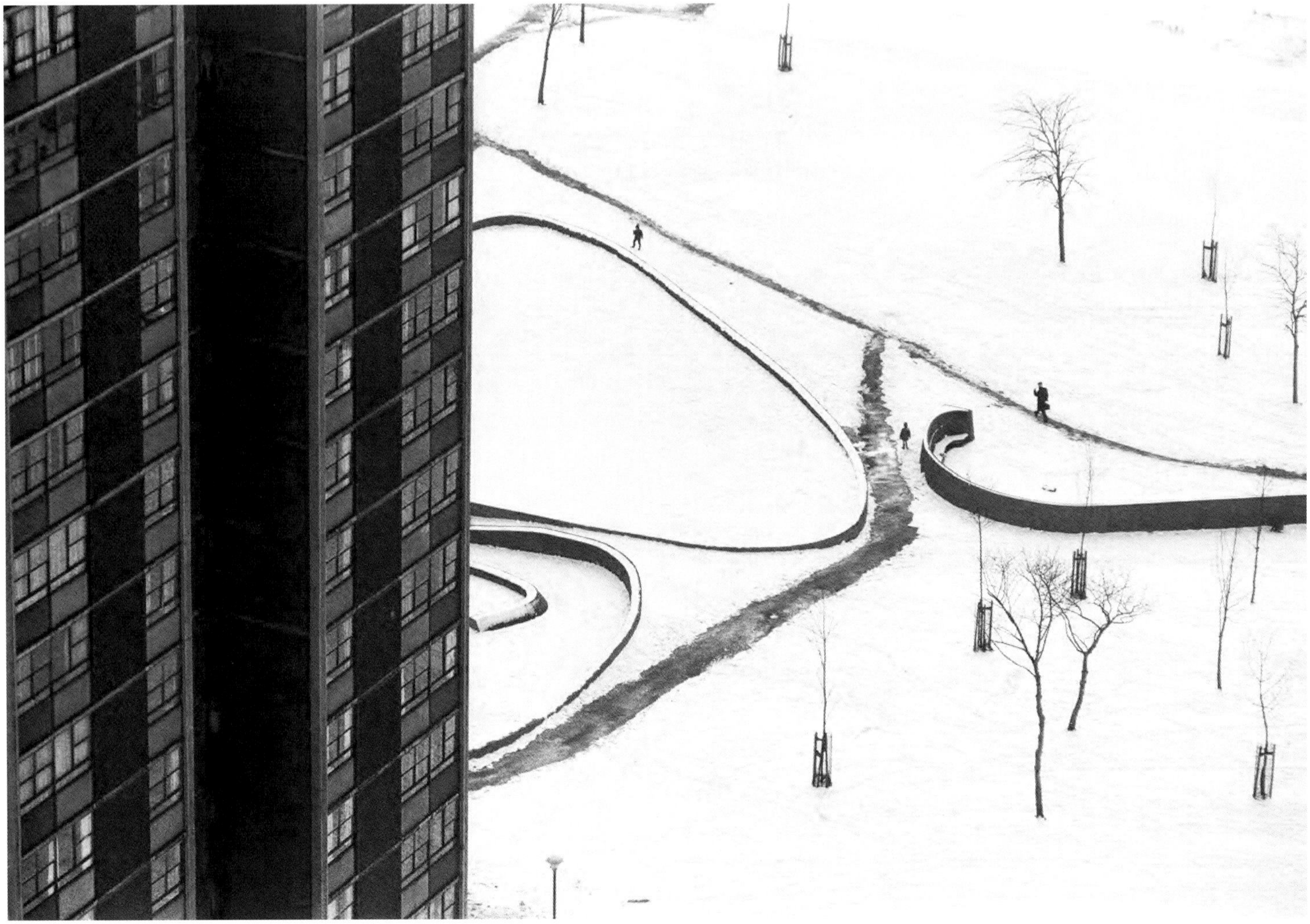

Newcastle-upon-Tyne. Tower blocks in West End, 1969.

ENGLAND, MY ENGLAND

A Magnum Photographer's Portrait

Chris Steele-Perkins

Introduction by David Elliot

Published by McNidder & Grace
21 Bridge Street
Carmarthen SA31 3JS Wales, United Kingdom
www.mcnidderandgrace.com

Original paperback first published 2023
First published in hardback in 2009, ISBN 9781904794387

A catalogue record for this work is available from the British Library.

ISBN: 9780857162410

Designed by Chris Steele-Perkins and Tabitha Palmer

PREFACE

Ever since I became a photographer England has been an important subject for me. Once I started to travel the world as a photographer I still returned to work on English themes, chipping away, trying to understand, in a small degree, what I was a part of.

A photographer is forced to interact with people and situations; to look at them carefully in order to take away some visual meaning. The photographer has to be there before sucking life through the lens into a photograph. This process of being thrown into unexpected situations, experiencing a world that is new and unfamiliar, learning about it and trying to create effective, elegant, occasionally beautiful images from those encounters, is what drew me to photography.

Over the time I've lived in England a massive change in English identity and ethnicity has taken place as it evolved into one of the most diverse countries in the world. When I came to England from Burma I was two and it was a white Anglo-Saxon country. Being a brown Oriental-looking child I did not feel properly English even though I had an English father, especially in the small West Country town where I lived, where everyone else was white. Perhaps this sense of distance colours my work.

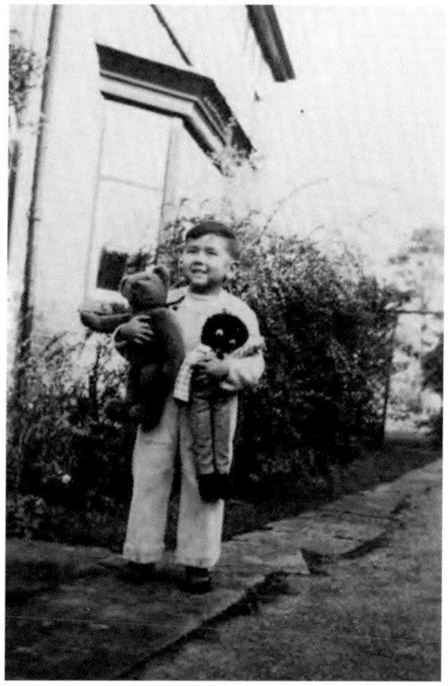

My first year in England.
Burnham-on-Sea, Somerset.

As I grew up, foreigners, many from the old Empire, came to England in increasing numbers, insistent in the face of violence and discrimination as well as, from other quarters, tolerance and understanding, that they had rights; that they and their religion and their culture had a place here; that they too could be English.

The old England of my childhood has not disappeared for the roots are far too deep and rich and ancient, but has changed, evolved and grown numerous new aspects. England is a concept beyond cartography and race, not amenable to precise definition. It is always in flux and the definition differs depending on where you stand and by what prejudices you are bent.

These photographs are a personal selection of images that I have taken over 40 years of photographing in this country. Some are drawn from books I have made on English themes, others from stories I have worked on, from pictures of family and friends, from random events encountered. They are not about celebrity or fame, but of everydayness and how that can be special.

It has been interesting for me to see some themes emerging as I started to put this work together, themes that haven't always been consciously pursued, yet echo those so important to English art: the absurd, violence, family, homelessness, humour, loneliness, identity and the grotesque. They don't dissect and analyse these conditions and situations; they do what photographs do; they describe and particularise them, and maybe heighten them if the photographs have been successful, and like a mosaic, if you take enough pieces and stand back a larger picture begins to emerge. Some kind of truth can be reached from the sum of the parts: an honest testament to this odd and redoubtable country, the England of the people, the country to which I owe so much; my England.

Chris Steele-Perkins, 2023

INTRODUCTION
JUST A BLOKE AT A ROCK 'N' ROLL PARTY...

David Elliott

...a night out with the Teds was generally a good crack – sometimes some violence, some vomit on the carpet, but generally a rock 'n' roll party. I wasn't a Ted, but it was easy enough to fit in. I was the bloke who took the photographs.[1]

...and the story does not end – or even begin – here. As well as a not-half-bad rock 'n' roll Party, Chris Steele-Perkins's England is an ant hill of complementary and conflicting images. In this challengingly idiosyncratic view of a minuscule fragment of the husk of this planet, Teds jostle with skinheads, punks with old people, stocking tops, racists, squaddies, buskers, hippies, wrestlers, pissing dogs, glum terraces, Geordies, seaside donkeys, homeless people, gerbils, games of cricket, punch-ups, gasworks, politicians, immigrants, knees-ups, babies, football, tattoos, wind breakers, fat cats, strippers, Buddy Holly, gurners, the chronically ill, squall-blown sand, cabaret artistes, the class system, hen parties, the CND, housing estates, a little bit of nature, miners, dead people, tits, reggae and dancing bears.

Unlike a number of recent books that have tried to dissect the anatomy of Englishness into past greatness, political and social development, or even anthropology,[2] we are faced here by a militantly unreductive and anti-hierarchical approach that, like some of the very best humour, from the stately maestros of the English Music Hall to the frenetic speed of Benny Hill, *Monty Python*, *The Fast Show*, Royston Vasey or *Little Britain*, takes on national clichés in order to turn them on their heads.

But unlike the comedians, there are no gags or punch lines here. Gentle humour, yes, stupidity, in spades, independence, sadness, bravery, also, as well as the stomach-churning, bitter-sweet scent of happiness cut with tragedy – versions of which all of us must recognise. The untrammeled delight of Amy, a young child with acute cerebral palsy, marvelling at the glowing 'stars' of the fibre optic lights suspended above her bed, made tears stream down my face. I quickly realised that these were not so much for her, she is obviously happy, but for the discrepancy she represents: an open embrace of wonder, in spite of the obvious disadvantage of her physical limitations. This instantaneously connected to something in me: I was crying not so much for her but for myself – for my petty dissatisfactions with life and my own incapacity for such wonder.

Funny stuff, photography, it can trigger things you don't expect. That's because it encompasses so many different viewpoints, visions – those of the photographer, the subject and the potential viewer – and within this mish-mash of associations and perspectives, strange things can happen. I am not thinking here, misty-eyed, about the history of photo-humanism or the grainy nostalgia of classic documentary, even though, at times, we are looking here at an England that has almost disappeared. Although aware of these traditions, and to a certain extent part of them, Chris Steele-Perkins has been able to maintain a creative friction and distance from what he portrays. This book is not a lament for the past, but merely a record and celebration of some of the things he has lived through, has been fascinated by, and survived.

One of the big surprises for me in flicking through these pages was the extent to which he has entered into an open-ended conversation with the work of both his predecessors and contemporaries. Thinking about it though, this seems perfectly normal. Photography has now developed to such an extent that images not only fall into genres, but also into families, rather like literary plots, jokes or comic situations. New images cannot but fail to take into account what has been made before and, if they are any good, add to this lineage through a simultaneous process of respect and challenge. In his black and white images of the 'grim' North, there are inevitable echoes of the visual research of Humphrey Spender and the Mass Observation Movement in the 1930s, of Bill Brandt's pre-war studies, as well as the work of the Exit Photography Group, of which he was a part, of Chris Killip's photo-documentaries, or the photography associated with Newcastle's Side Gallery during the 1970s and 1980s.[3] The people at rest and play shown here summon up different shades: some classic images by Henri Cartier-Bresson or Robert Doisneau, the 'innocent' pleasures of working people illustrated by Bert Hardy in the pages of Picture Post, Tony Ray Jones's more surrealistic take on the middle classes in the 1960s and Martin Parr's even more laconic view of the inequalities and absurdities of English life in the 1980s and 1990s.[4] This breadth of view increases the image's potential for shock of recognition and toughens the photographer's frame of reference.

But the real strength of this selection is its lack of contrivance. Unlike many other books on England or 'Englishness', there is no pretension here towards consensus or objectivity. This is unapologetically the photographer's *own* England and the beauty of it is that it never set out to be a portrait of a country, but was 'unconsciously' accumulated over a period of forty years, to be retrospectively selected and laid out in the sequence we see here. Chris Steele-Perkins is not only the photographer but also the picture editor of his work and the book is a more or less chronological montage of the different things that have taken and continue to take his eye.

Chris Steele-Perkins was born in Burma in 1947 and was taken to England at the age of two. His Burmese mother was not invited to accompany his father, and he was only to see her again at the age of twenty six. Apart from what must have been a traumatic separation, of which he apparently has little memory, he had a conventional middle-class English education. In 1970 he graduated in Psychology at the University of Newcastle-upon-Tyne and, by the early 1970s, had moved to London to work full-time as a photographer. There he began to concentrate on urban issues, particularly on the effects of poverty, and two early projects sketch out the scope of his subsequent development. In 1972 he travelled to the newly forged country of Bangladesh, the social fabric of which was reeling from its War of Independence from Pakistan, one year previously;[5] in 1975 he joined the Exit Photography Group in London, whose study of the, then derelict, dockland area of Wapping mushroomed into a much larger social project spread across the whole country that culminated in over 30,000 negatives as well as hours of taped interviews.[6] Since this time he has continued to move between Britain and abroad, covering wars and famines in Asia and Africa, as well as working on commissioned stories and his own projects.

Although, since the end of the 1990s, he has no longer covered conflicts or catastrophic events, the same range of interest and geography still informs his work. The fact that he is half Burmese suggests a certain detachment, although he feels himself to be 'mainly English' as that is where he was brought up. But looking through the images in this book, as well as through the whole span of his work, I cannot help but feel that a fundamental sense of difference, even distance, leads him to search for the sustenance of community or 'family'through photography, and sometimes – as in any picture album – this is expressed literally.[7]

The ability to be both a part of something yet separate from it, is precious to any artist. When working with people and their lives, it is a necessary inoculation against the self-indulgent viruses of either sentimentality, through provincial identification, or sensationalism, through callousness. The work we see here is neither. "The camera," in his own words, "allows me to enter other people's lives. It is an extraordinary tool to record experiences in the world. We used to think that everything was possible through photography. I still use it ... to understand the way things are, to learn about the things I do not really know."[8] Balanced on a tightrope between engagement and detachment, his process of 'understanding' and 'learning' is energised by empathy.

The particular ability to share the feelings of others and, from this, to project oneself in their position while still retaining an aesthetic distance, gives Chris Steele-Perkins the possibility not only of dodging the brutalising effects of violence wherever it may occur, but also of not slipping on the vomit on the carpet, however metaphorical it may be. Rare talents indeed! As we see here, they make him so much more than just 'the bloke who took the photographs' at a rock 'n' roll party a long time ago.

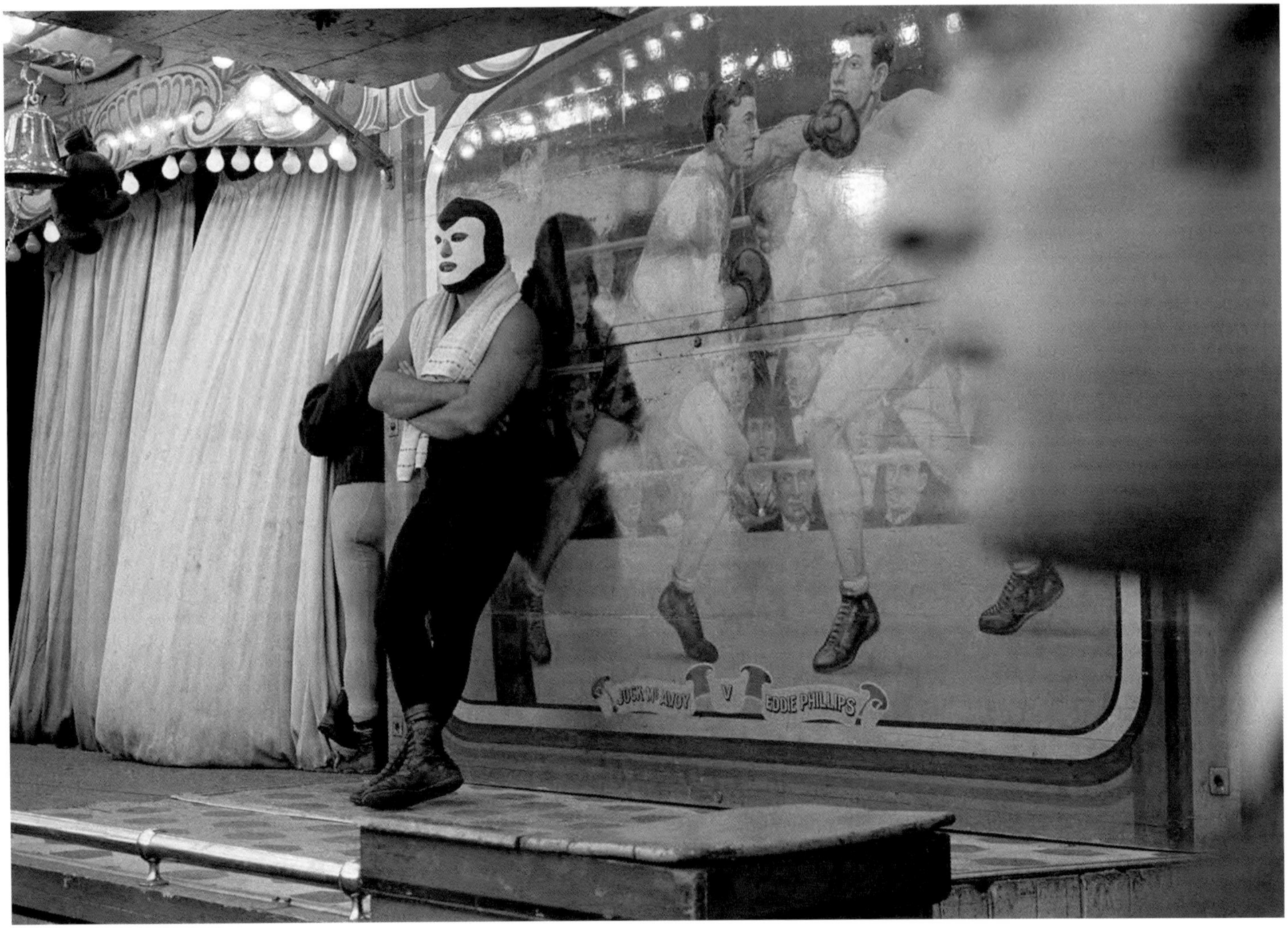

Newcastle-upon-Tyne, fairground boxing booth, 1969.

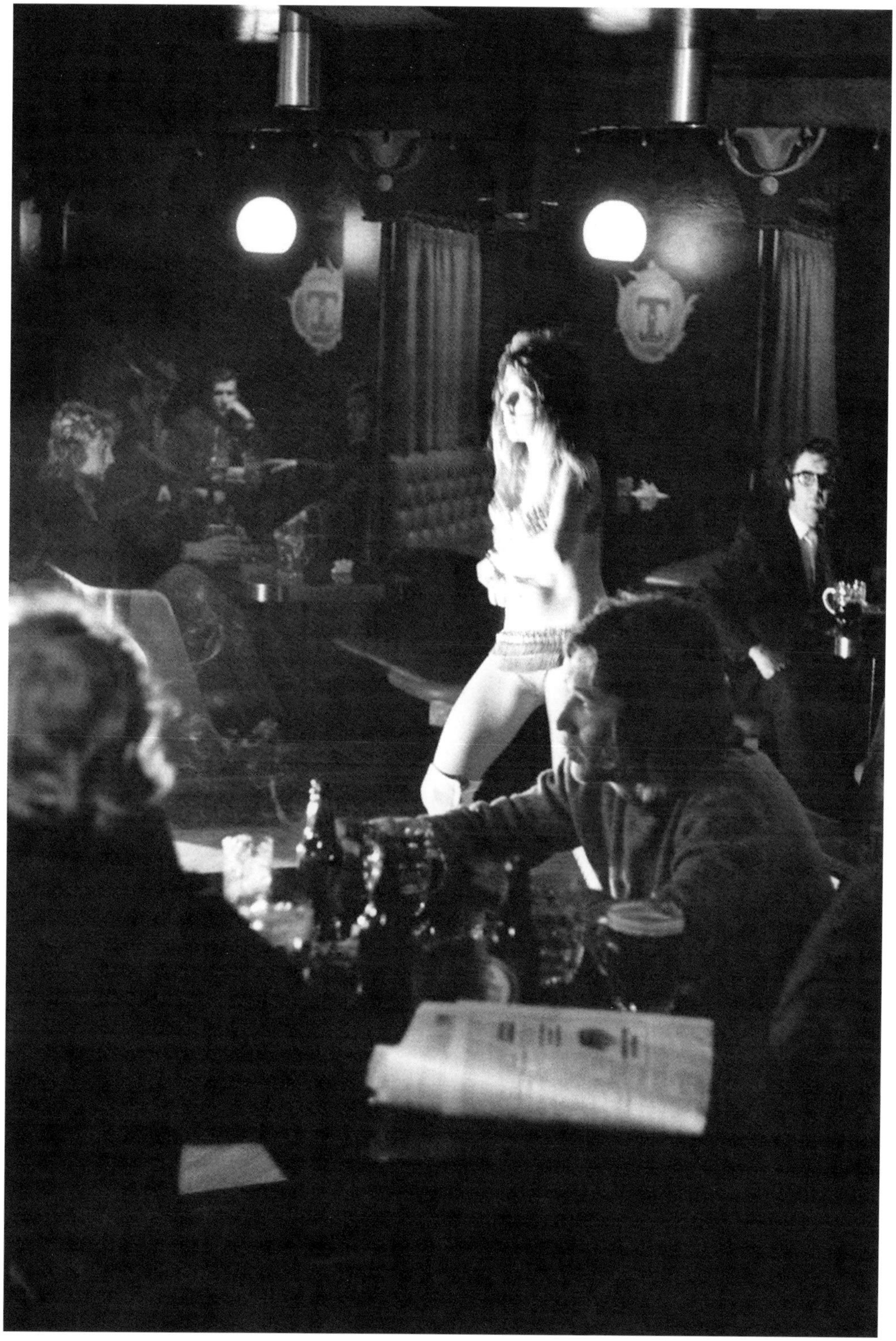

Dancer in a London pub, 1974.

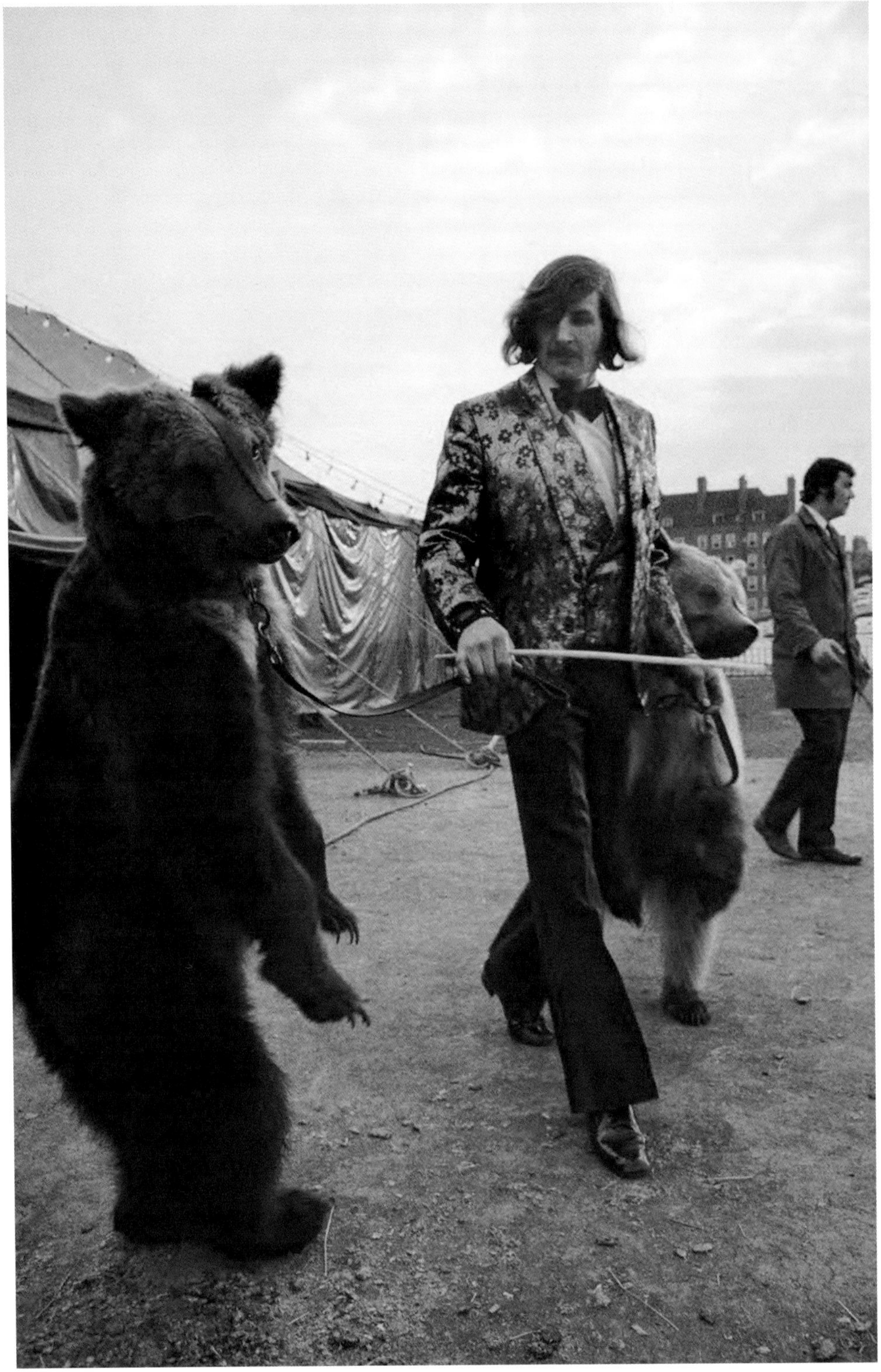

London. Circus Hoffman, 1973.

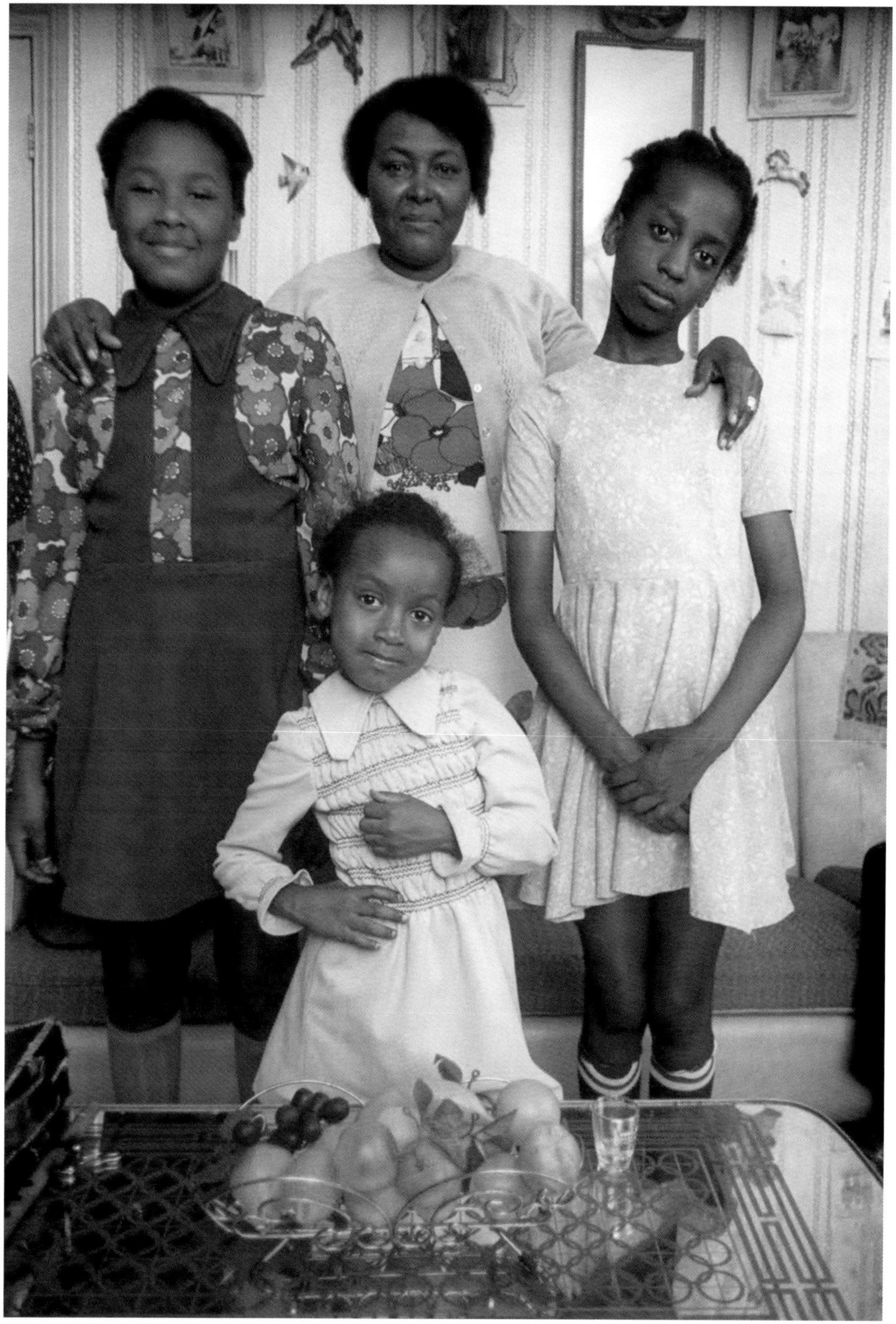

London. Family in Brixton, 1973.

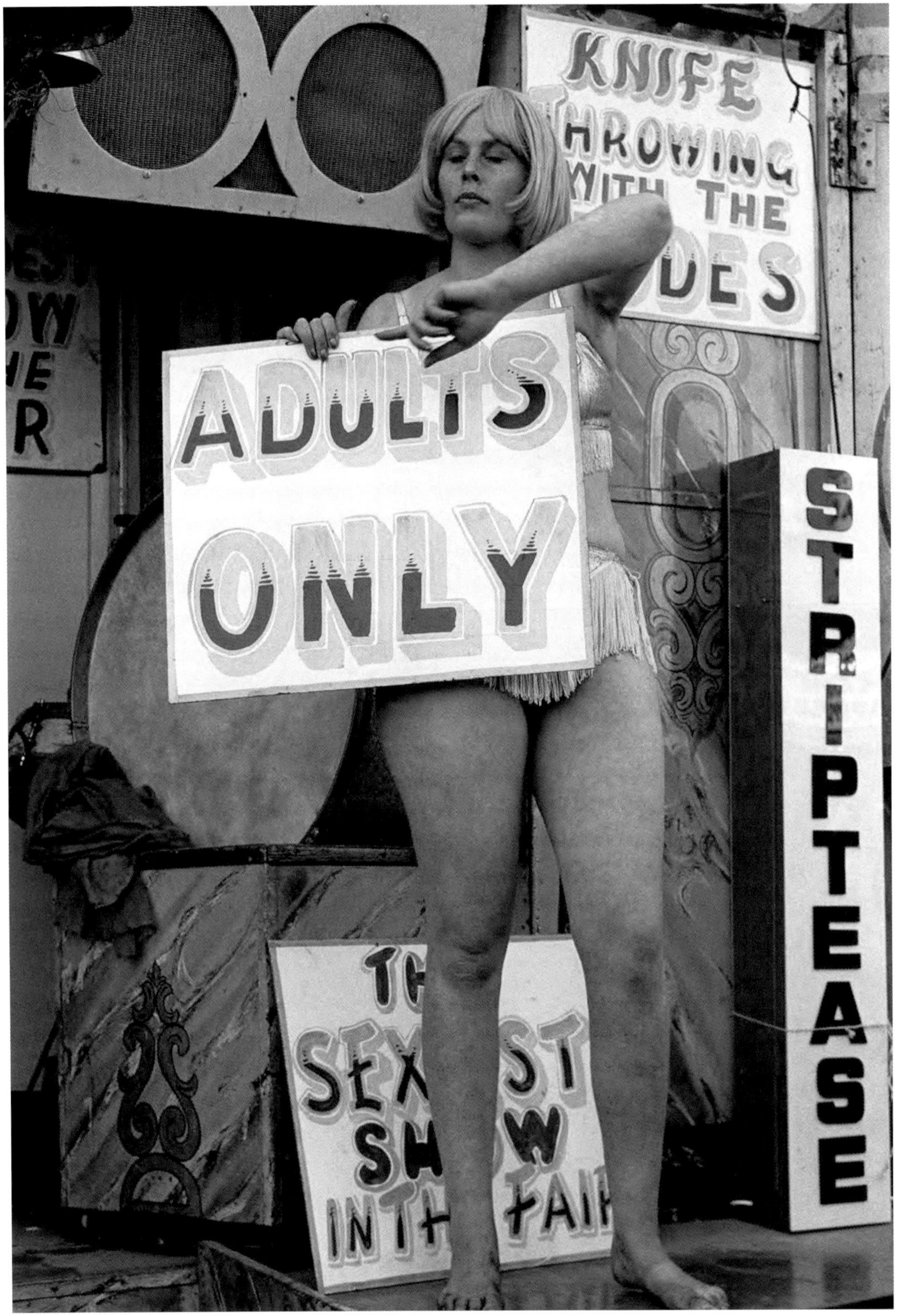

Fairground attraction. Newcastle-upon-Tyne, 1973.

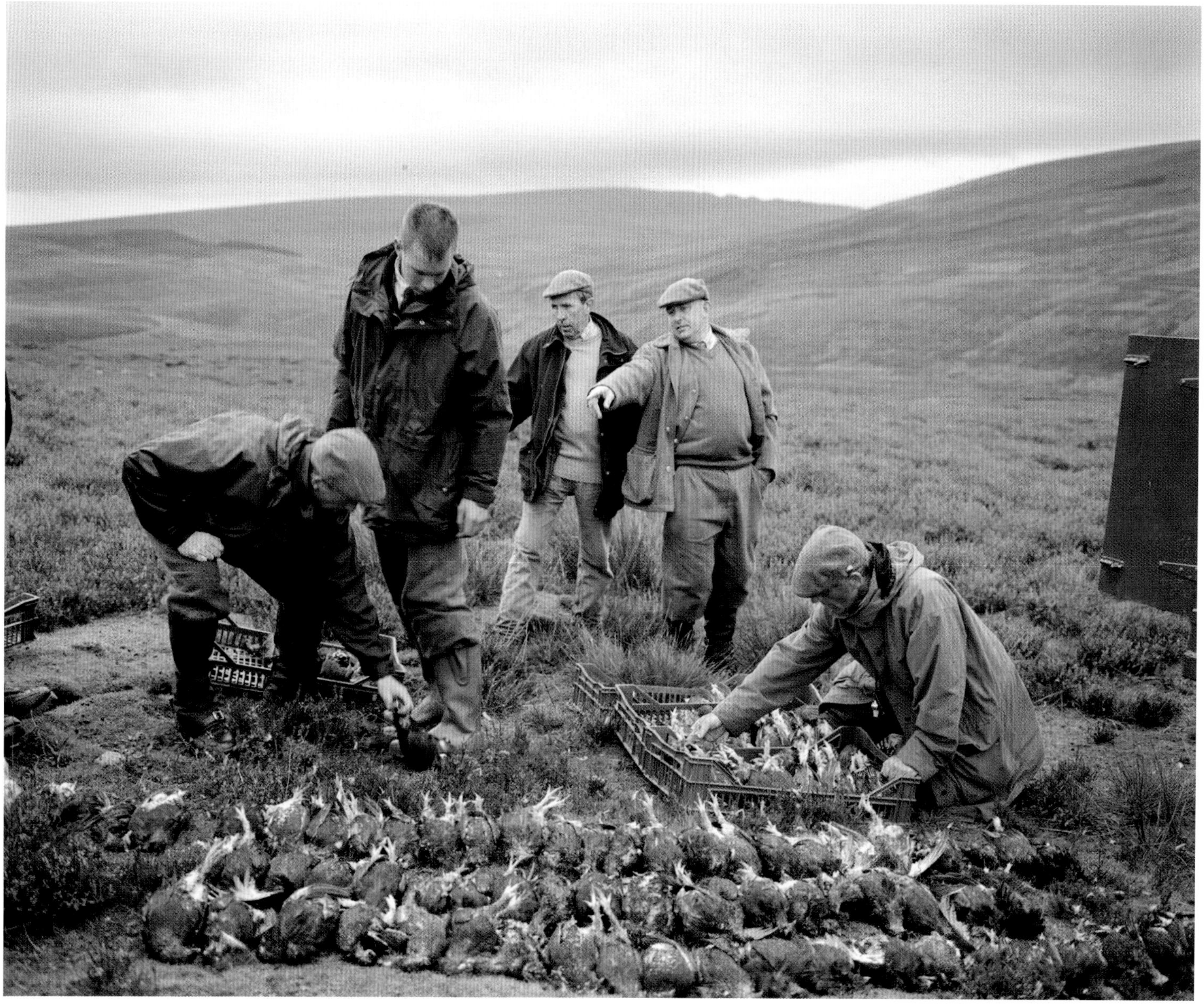

Grouse shoot in County Durham.

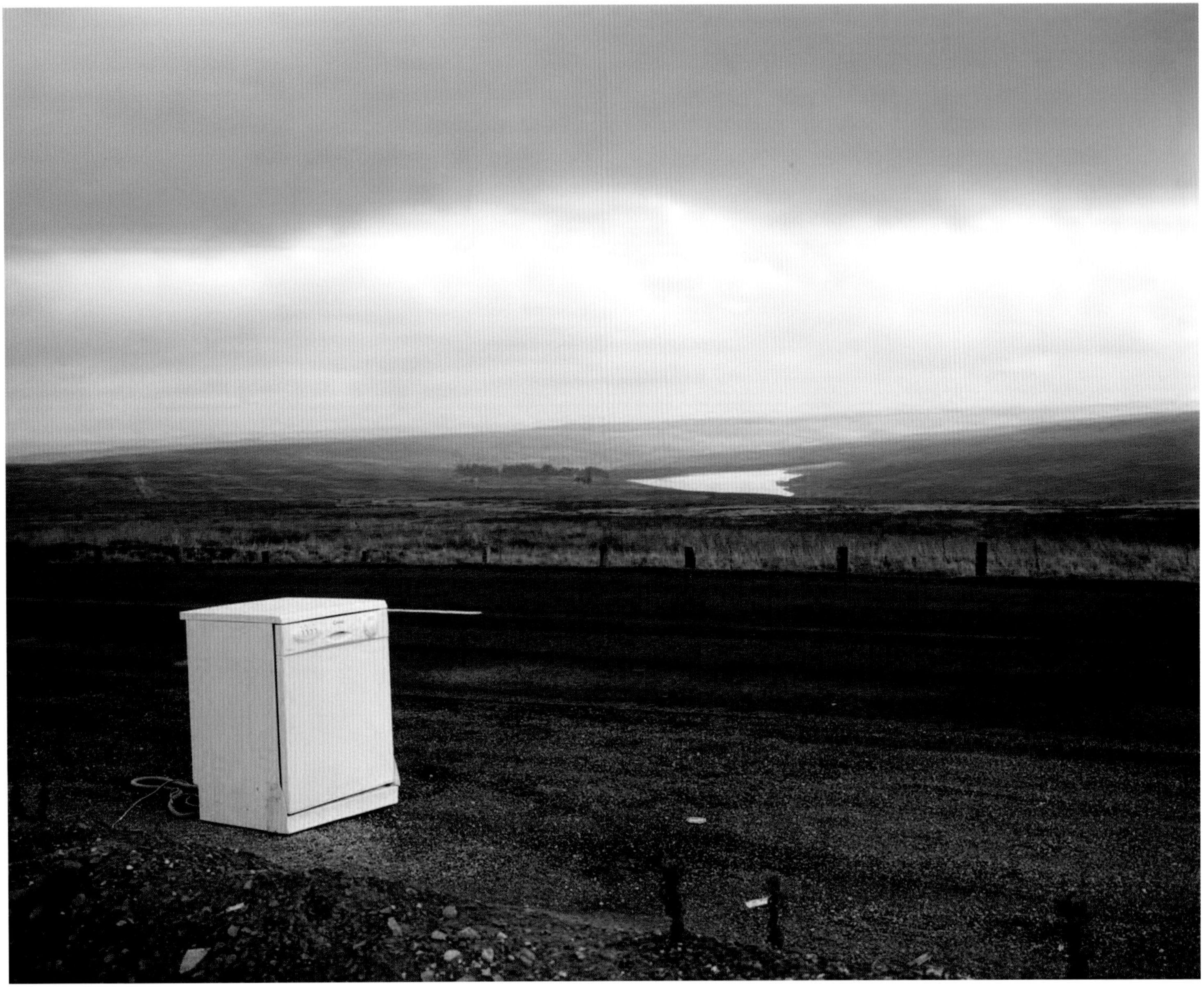

Dishwasher dumped on road.

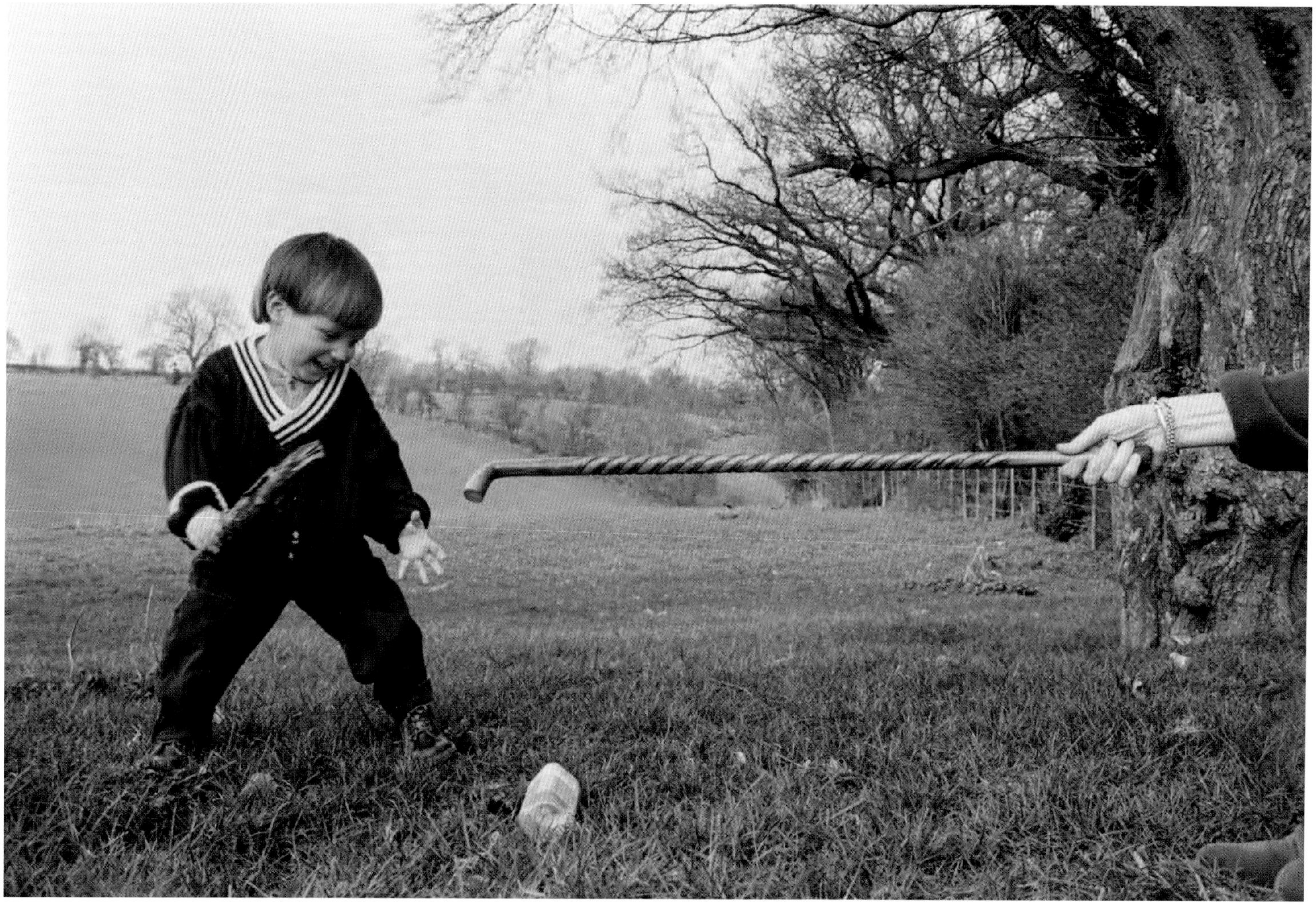

Cedric with a stick.

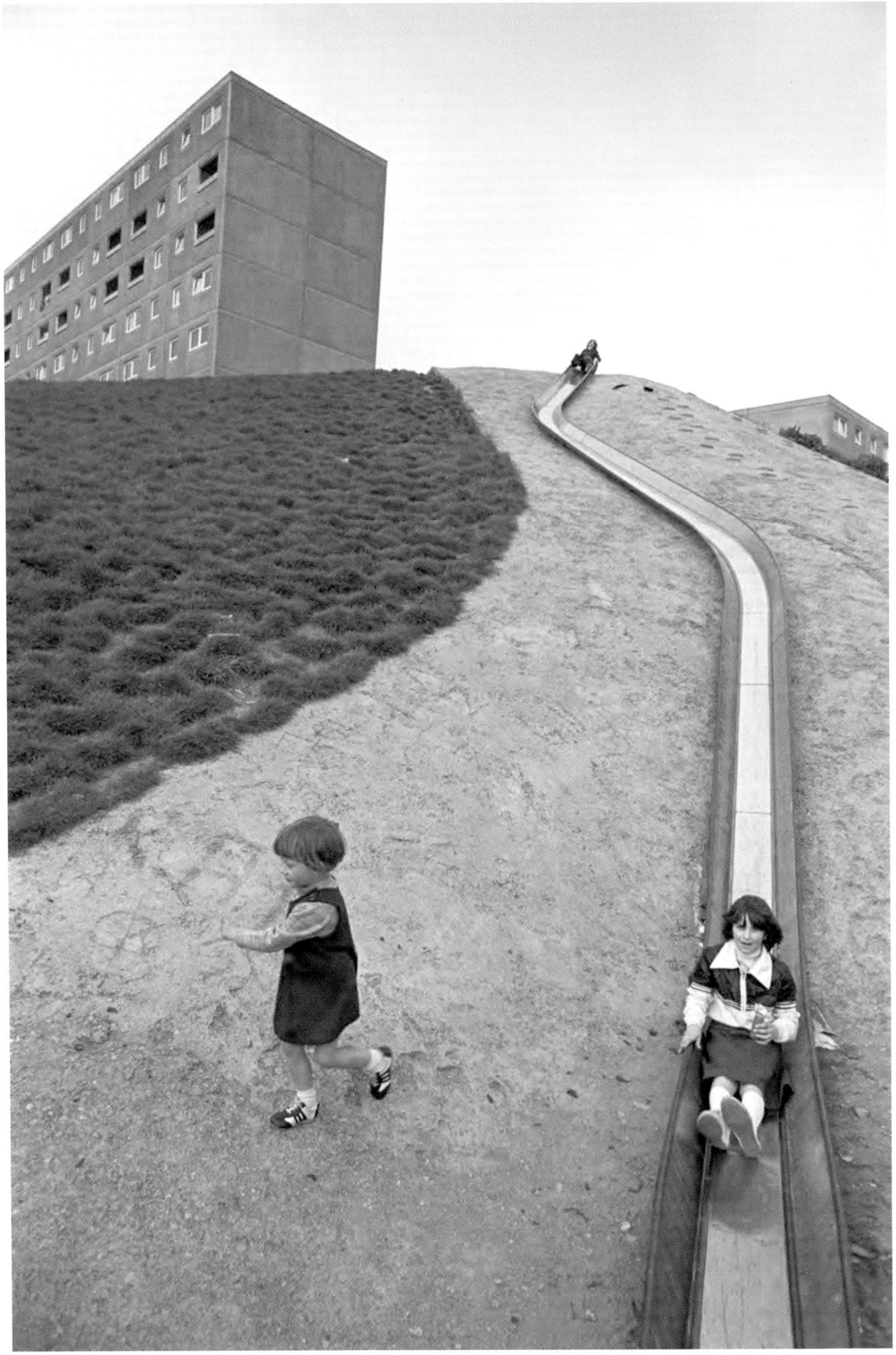

Children playing.

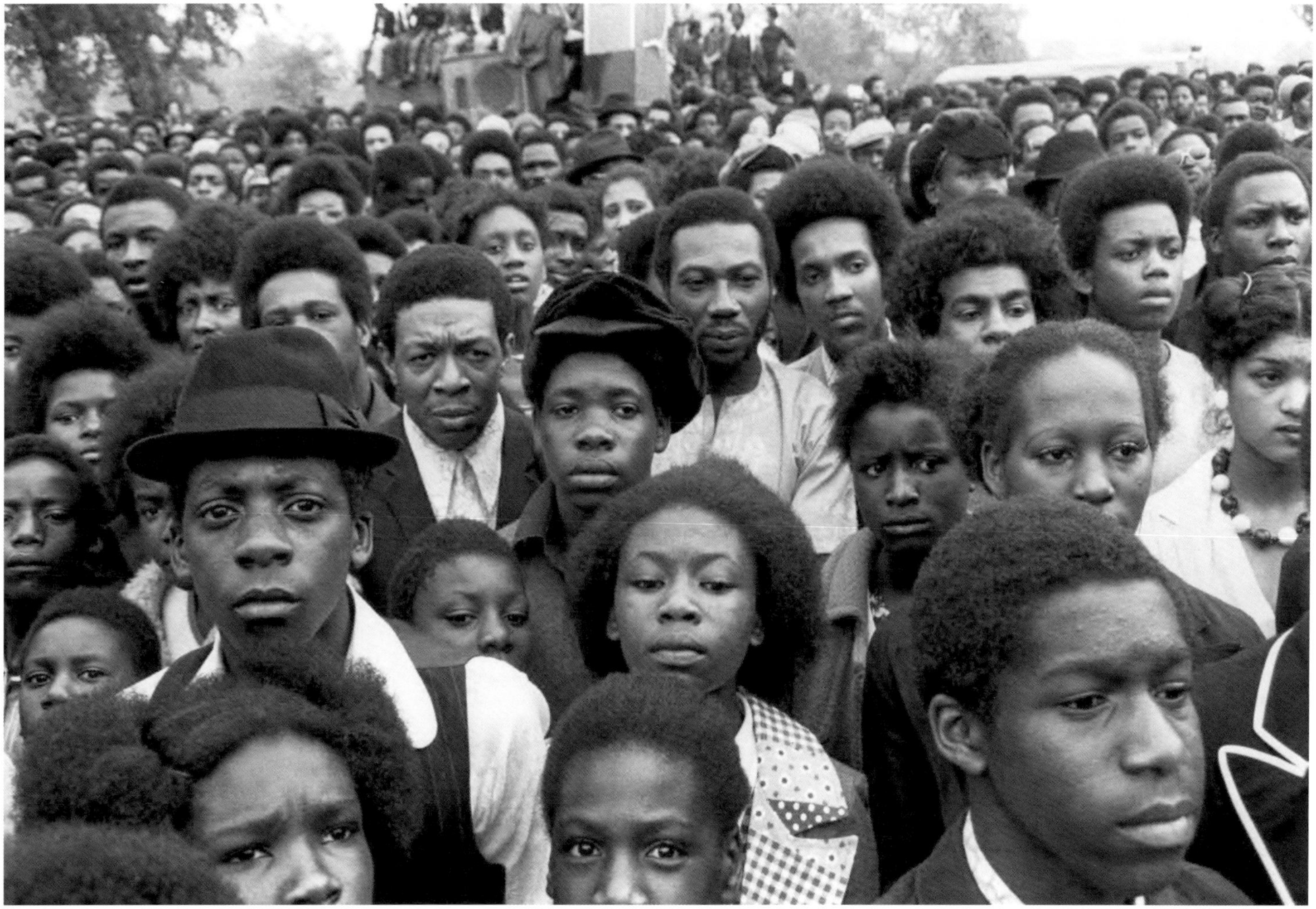

Brixton, London. Reggae Festival, 1974.

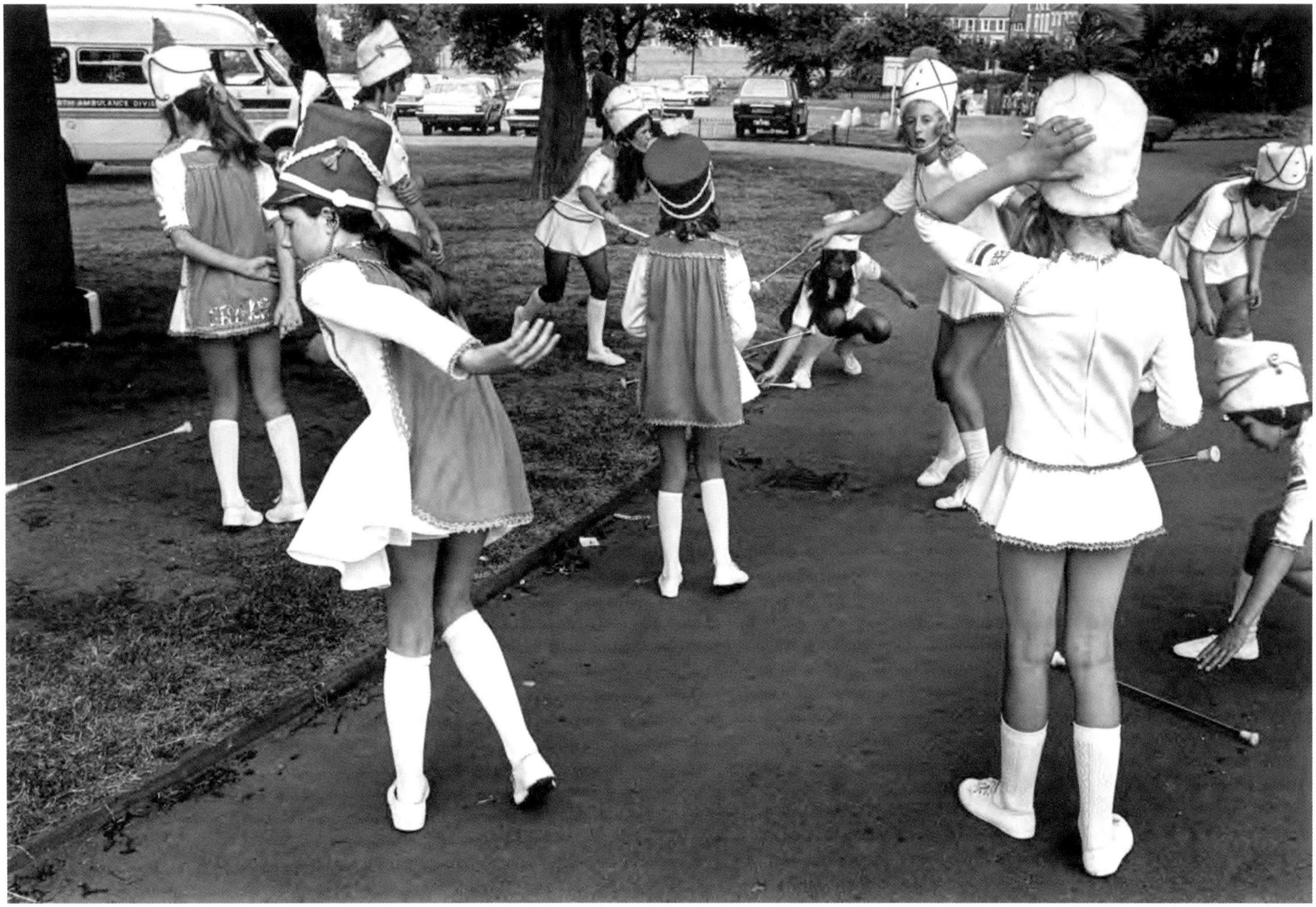

Drum majorettes in Brockwell Park, London, 1975.

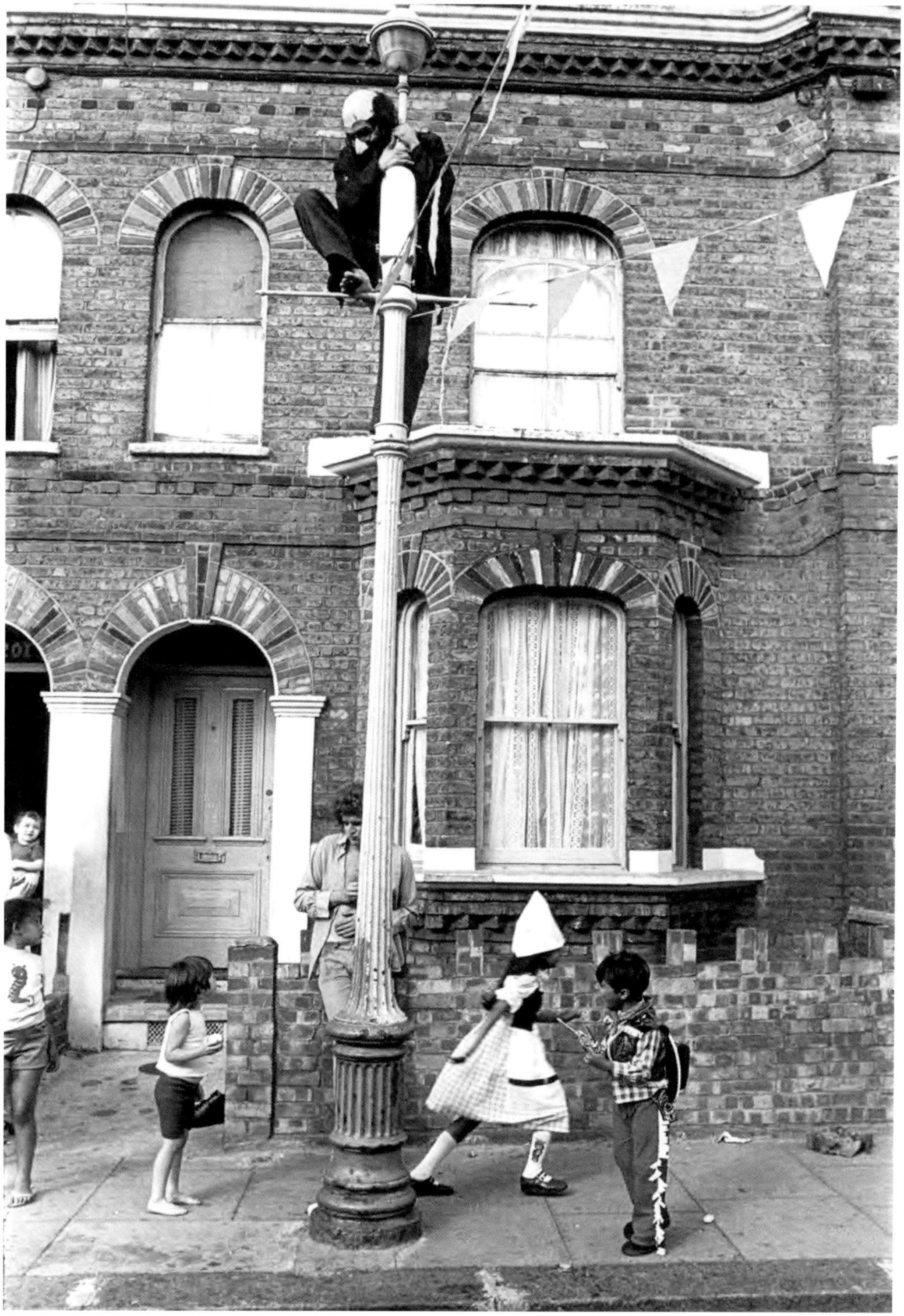

London. Community Festival in Brixton, 1975.

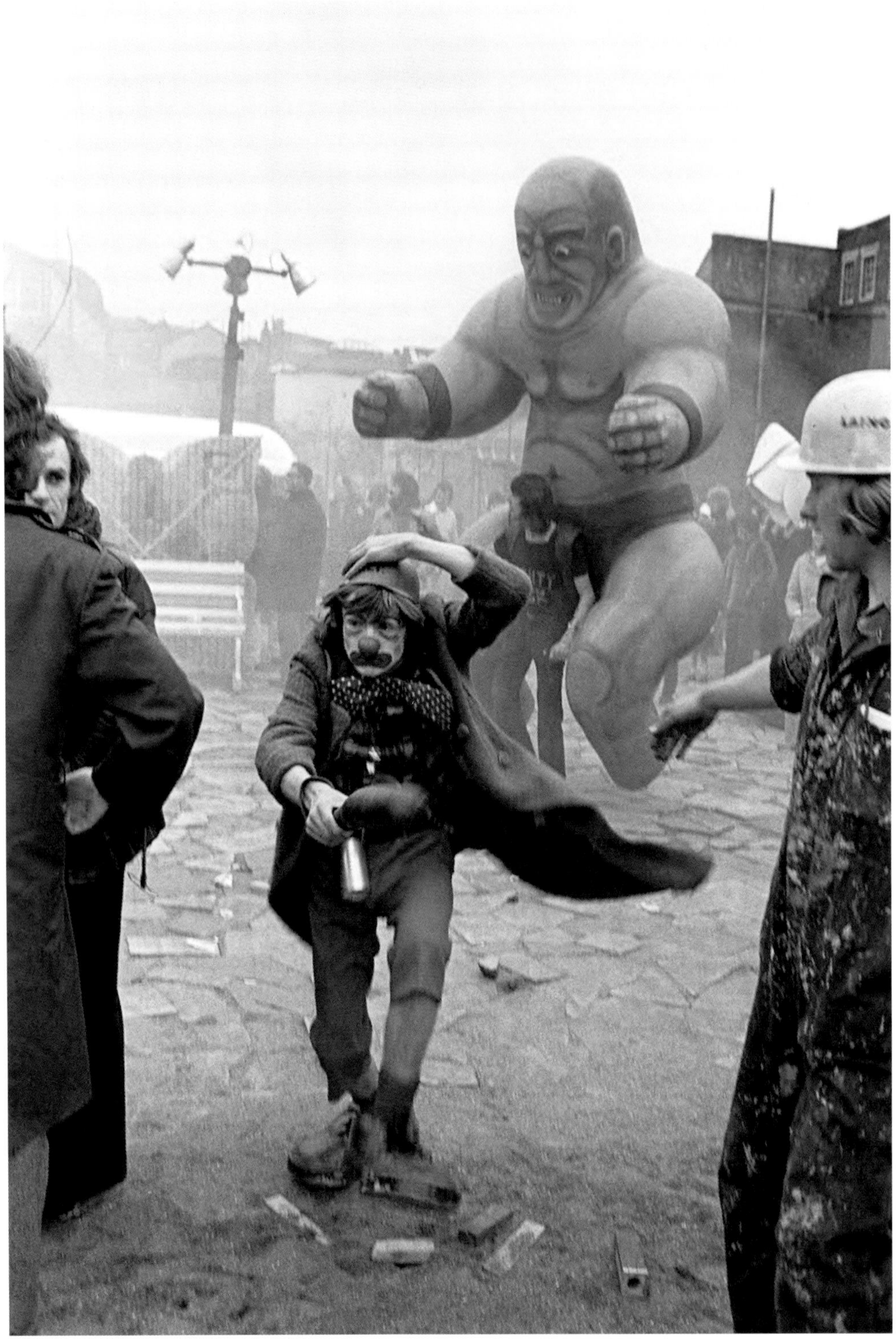

London. East End street festival, 1975.

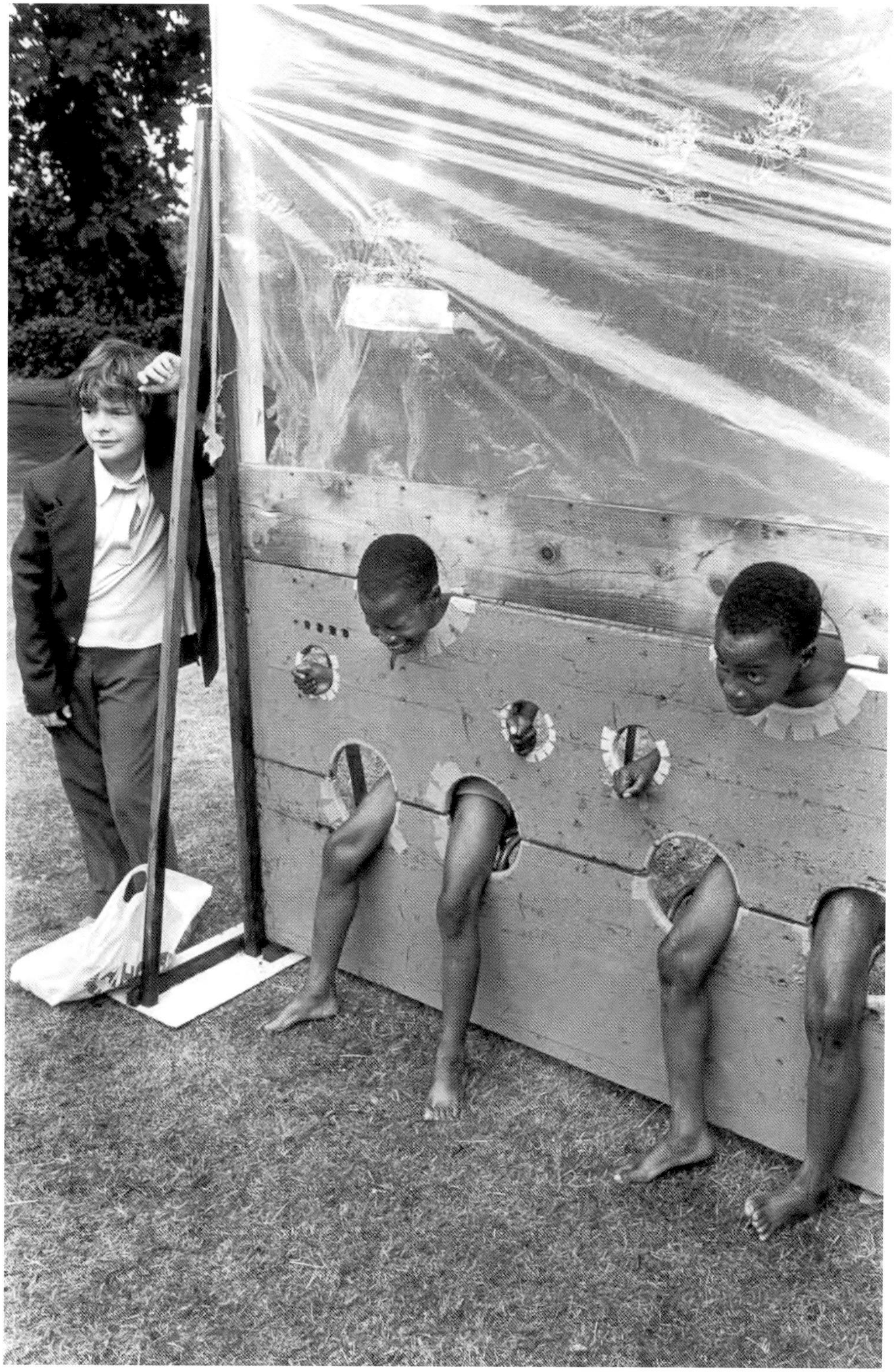

London. Lambeth Palace charity event, 1975.

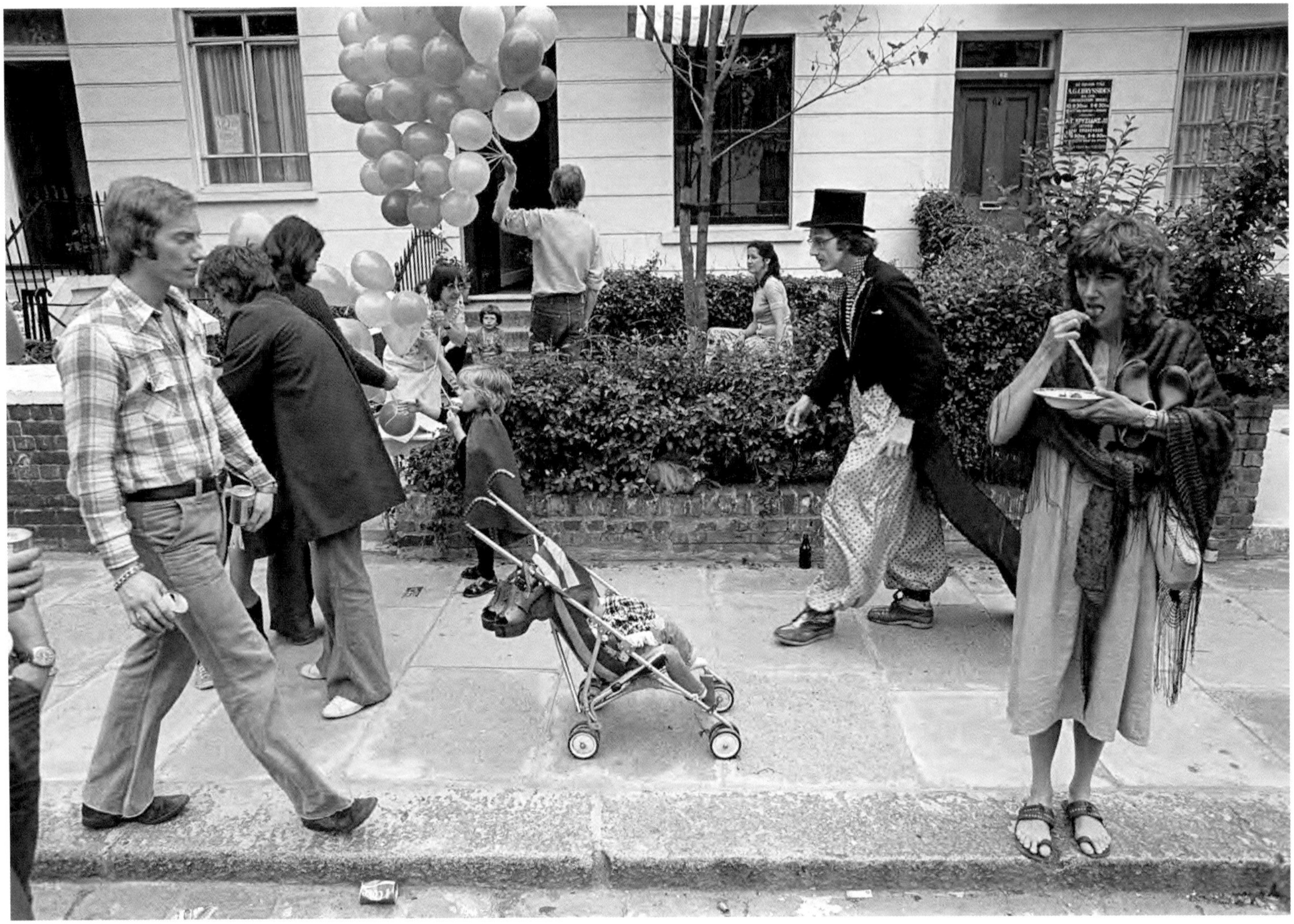

London. Street festival in Camden, 1975.

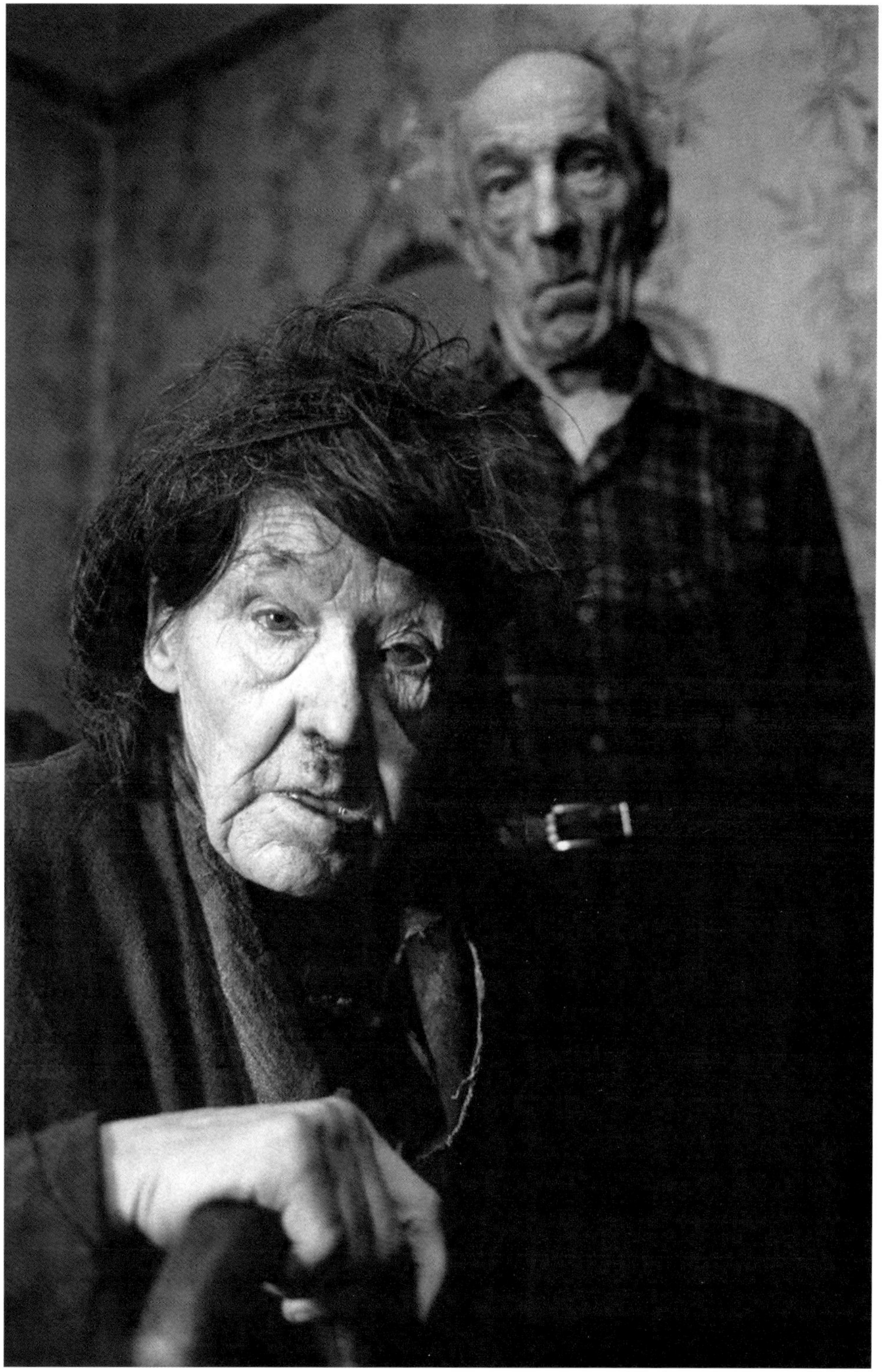

Newcastle-upon-Tyne. Couple, 1975.

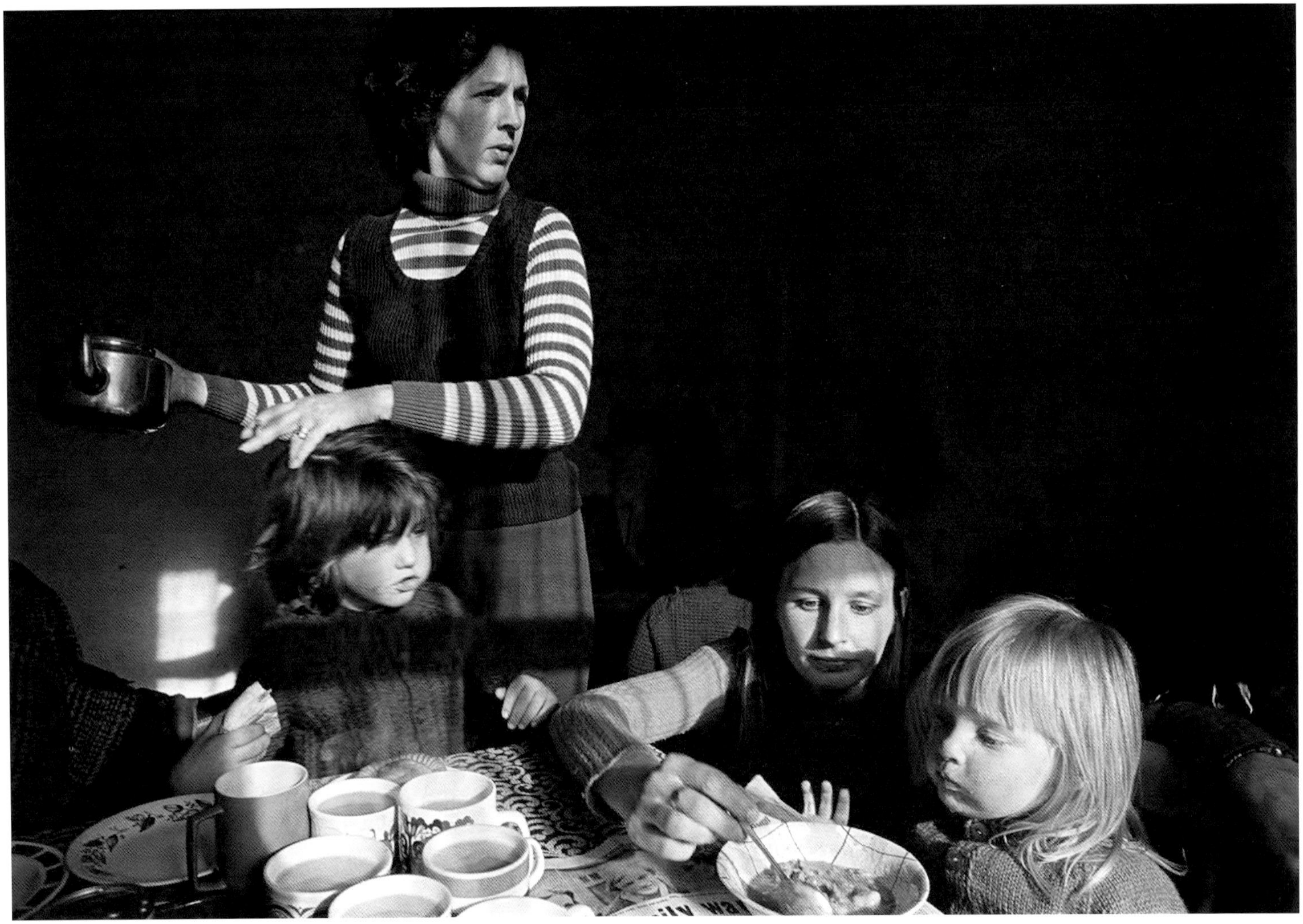

Women's refuge in Newcastle-upon-Tyne, 1975.

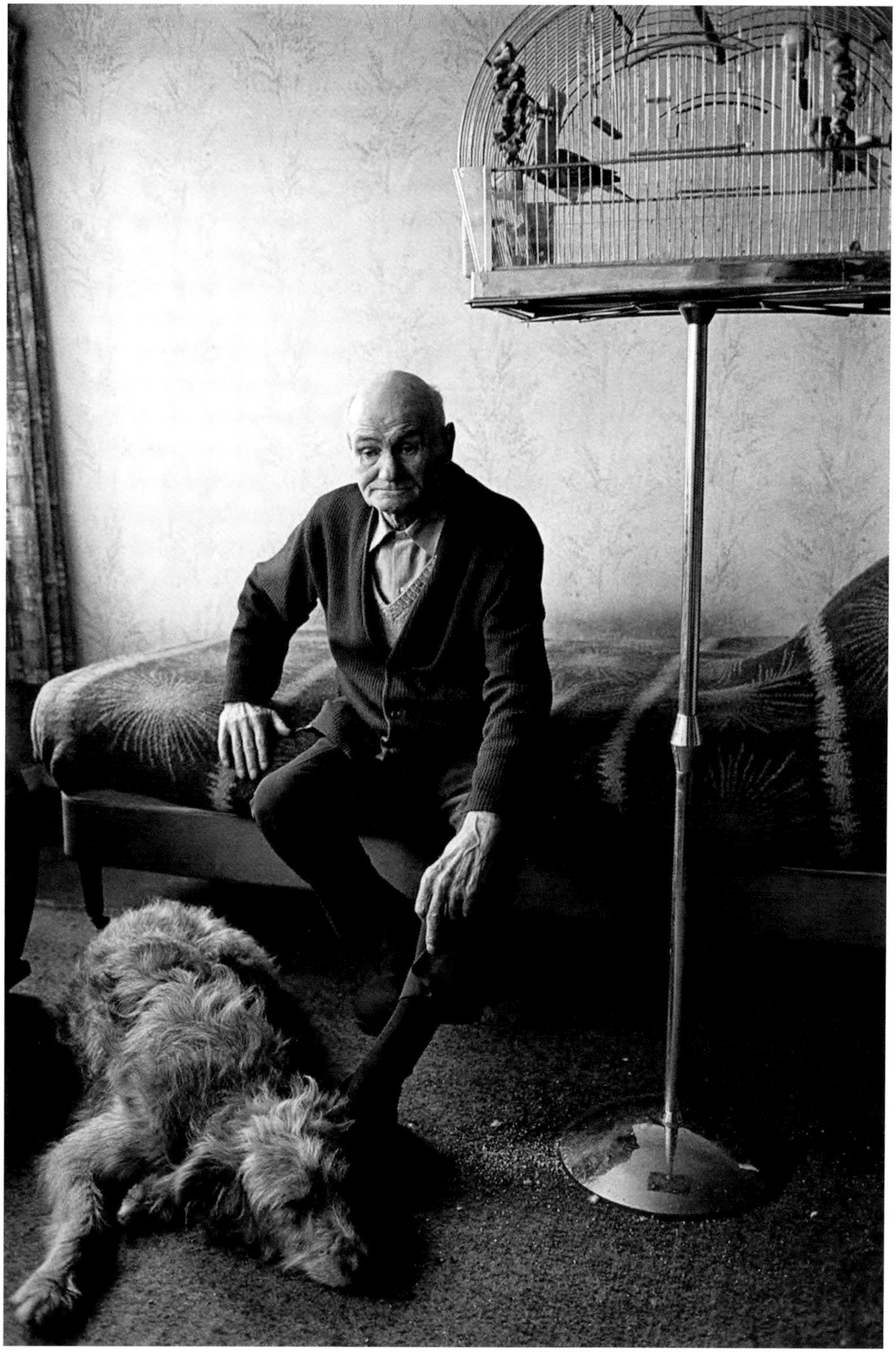

Middlesbrough. Pensioner with his dog, 1975.

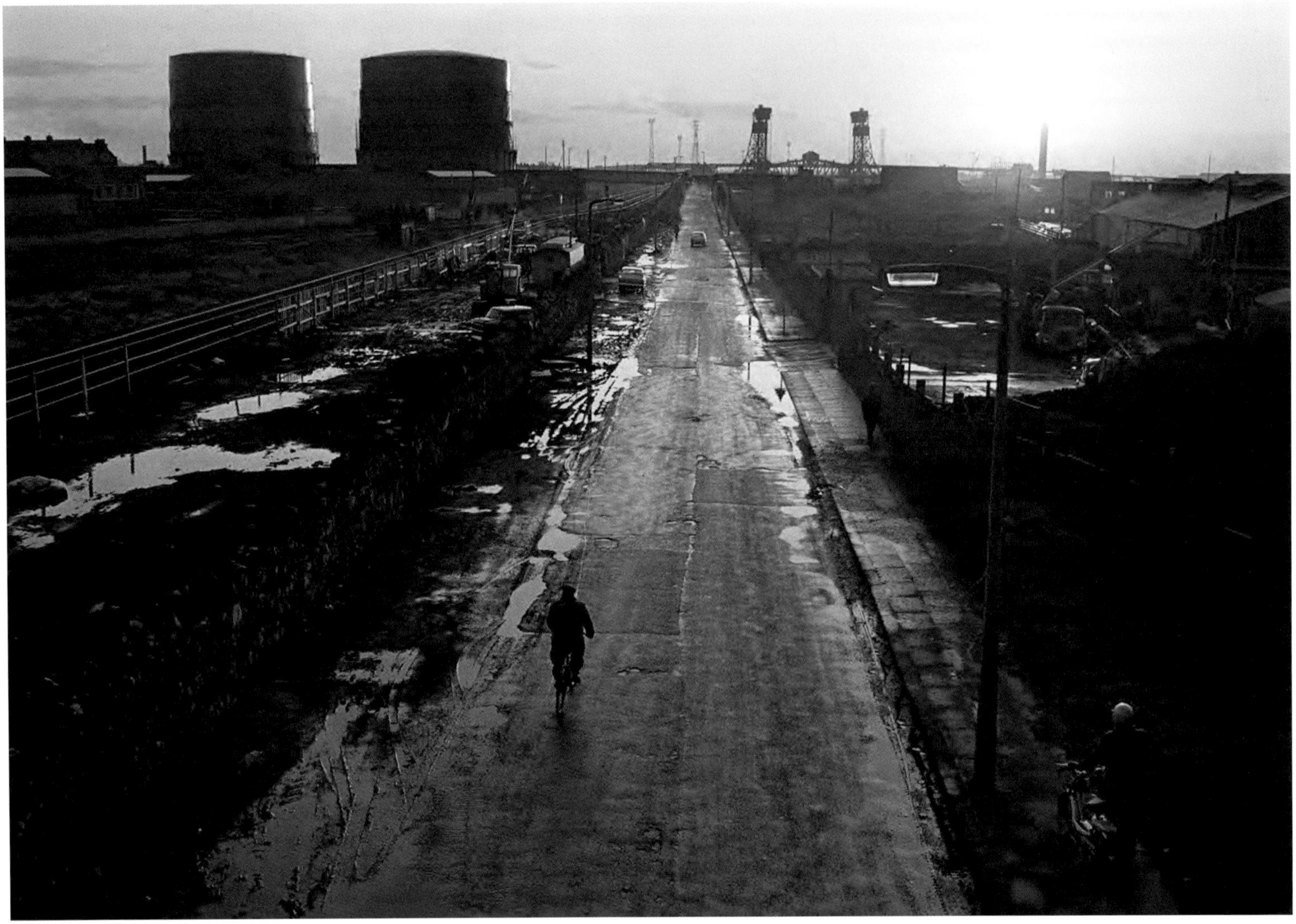

Middlesborough. Clearance area, 1975.

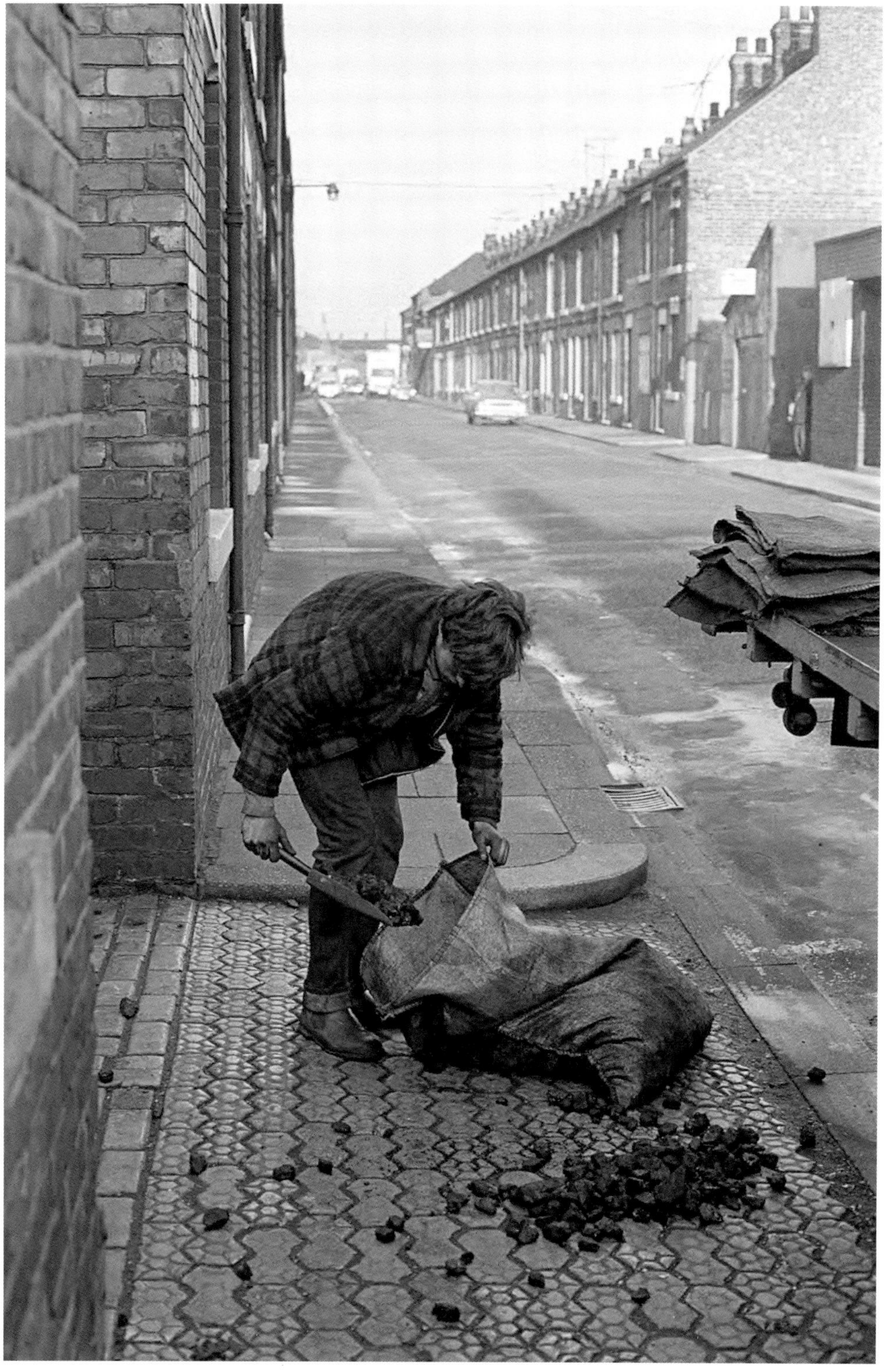

Coal delivery in Middlesbrough, 1975.

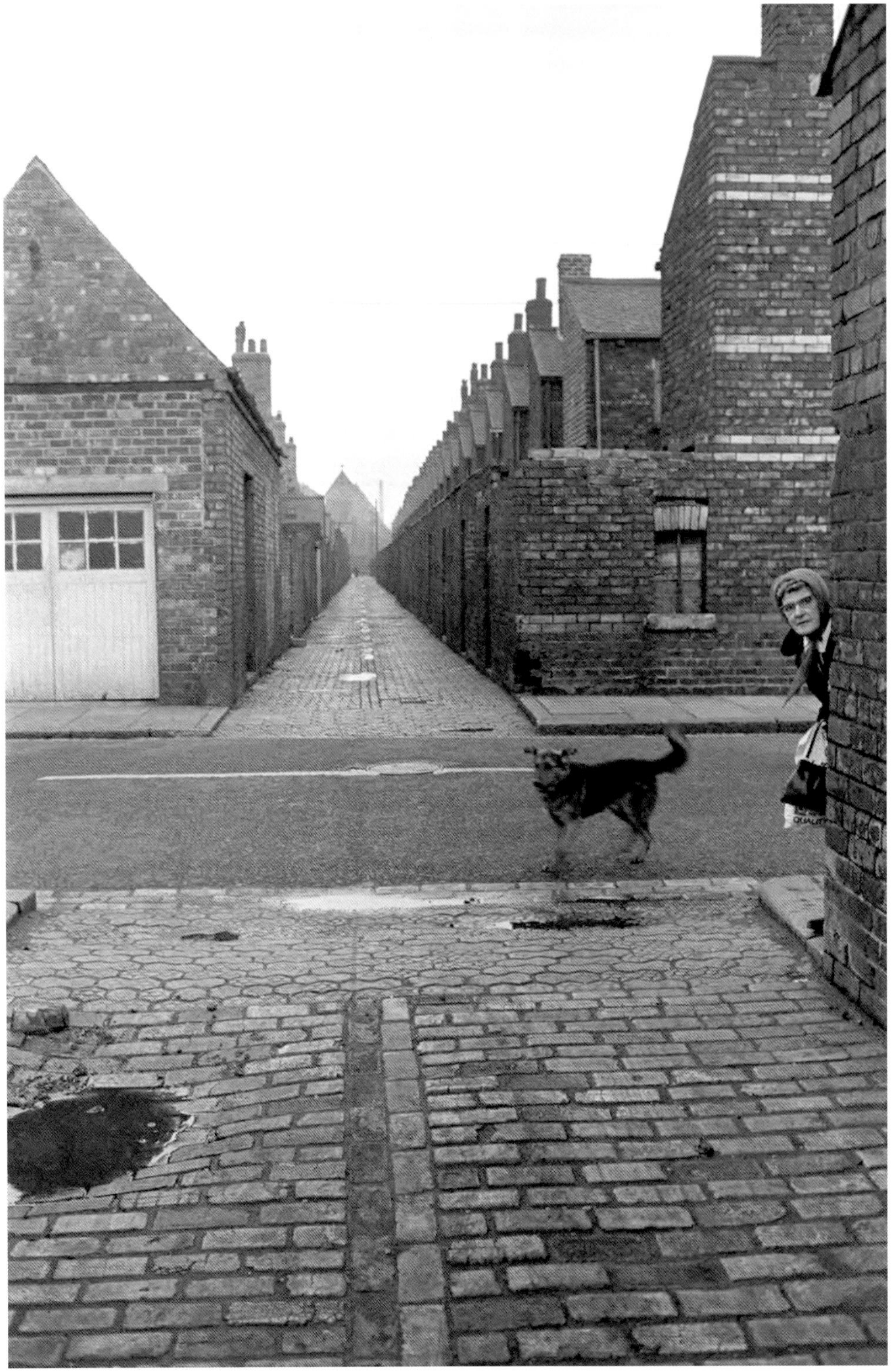

Middlesborough. Back alley, 1976.

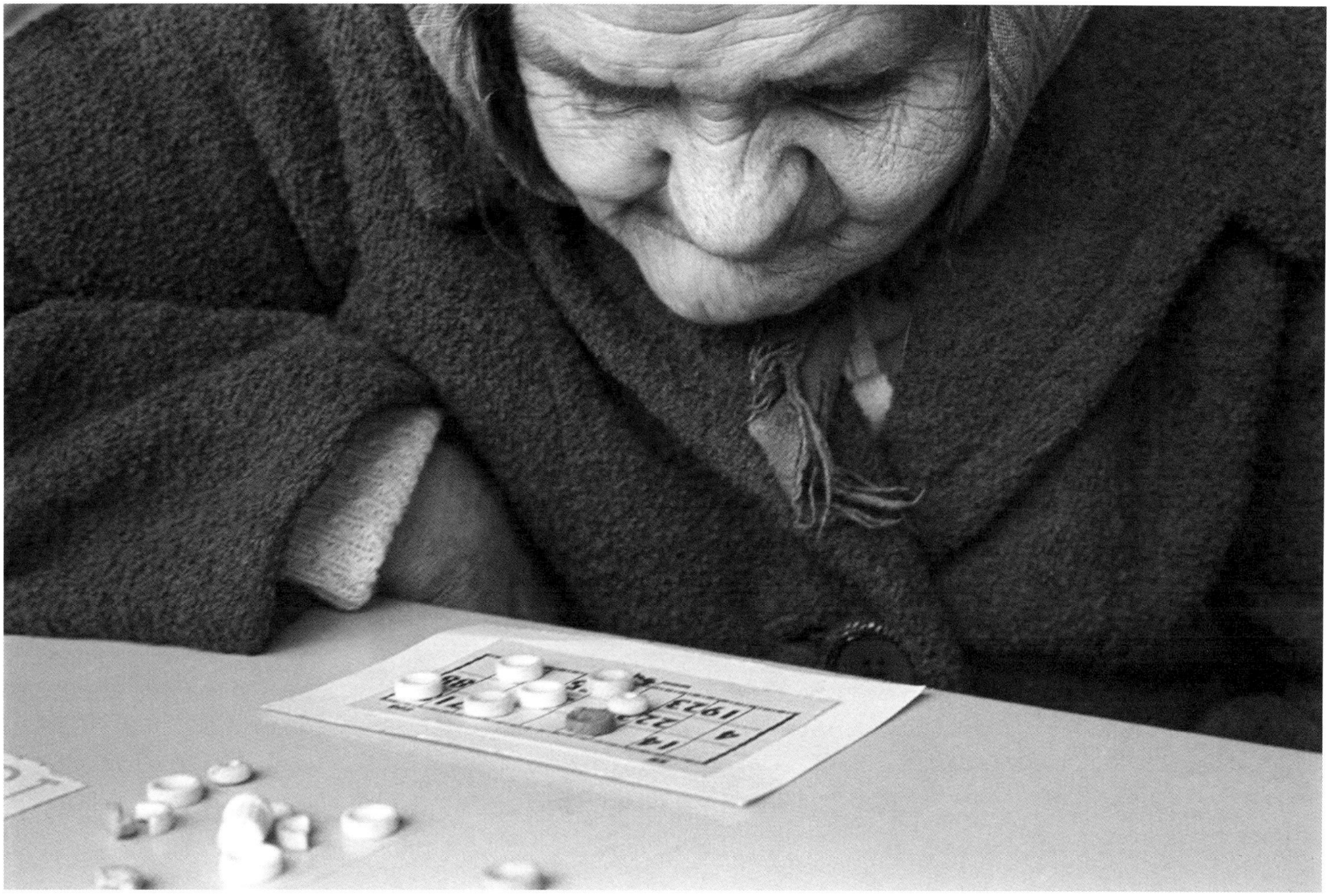

Middlesborough. Bingo in a pub, 1975.

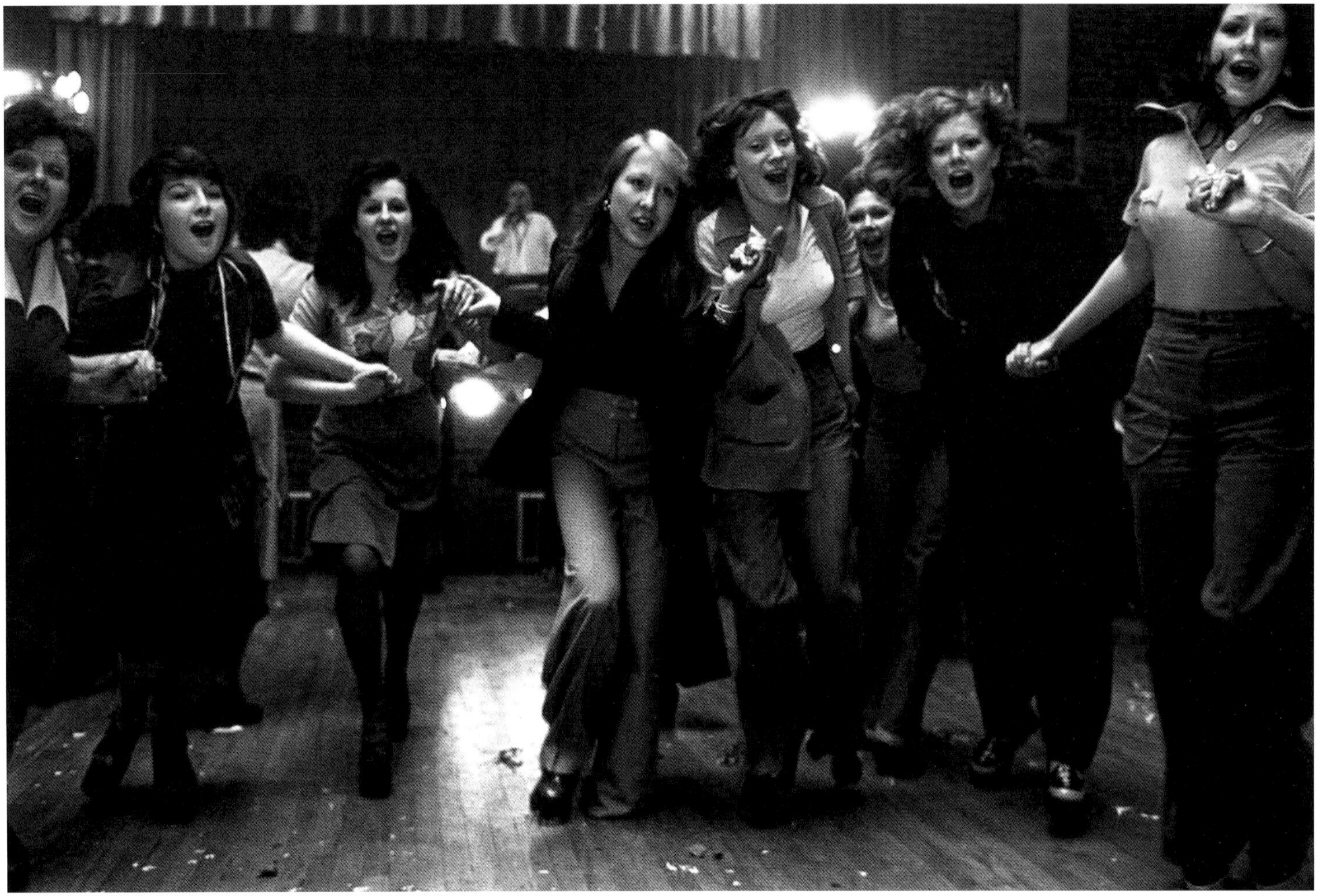

Middlesborough. Party at a community centre, 1975.

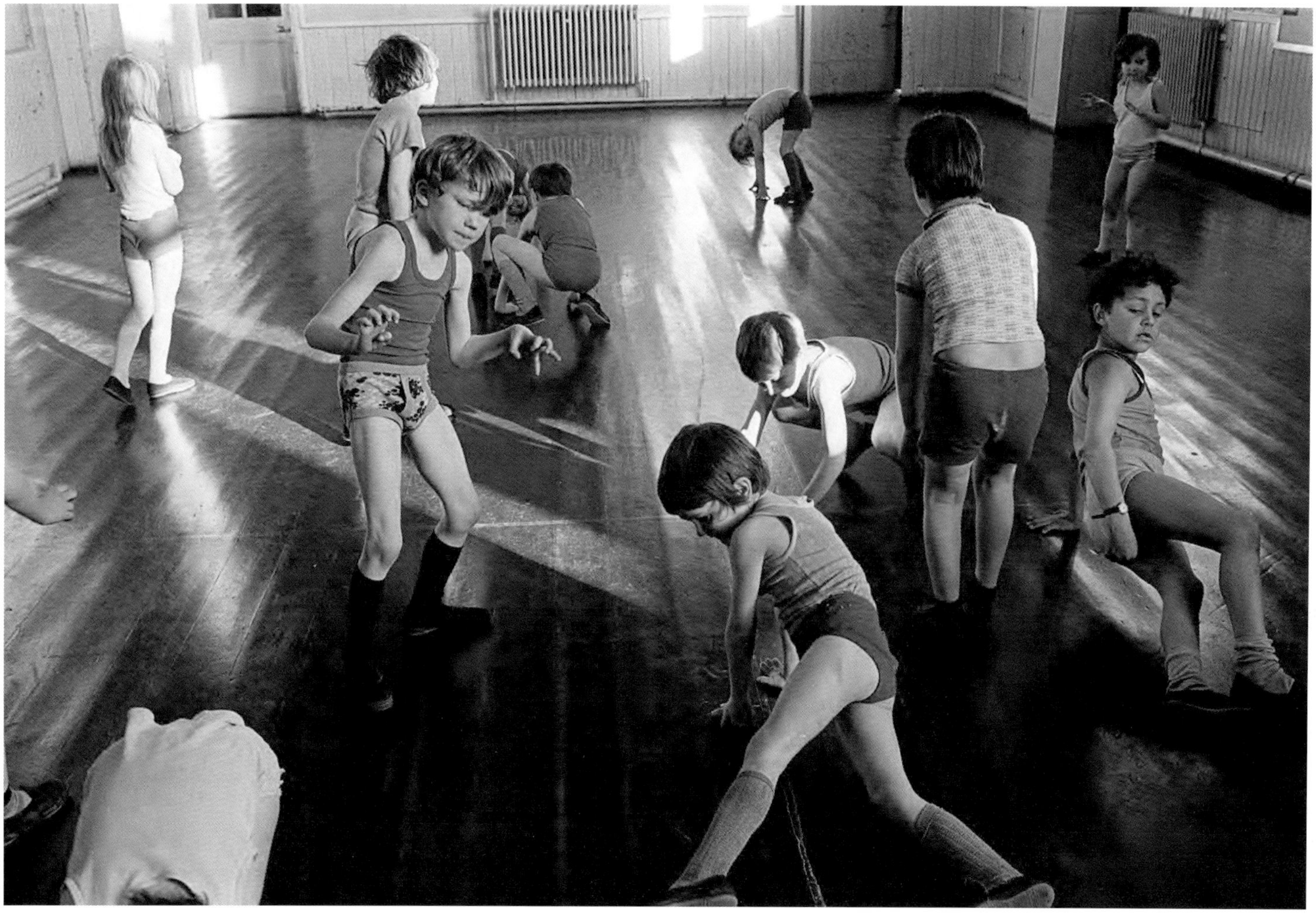

Exercise class in a school in Middlesbrough. 1975.

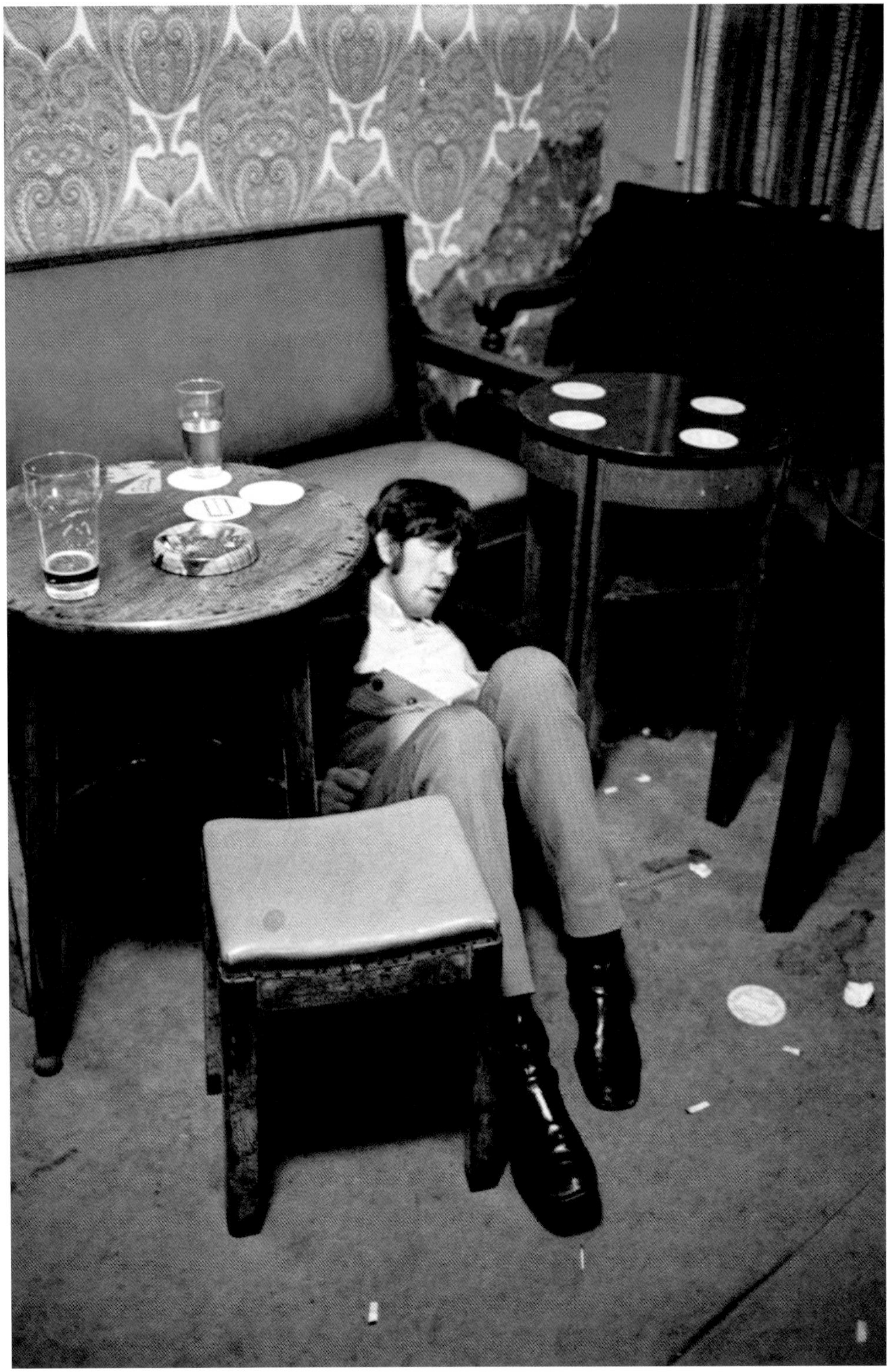

Pub in Middlesbrough, 1975.

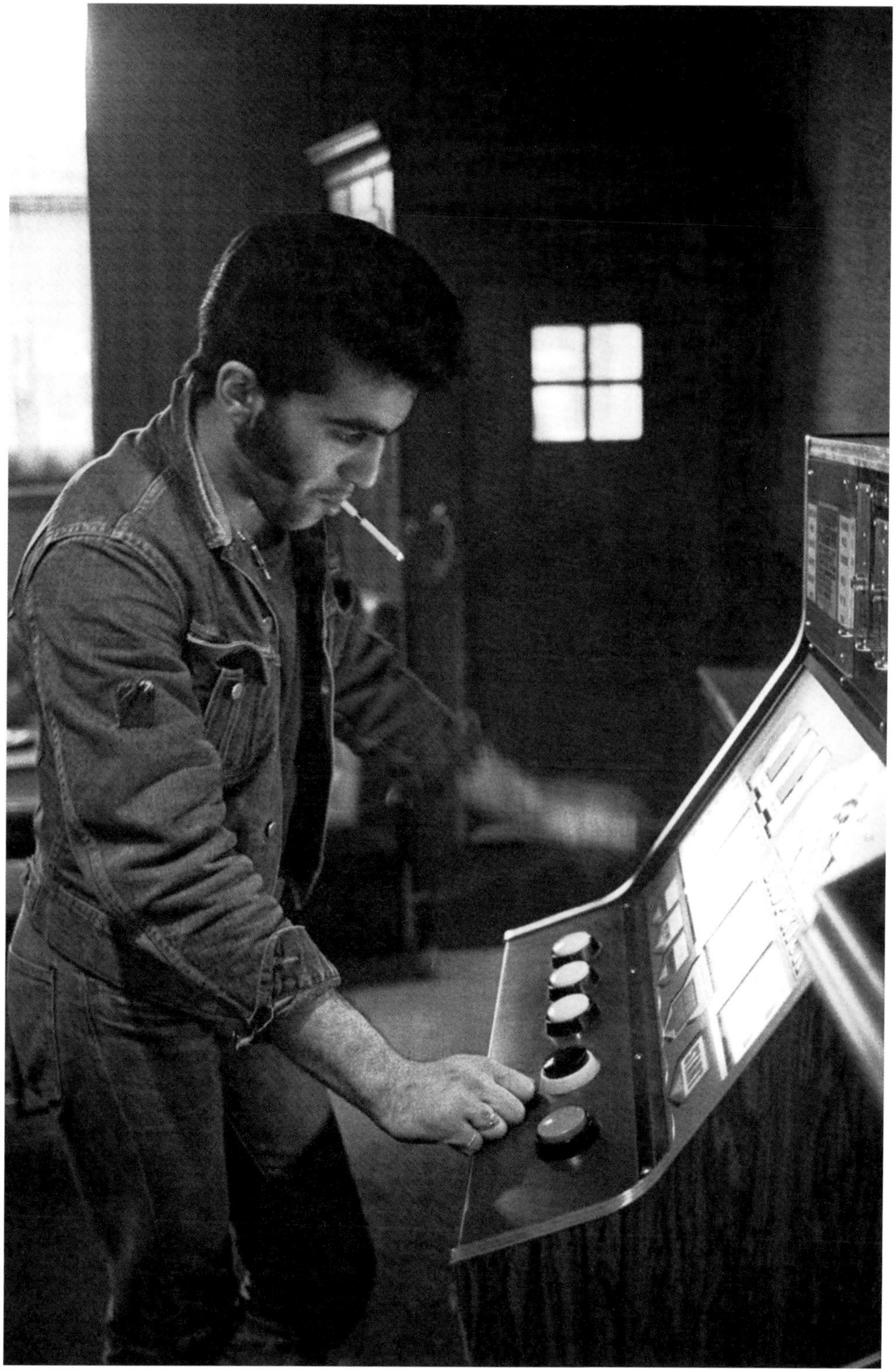

Playing a fruit machine in London pub, 1976.

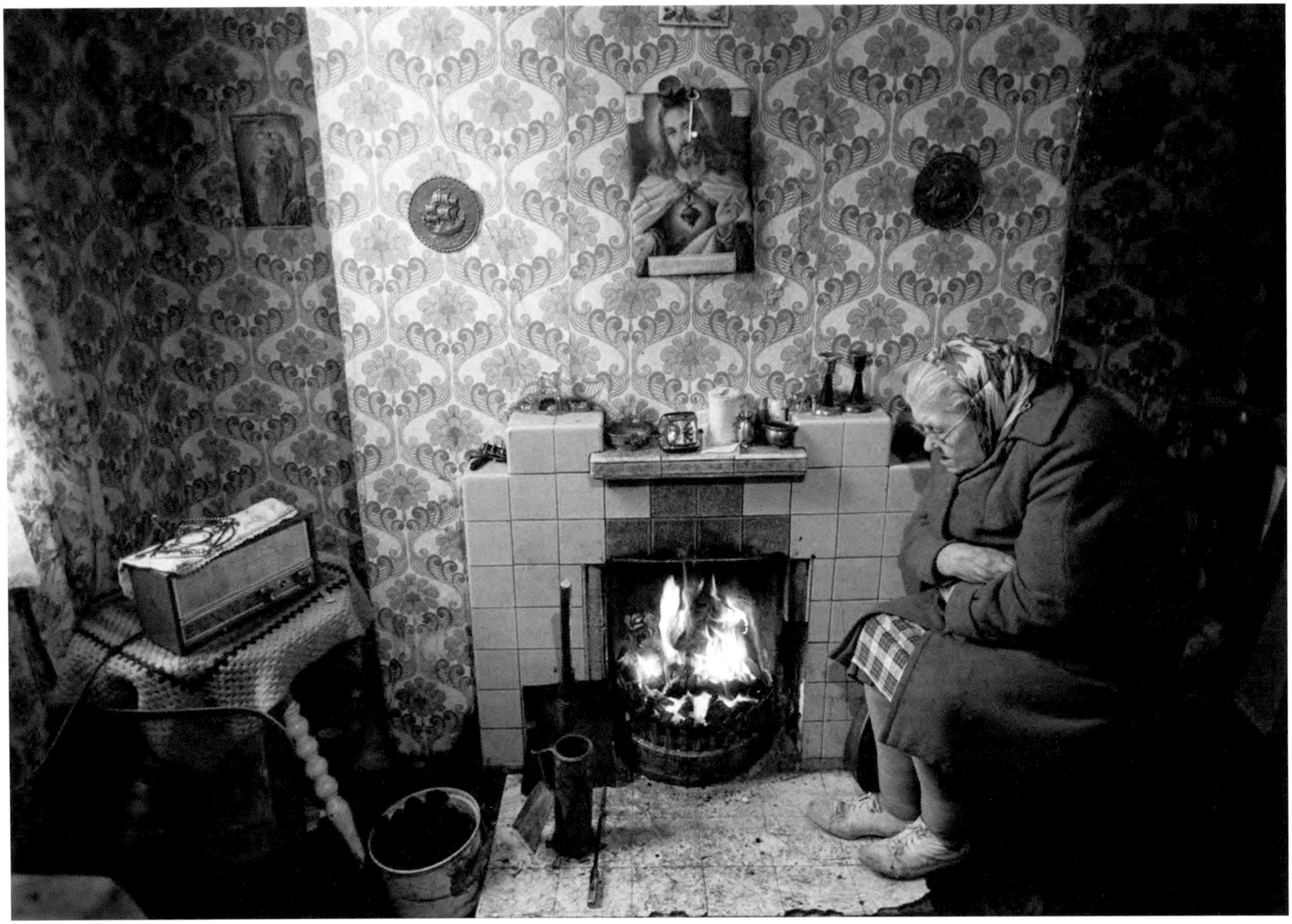

Old lady living alone. Middlesbrough, 1976.

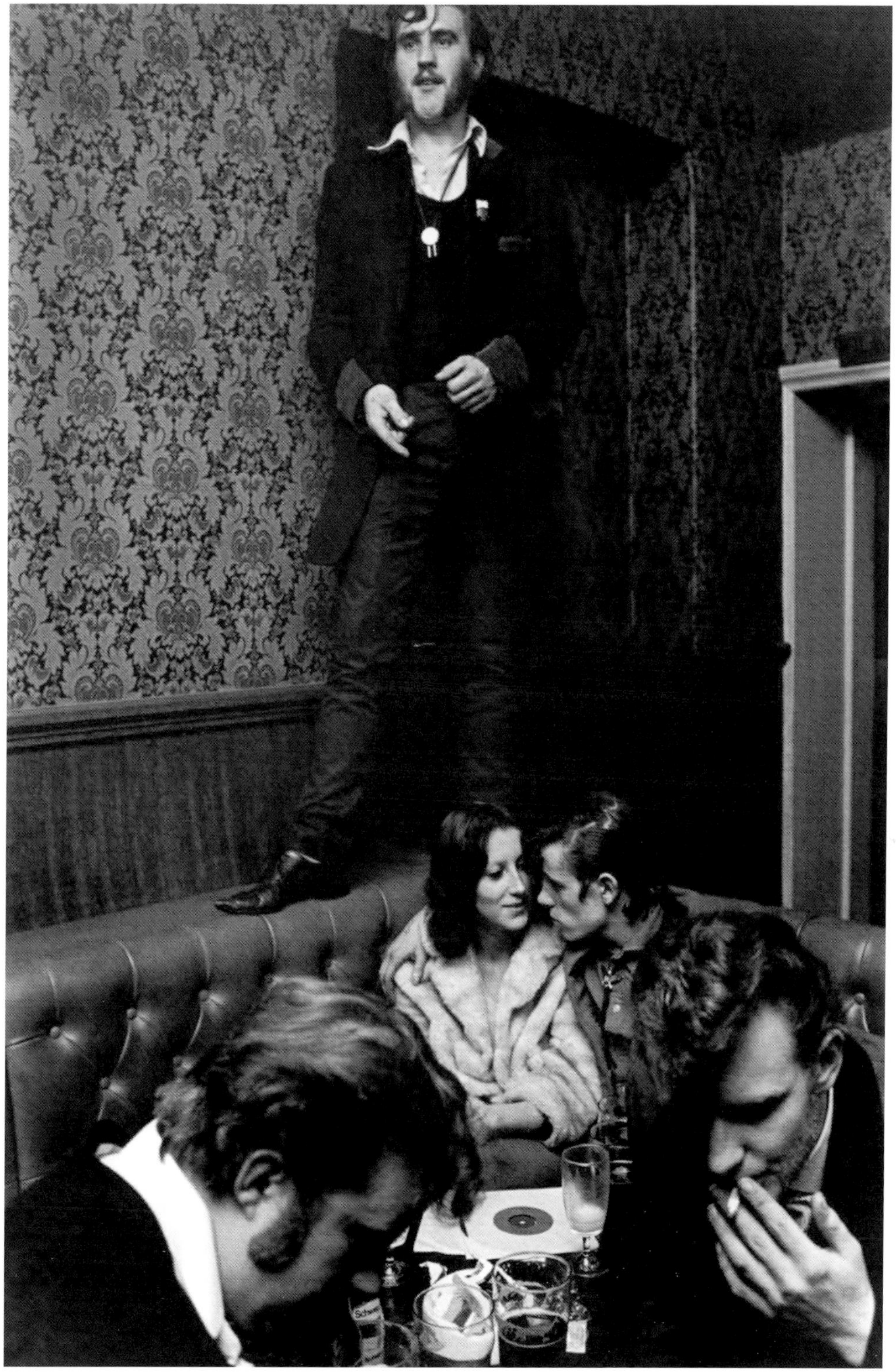
London. Barry Ransome in The Castle, Old Kent Road, 1976.

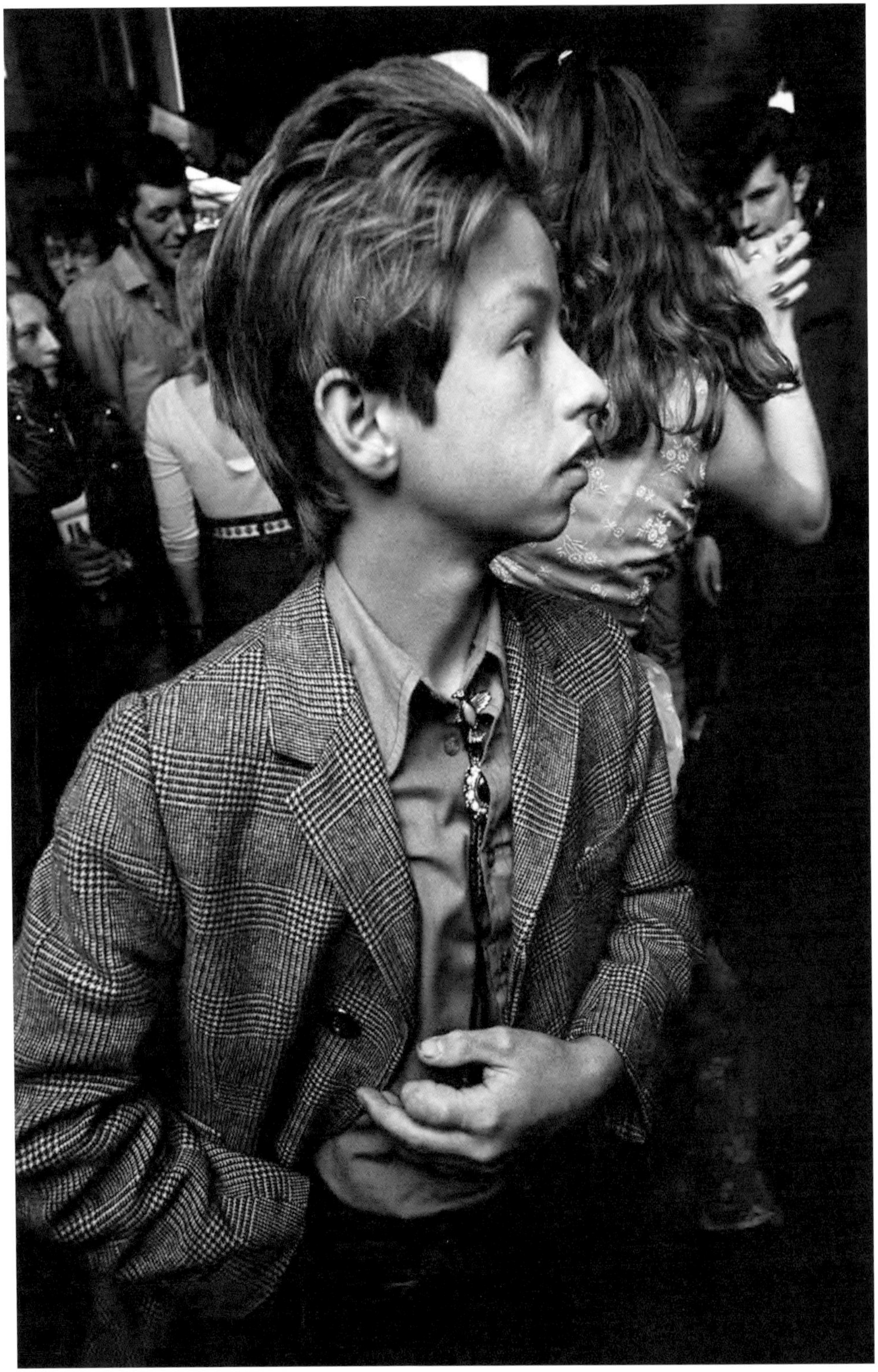
Kenny, a young Teddy Boy in a London pub, 1976.

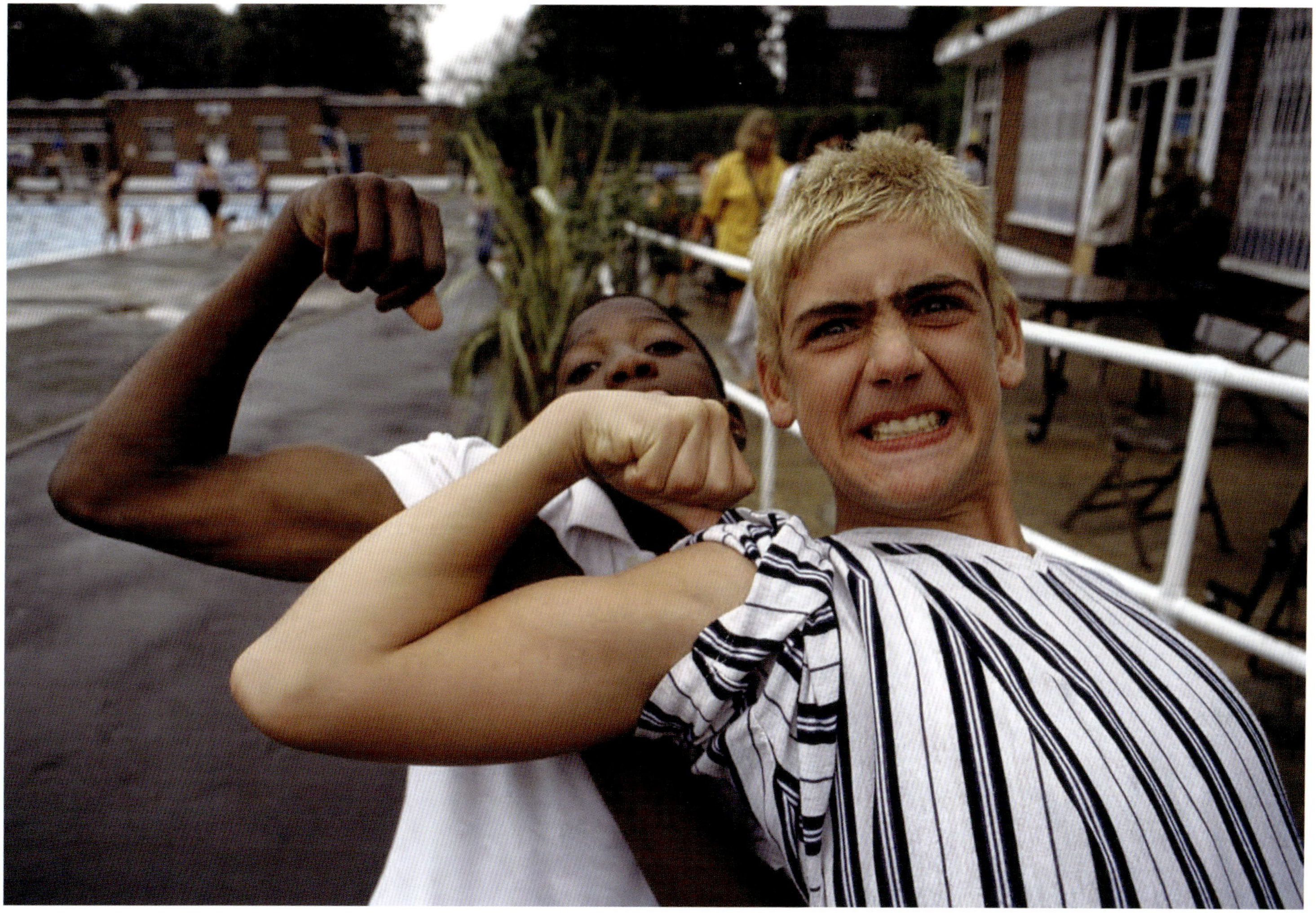

London. Kids at Brixton Lido, London, 1995.

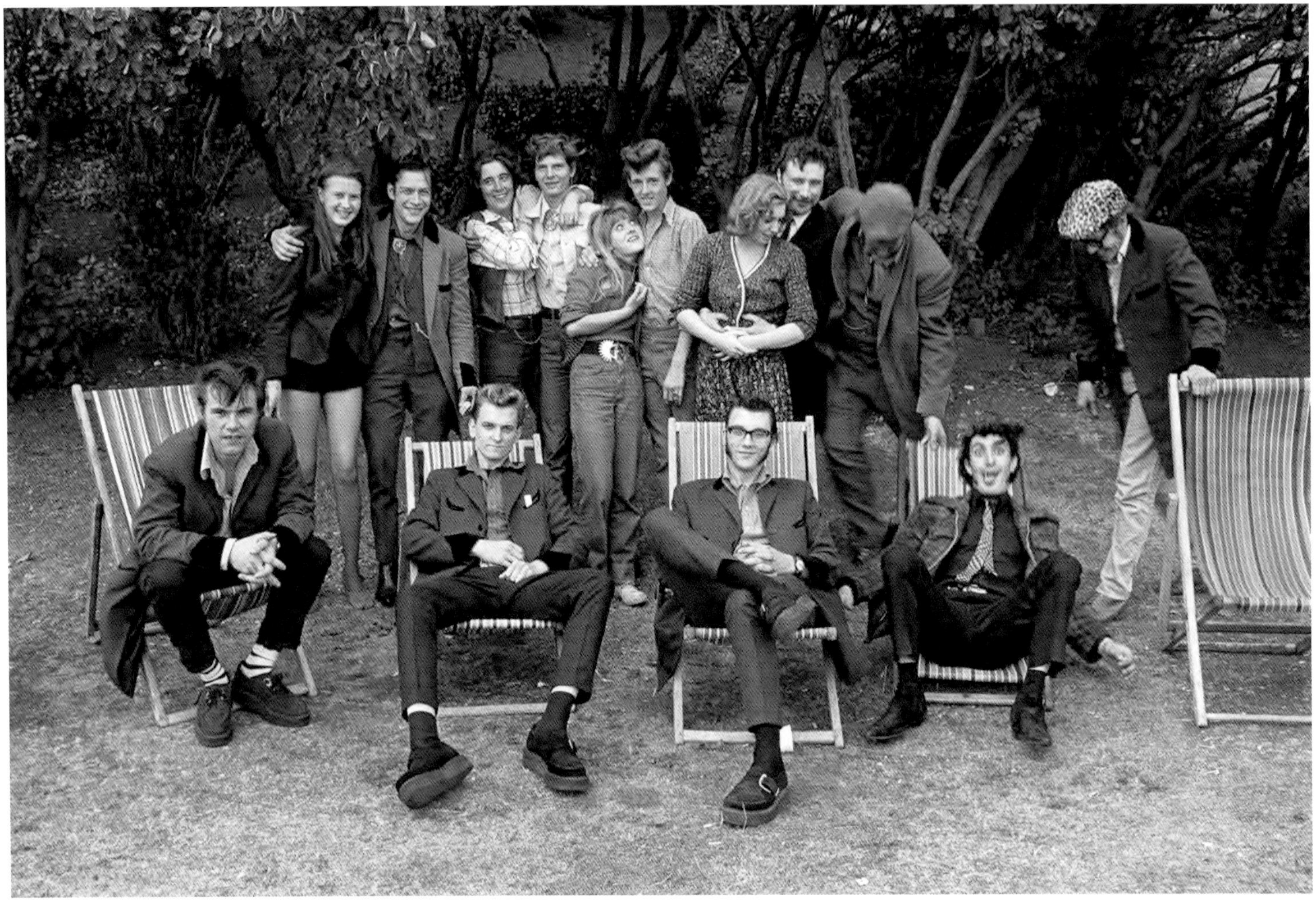

Southend. Teddy Boys on Bank holiday, 1976.

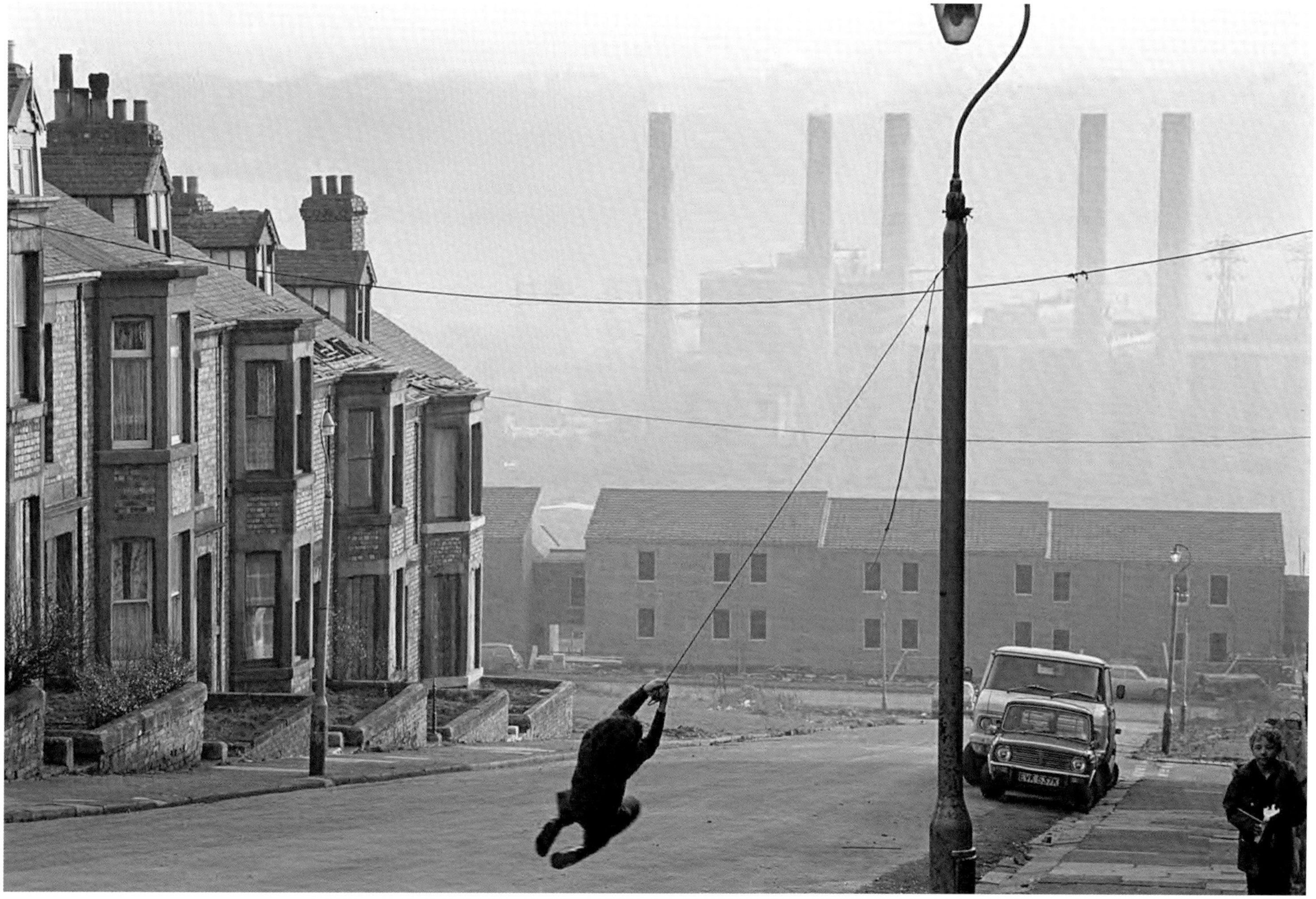

Swinging on a lamp post in West End of Newcastle-upon-Tyne, 1975.

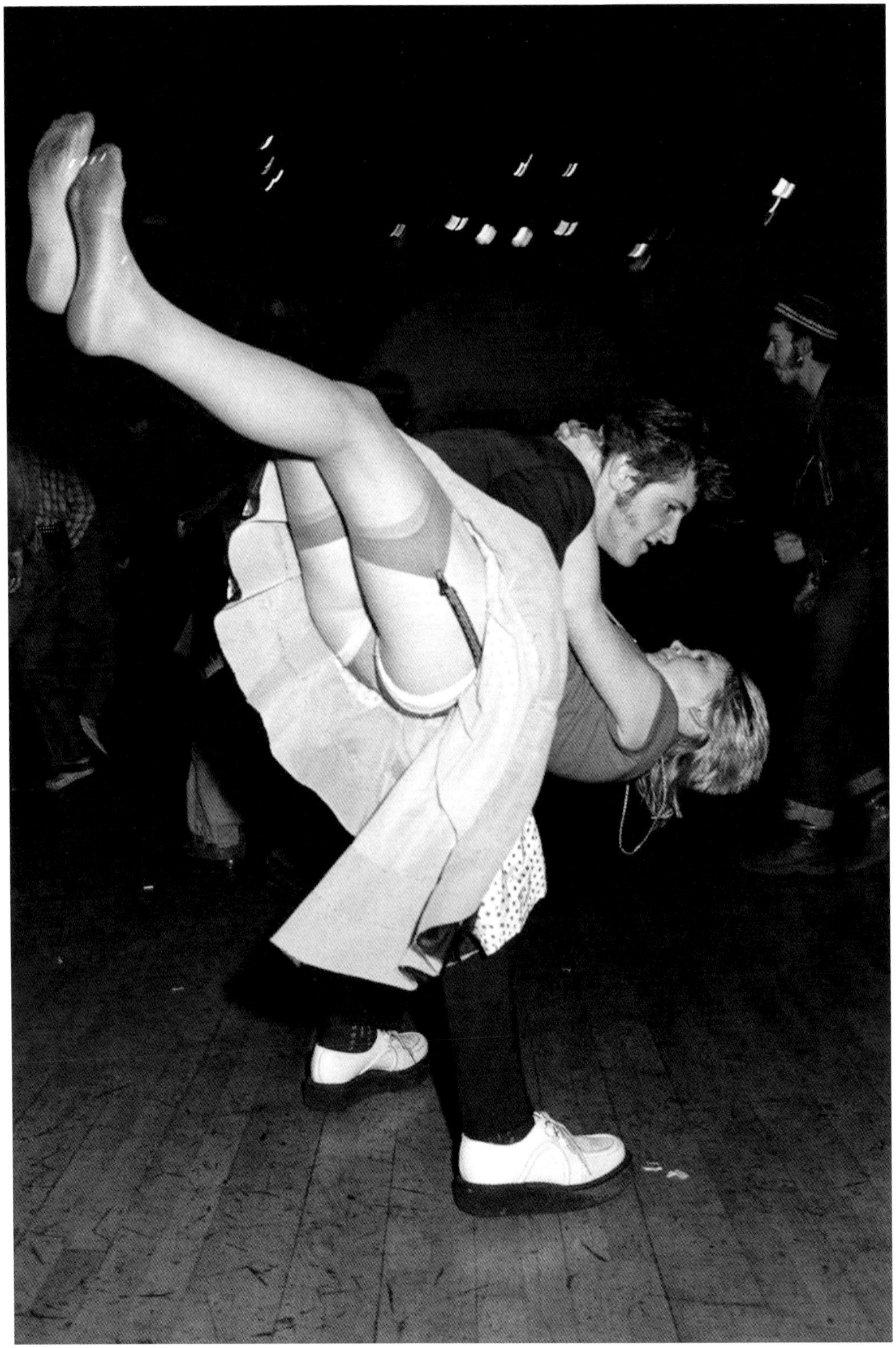

Dancing in the Lyceum Ballroom, London, 1976.

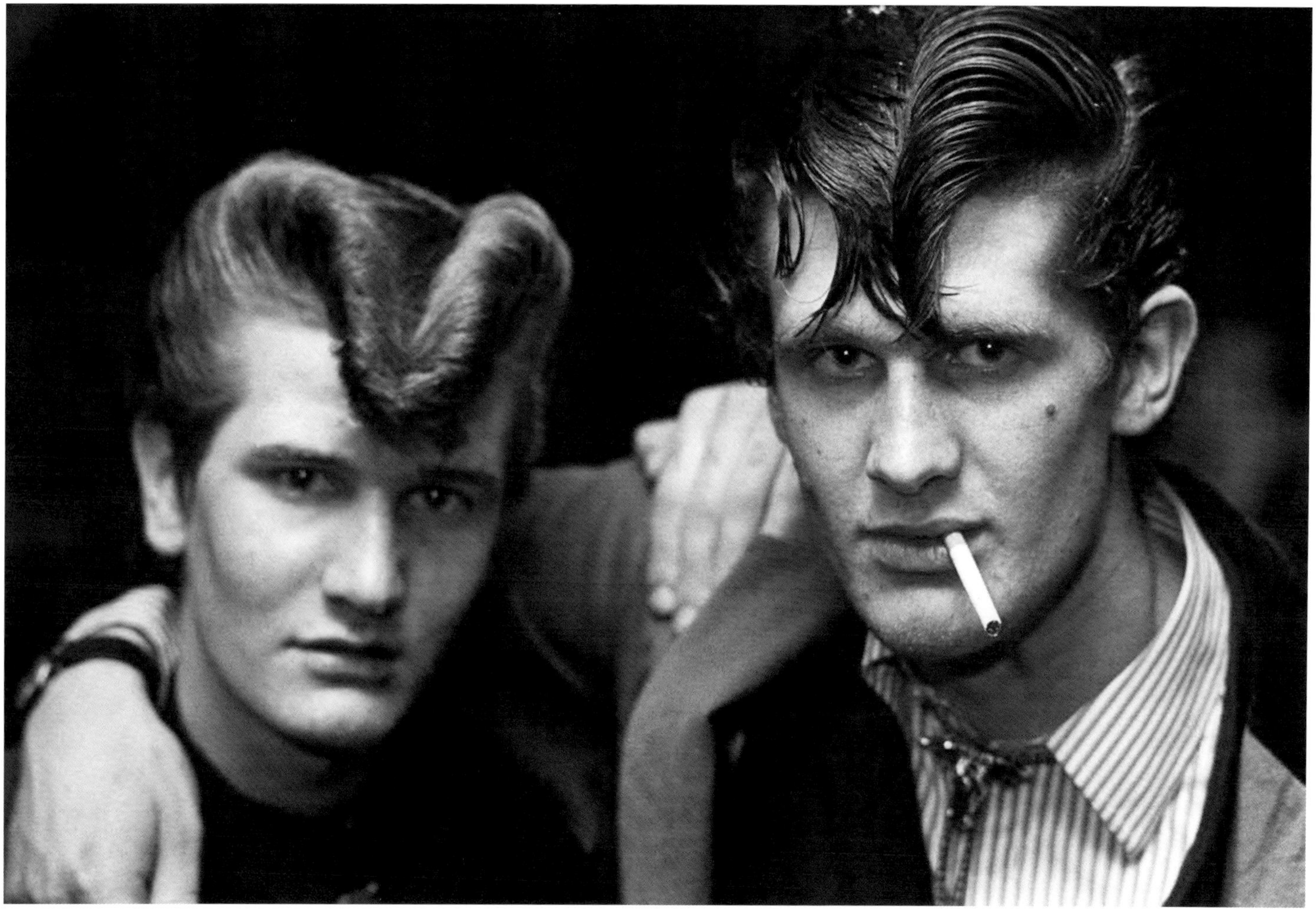

Two brothers in Red Deer, Croydon, 1976.

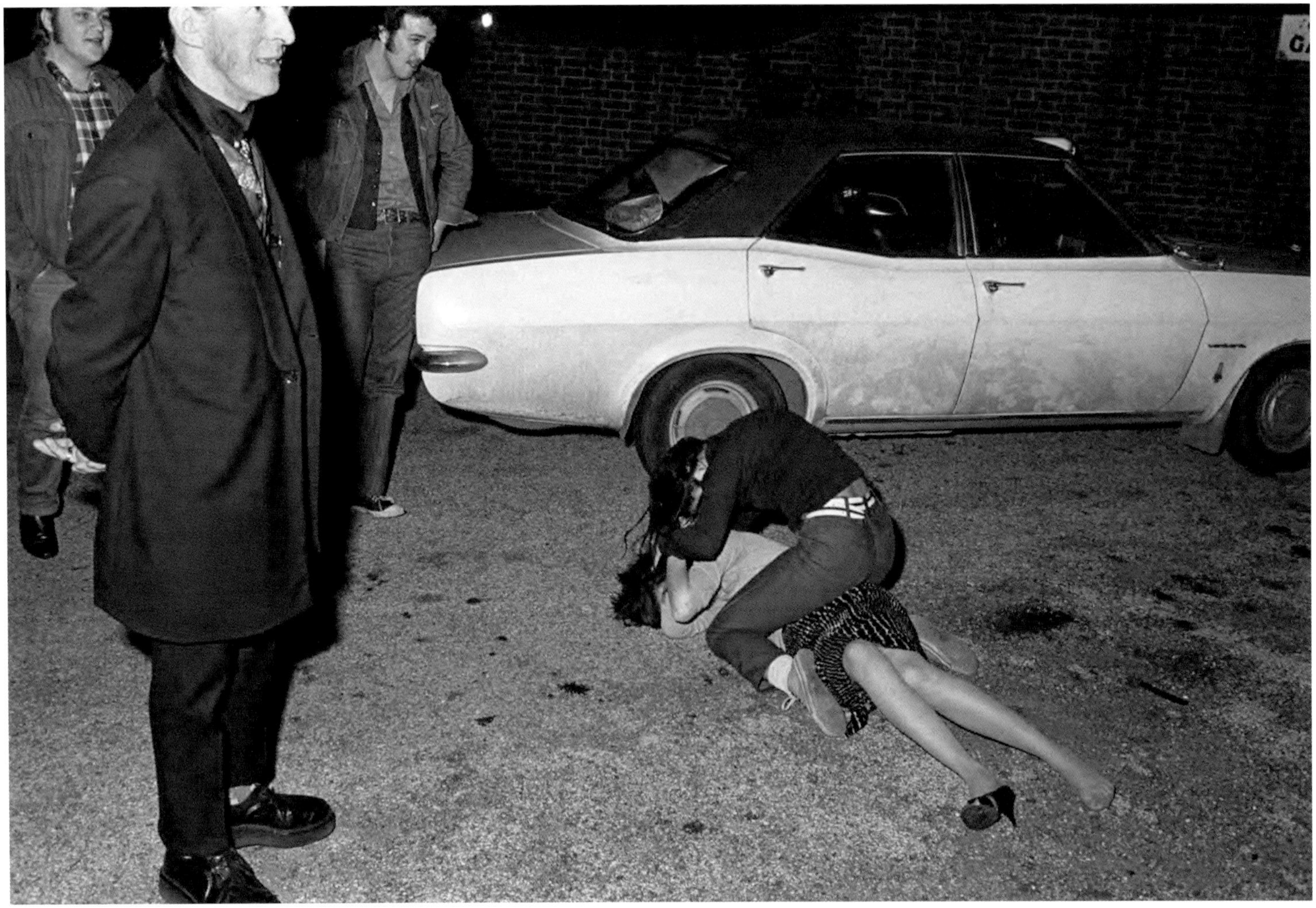

London. Girls fighting in the car-park of The White Hart, Willesden, 1976.

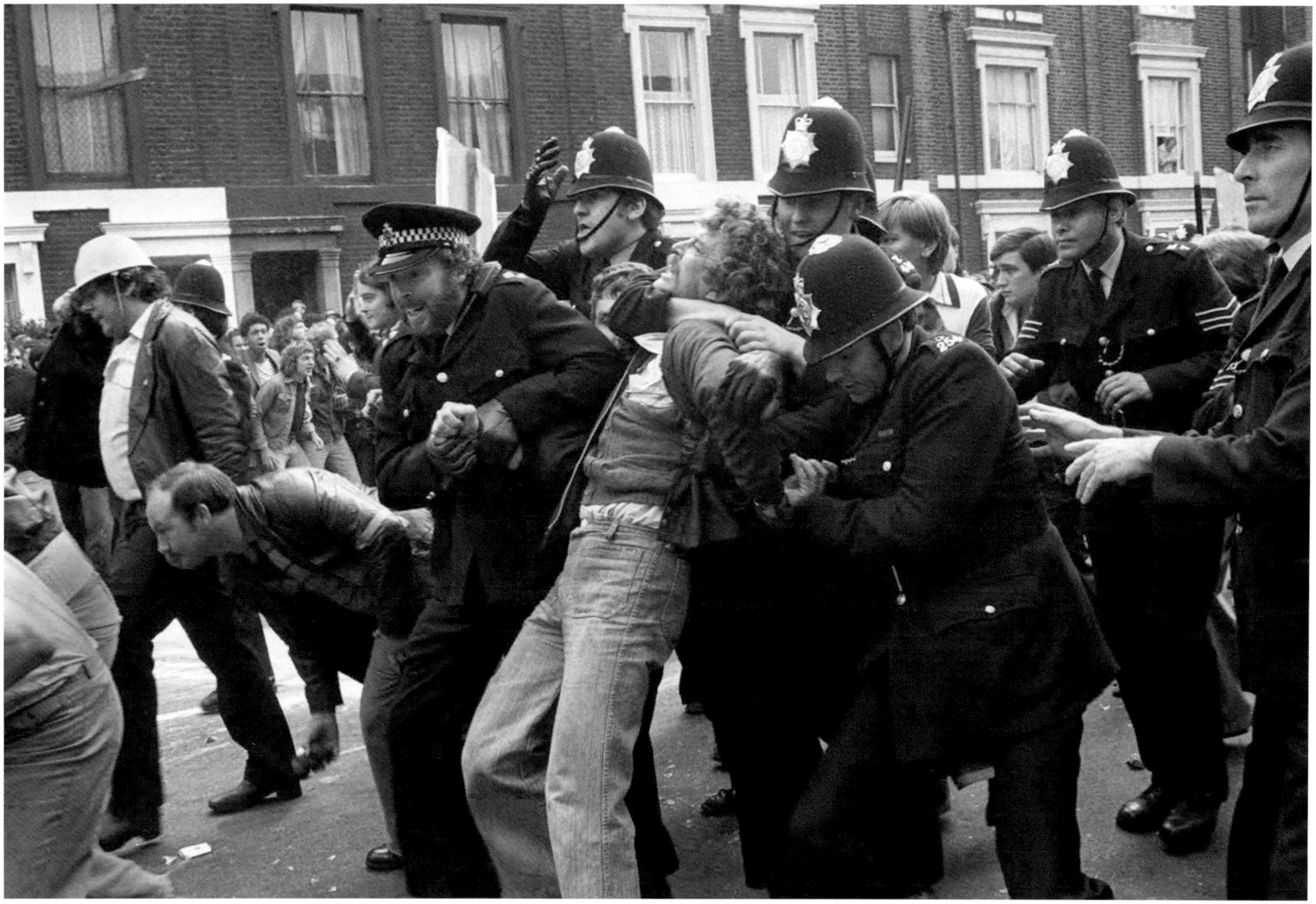

London. Anti-nazi demonstration in Lewisham, 1977.

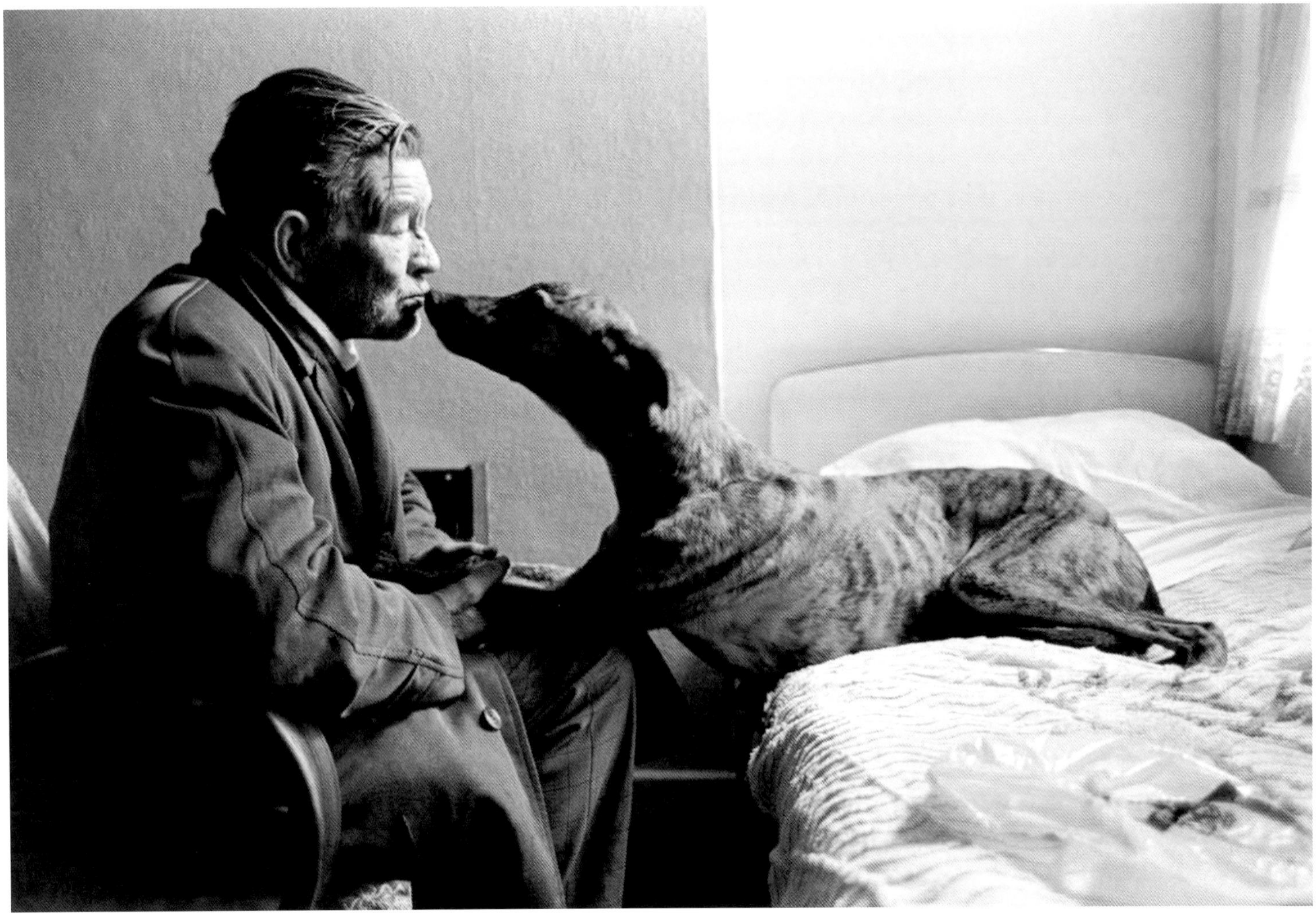

Birmingham. Alcoholic living alone with his dog, 1978.

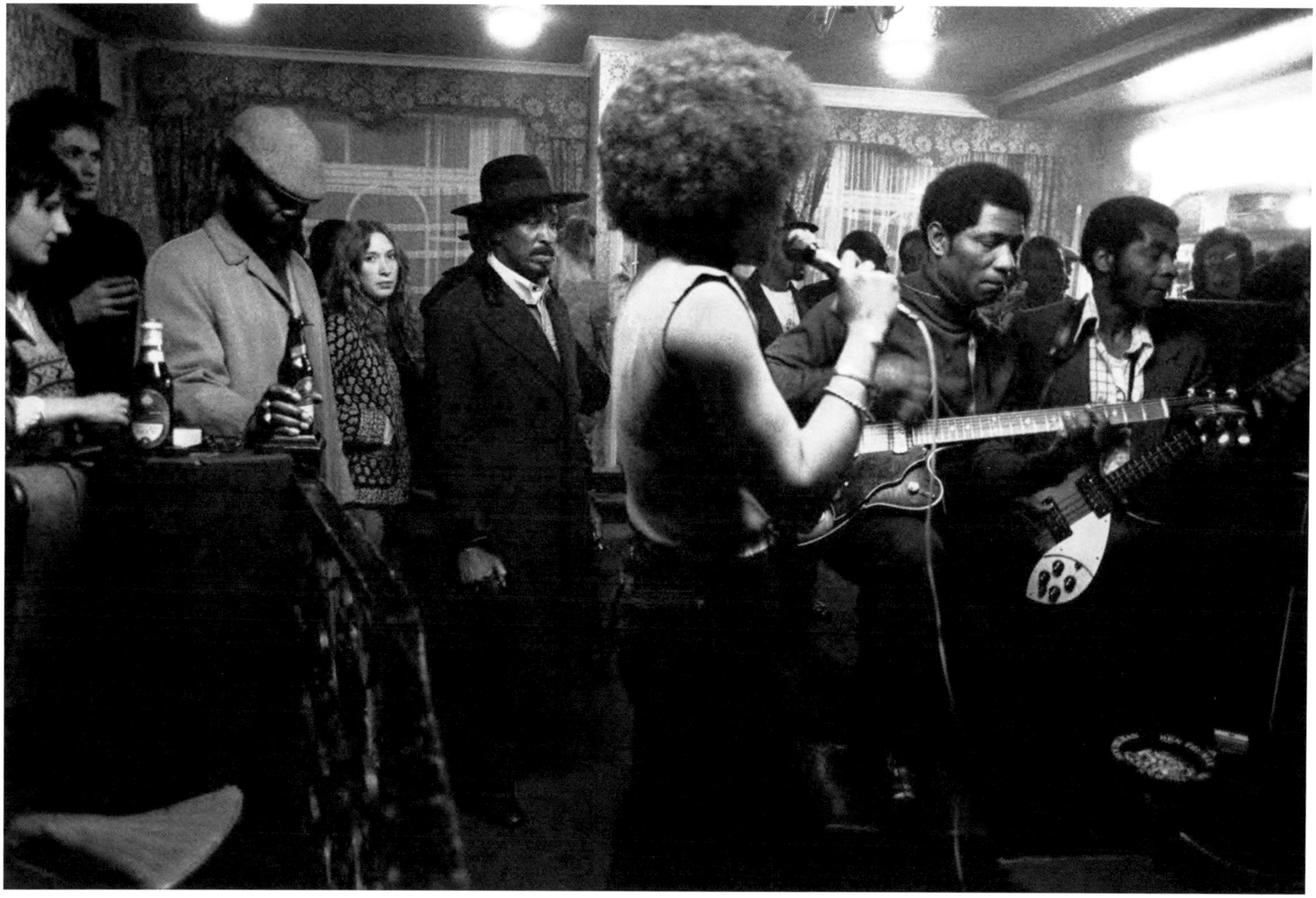

London. The Coach and Horses pub in Brixton, 1978.

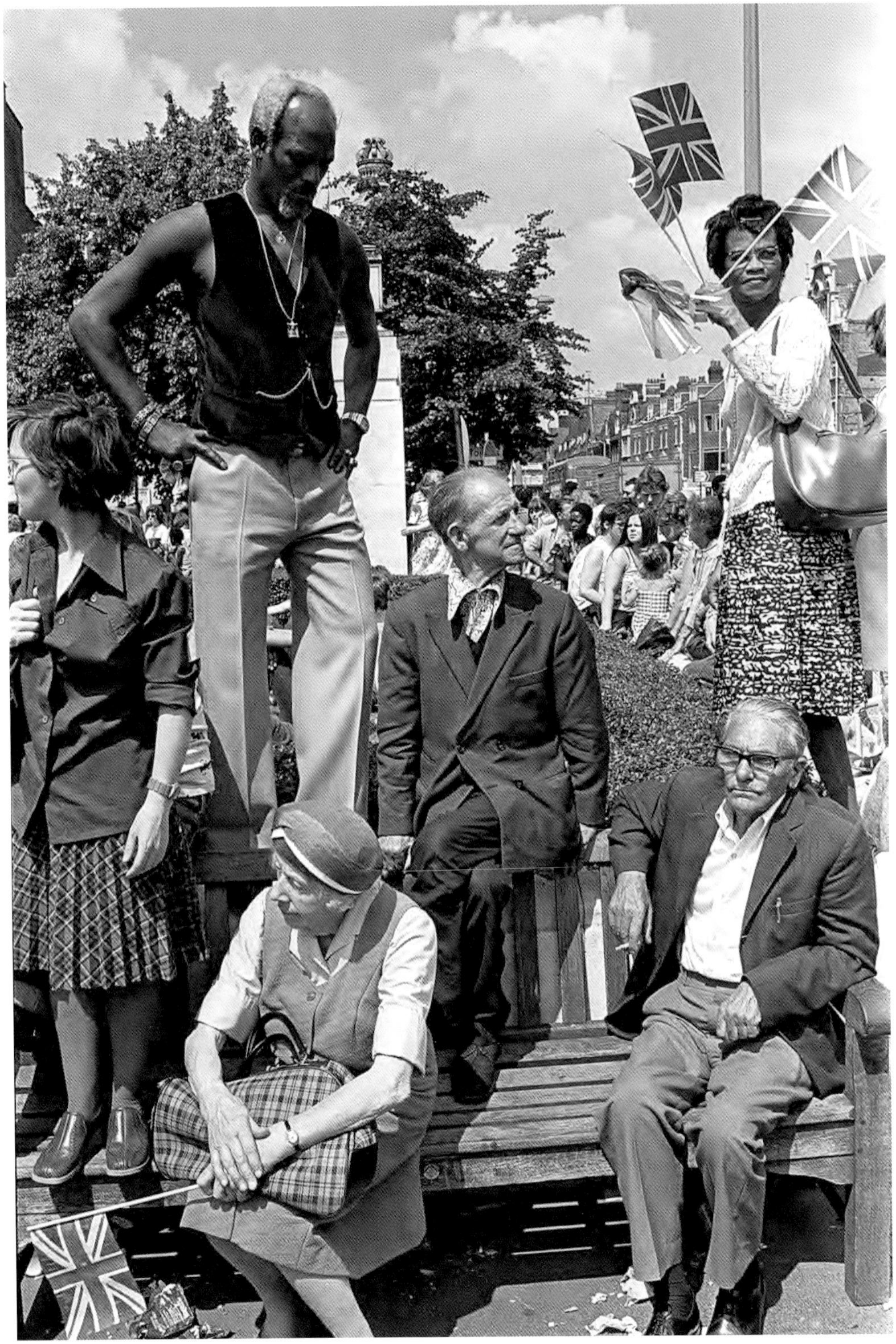

The Queen's Silver Jubilee. London, 1977.

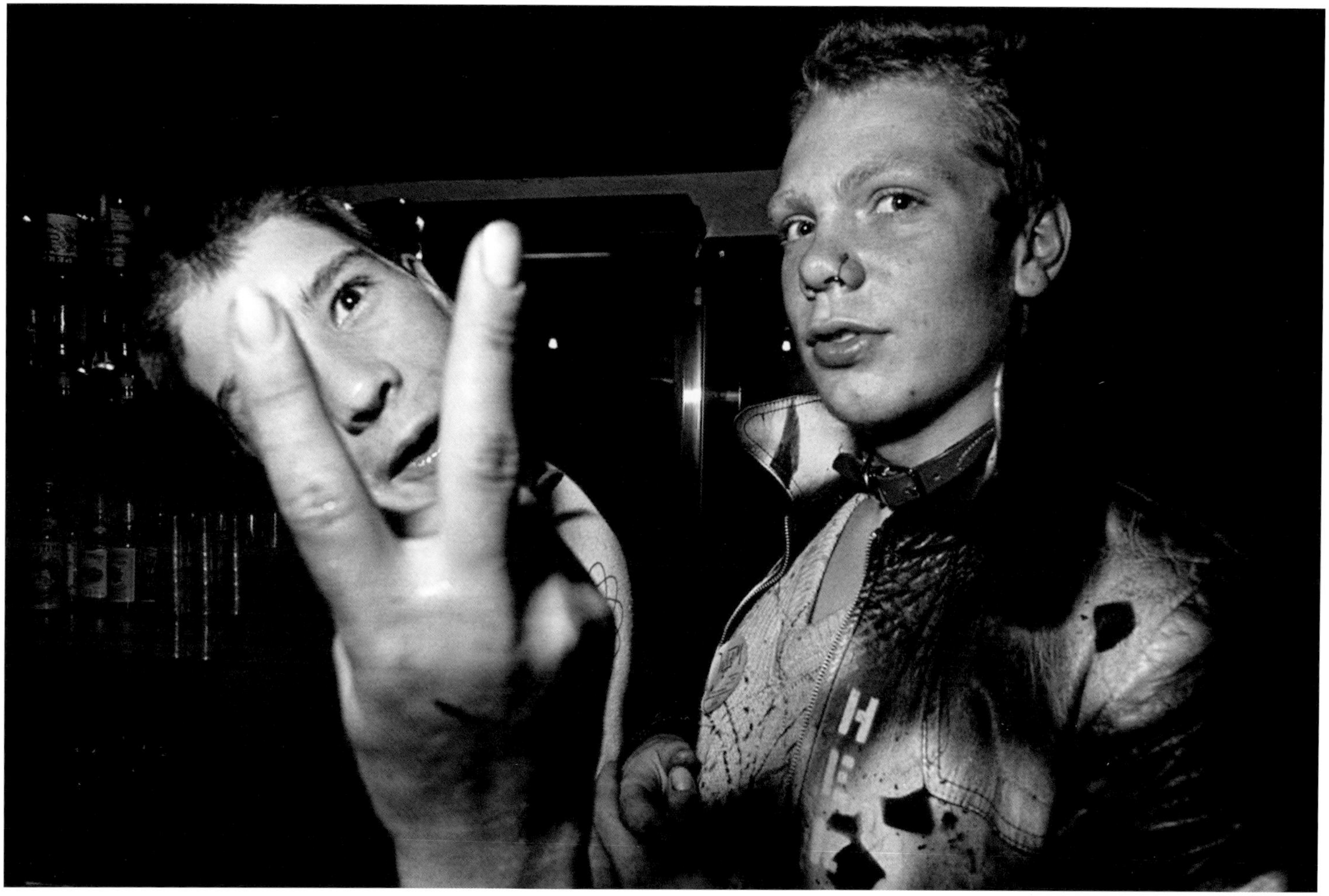

Punks in a London club, 1978.

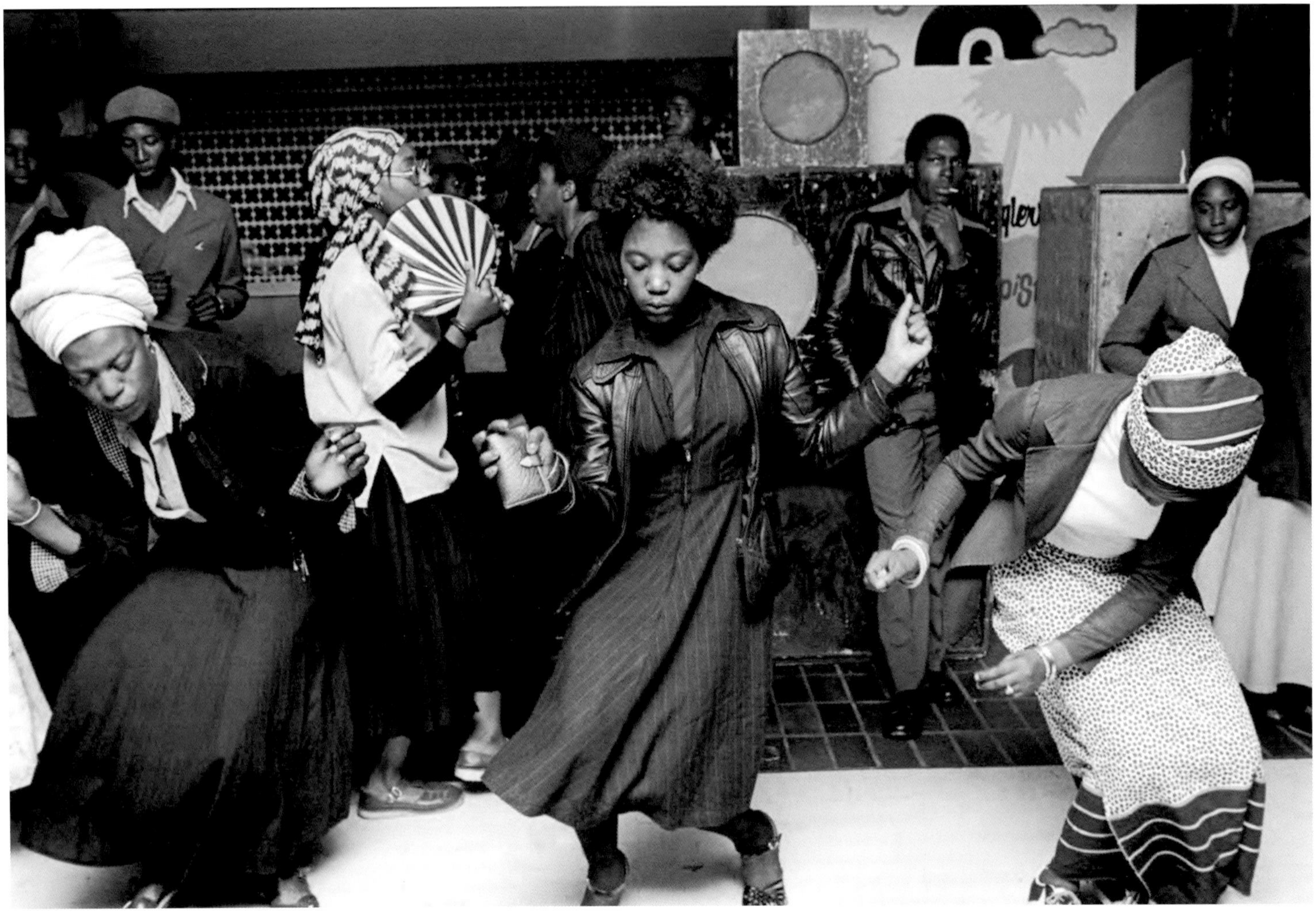

Wolverhampton youth club disco, 1978.

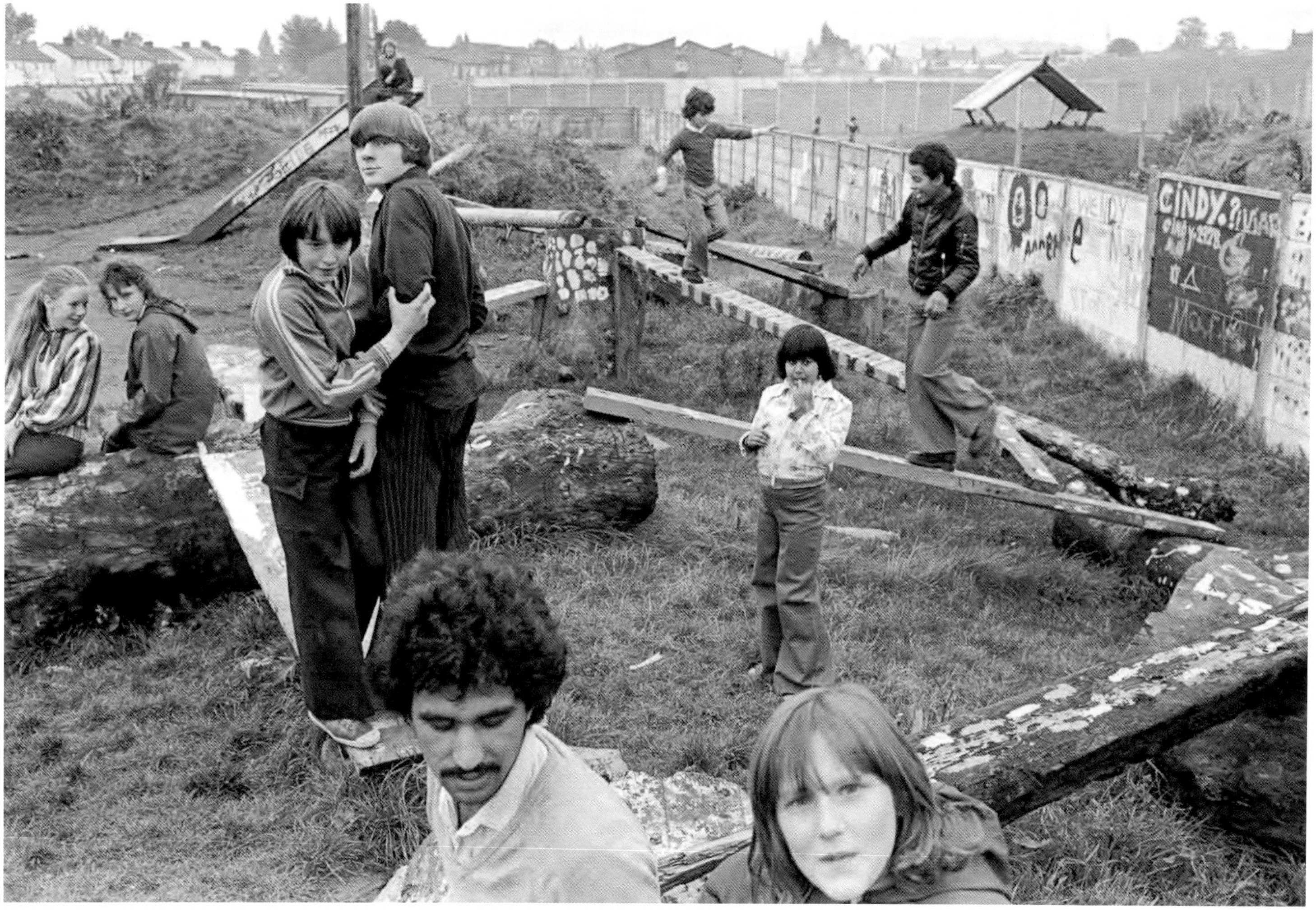

Wolverhampton. Adventure playground, 1978.

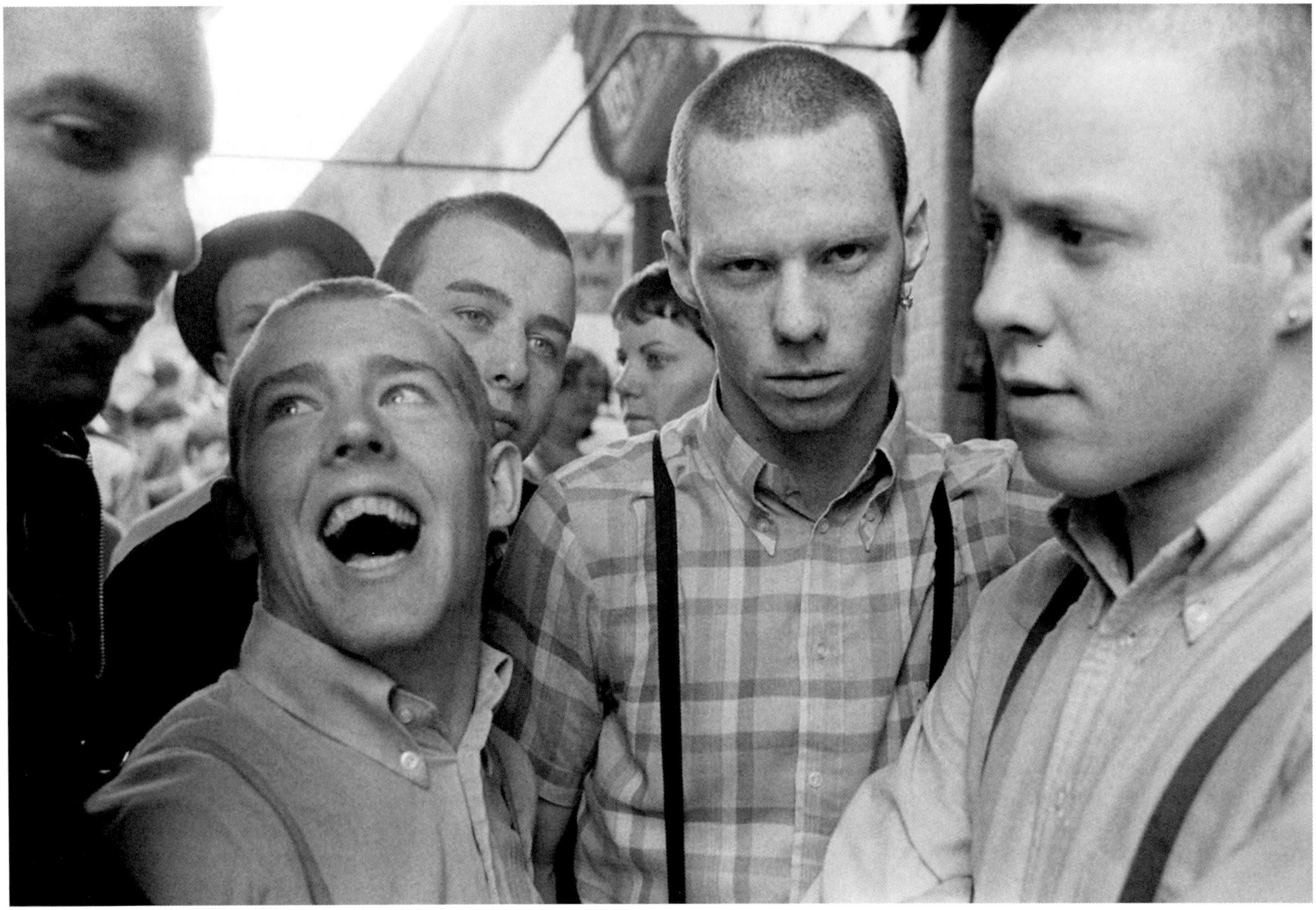

Skinheads in Hackney, London, 1979.

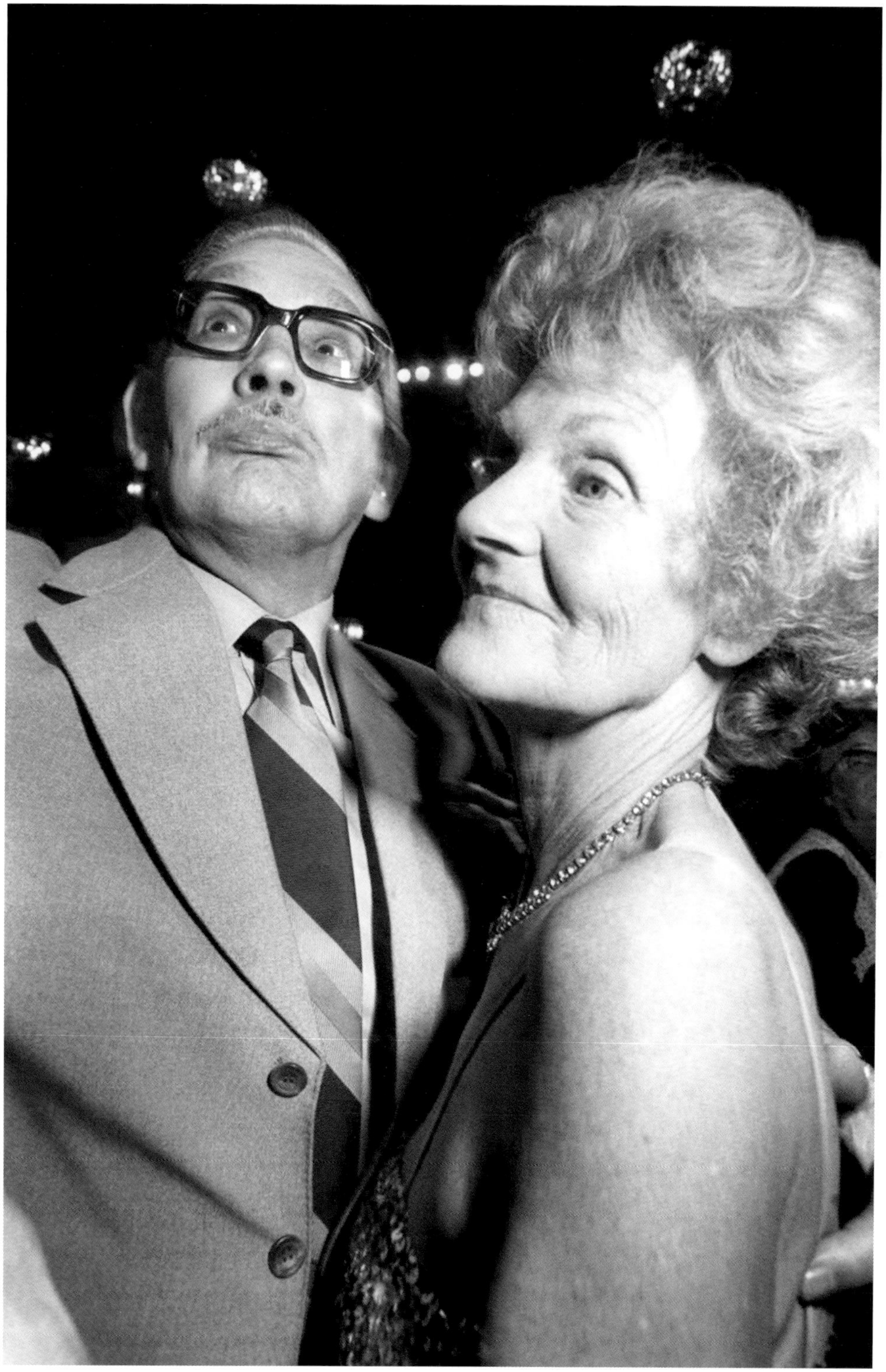

Blackpool. Conservative Party Conference Ball, 1979.

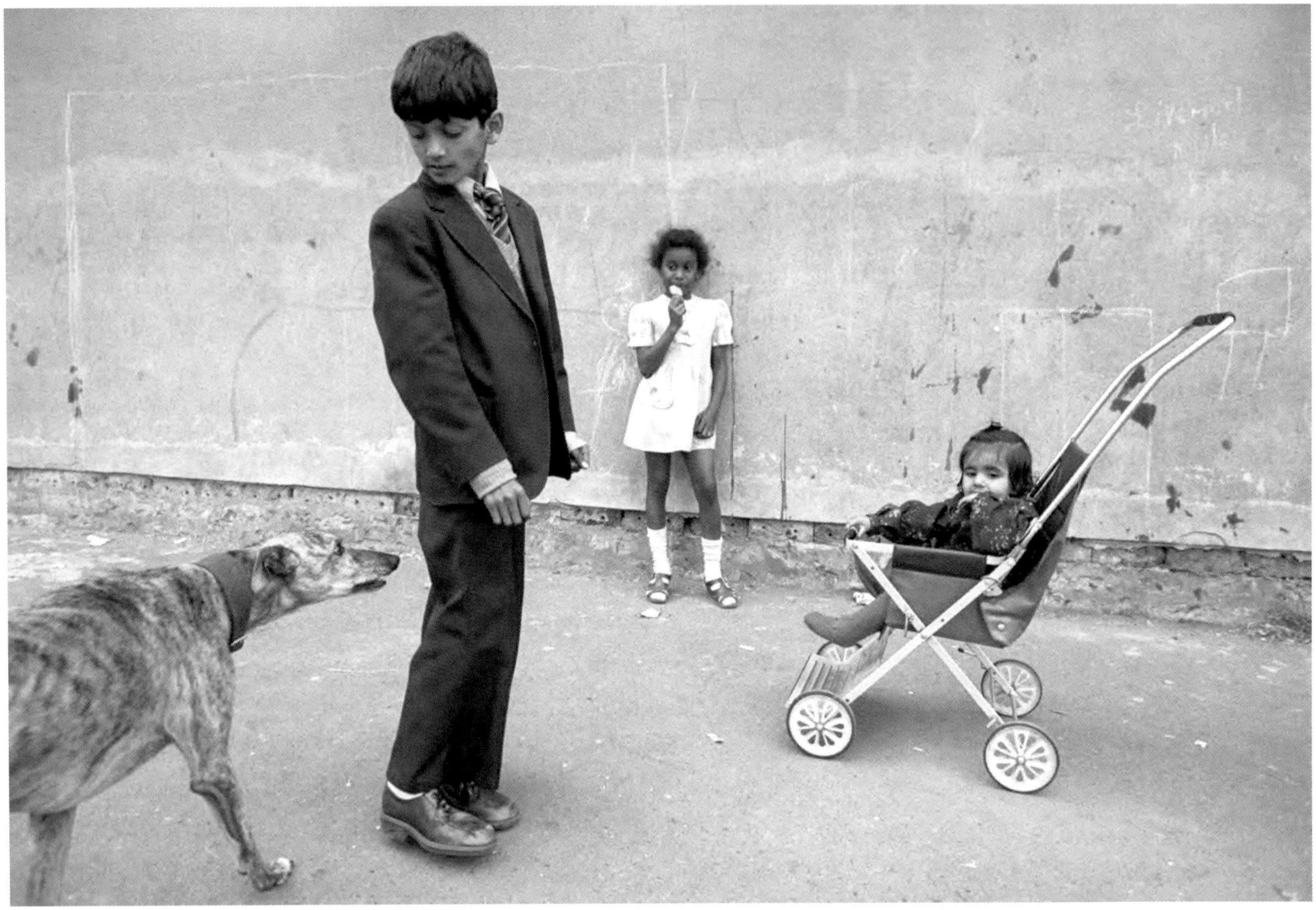

Wolverhampton. Children with sniffing dog, 1979.

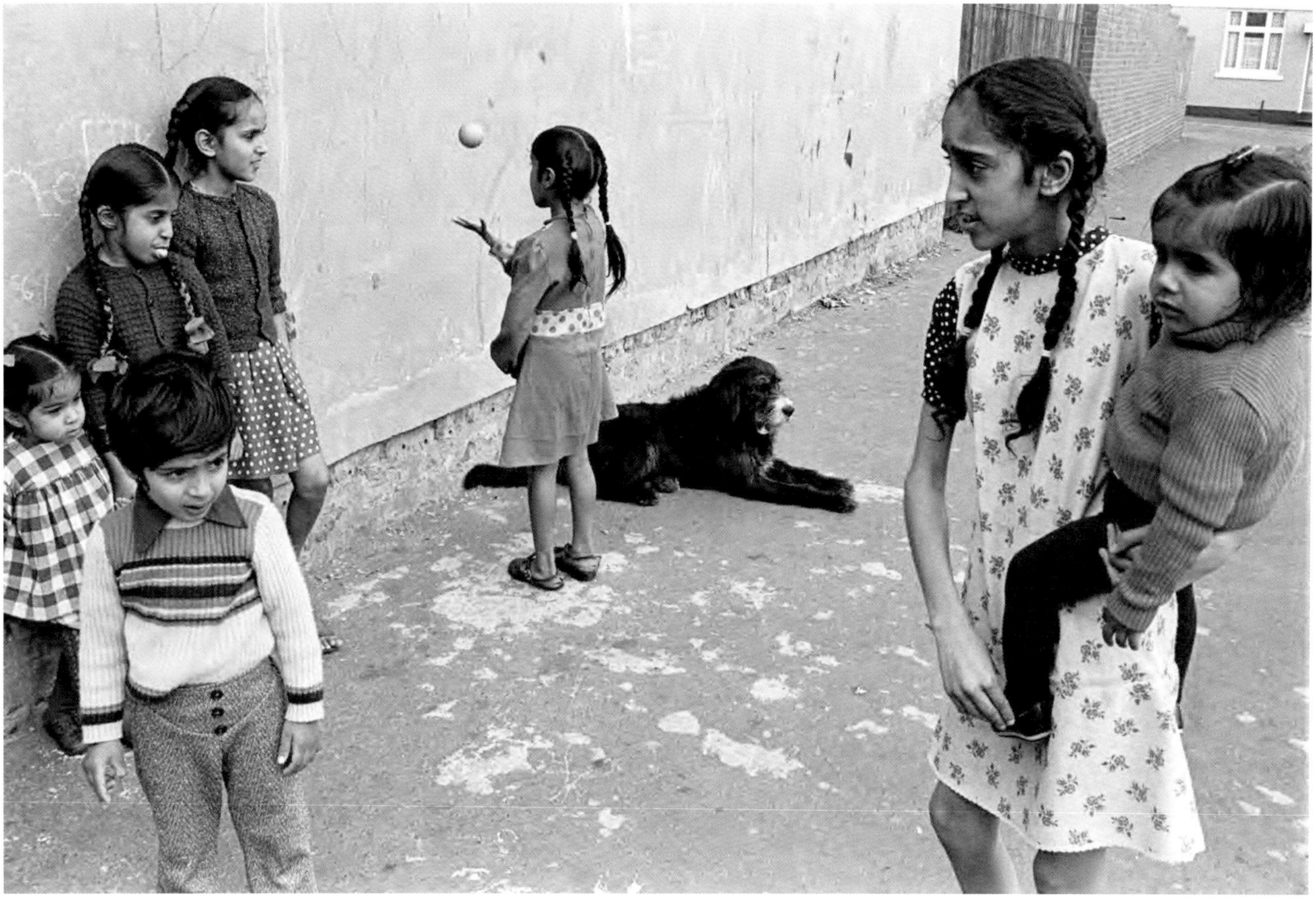

Wolverhampton. young children playing in the street, 1979.

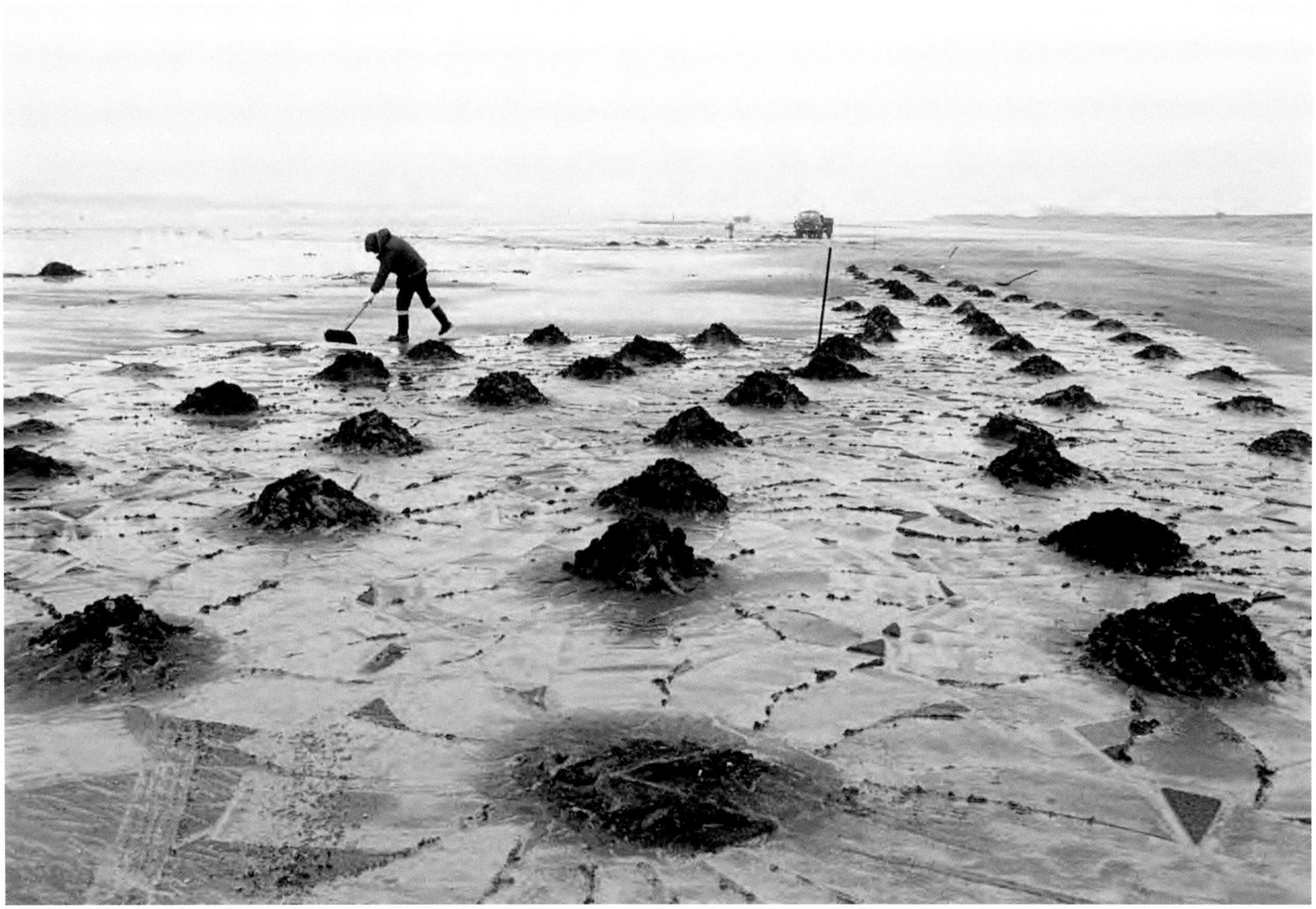

Hartlepool. Collecting sea coal on the beach, 1982.

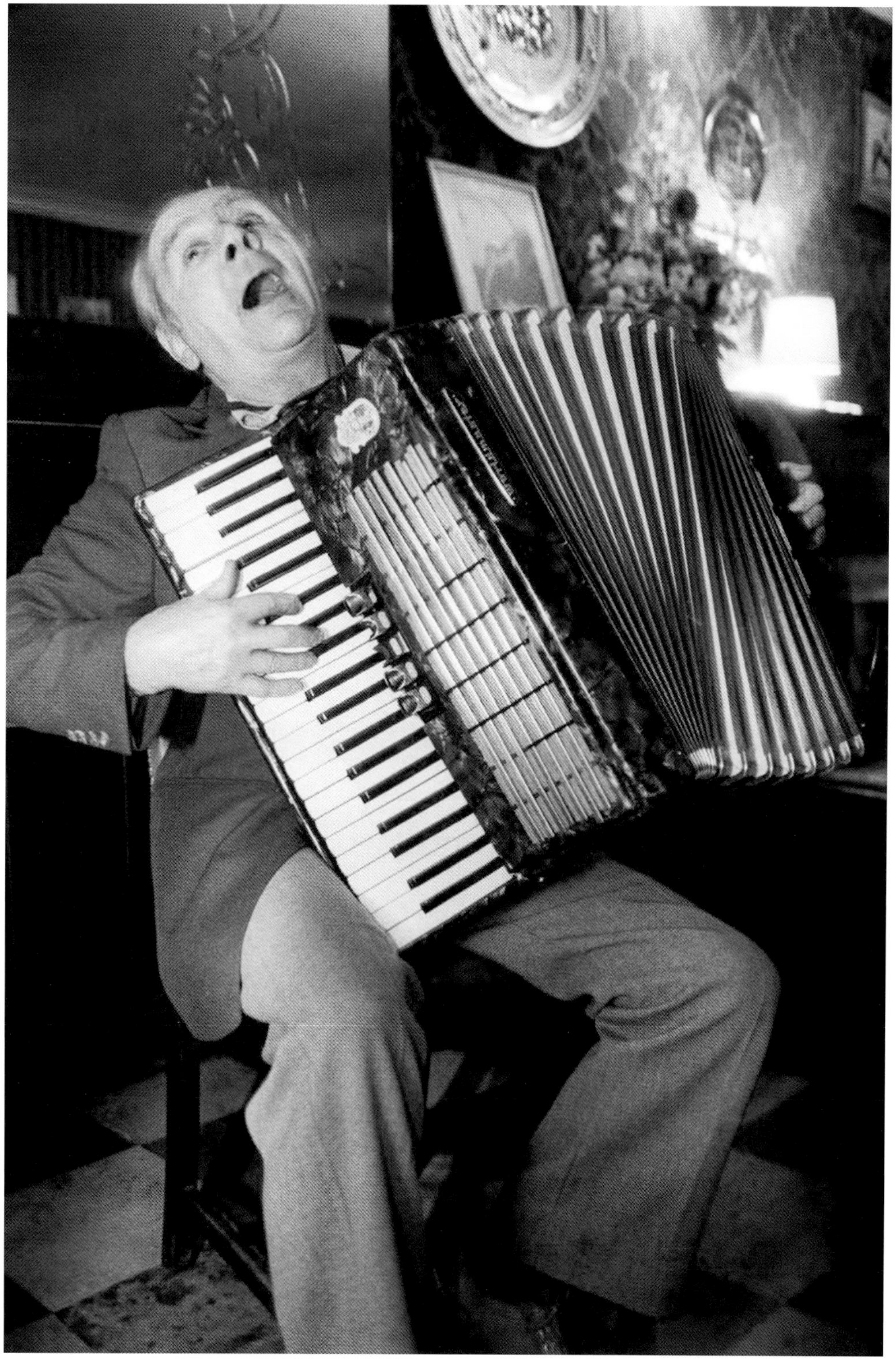

Accordianist in East End pub, London, 1987.

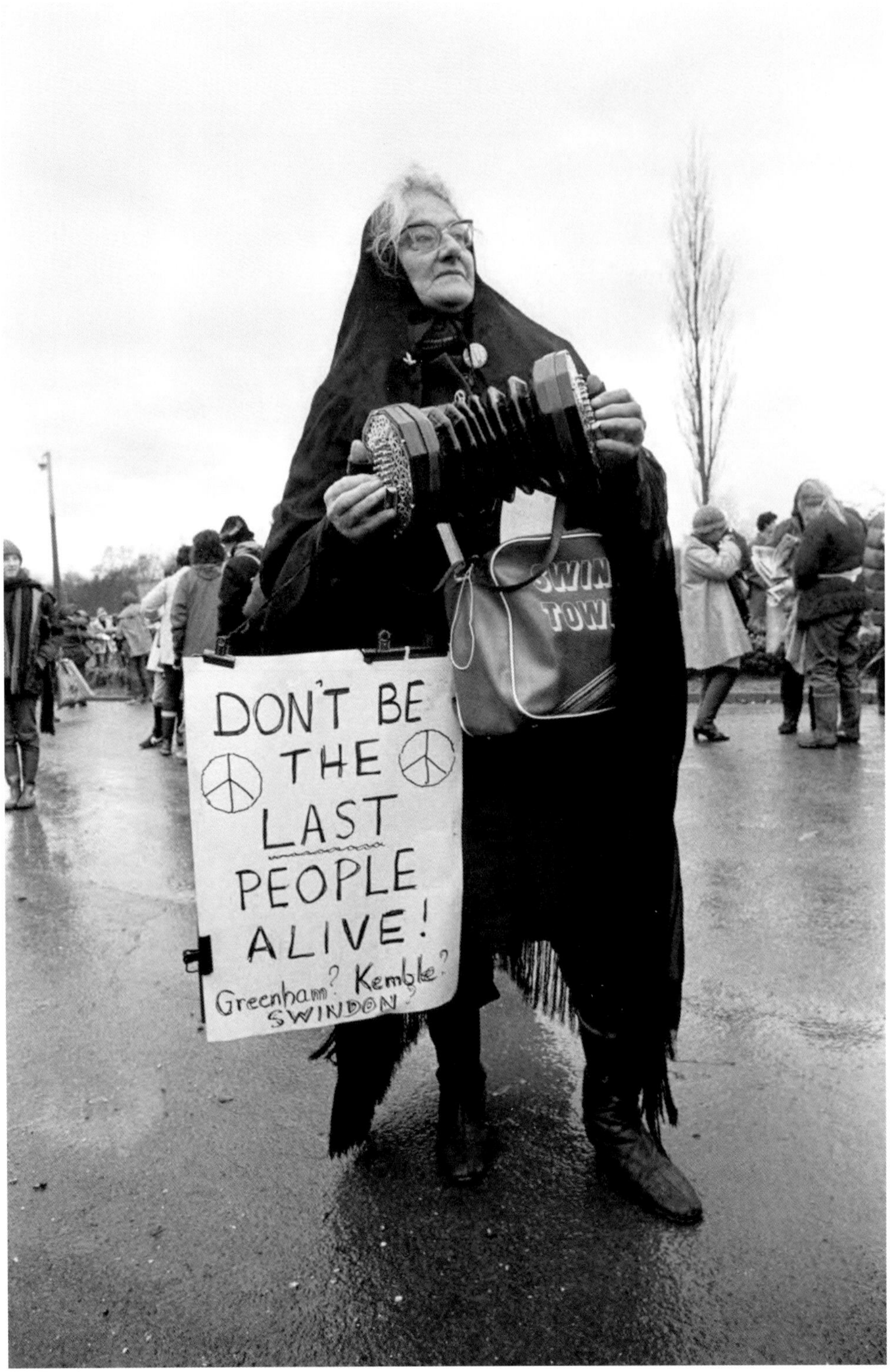

Anti-nuclear weapons protestor at Greenham Common, 1983.

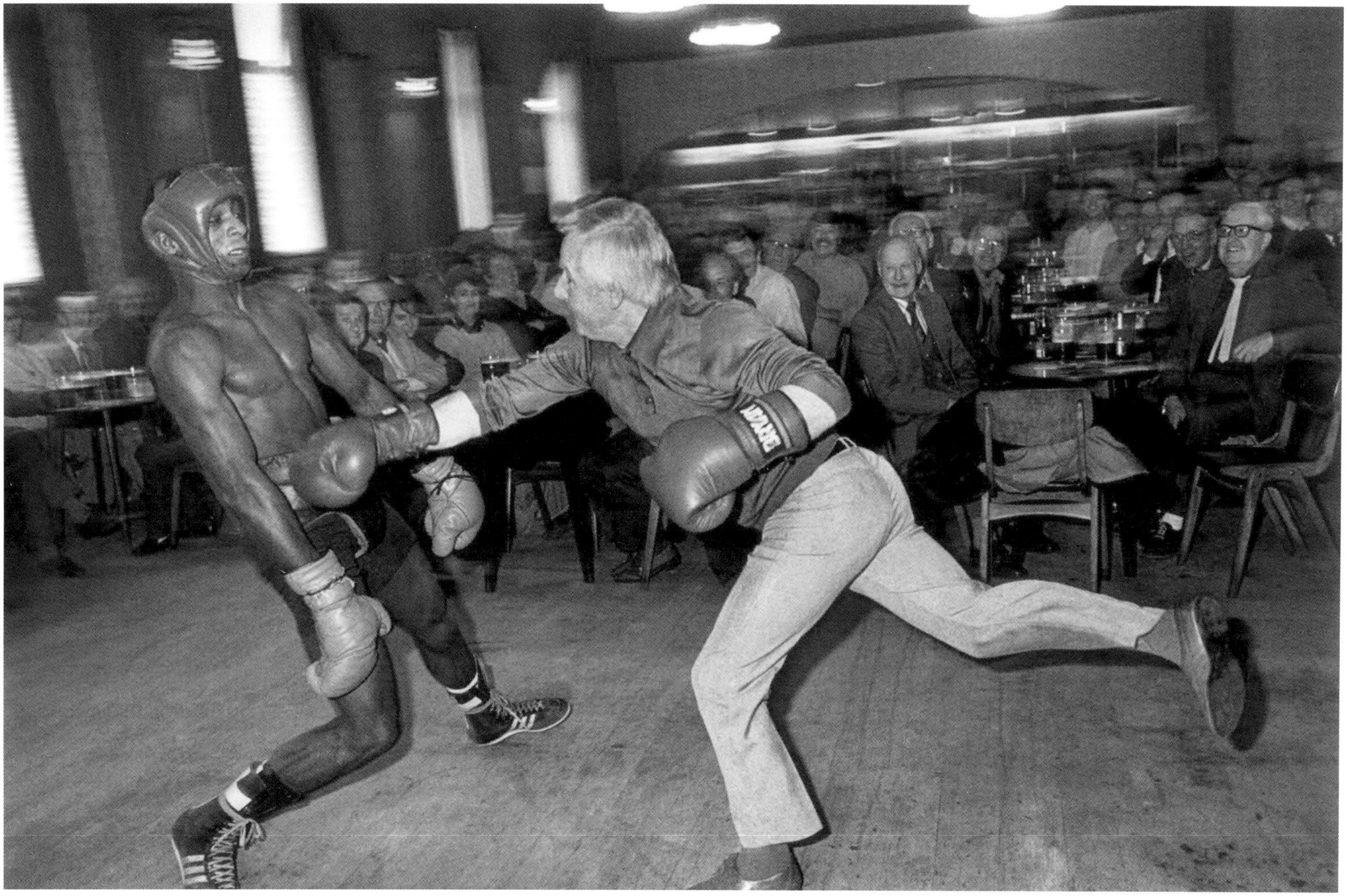

Sheffield. Middleweight boxer Herol Graham in a working men's club, 1986.

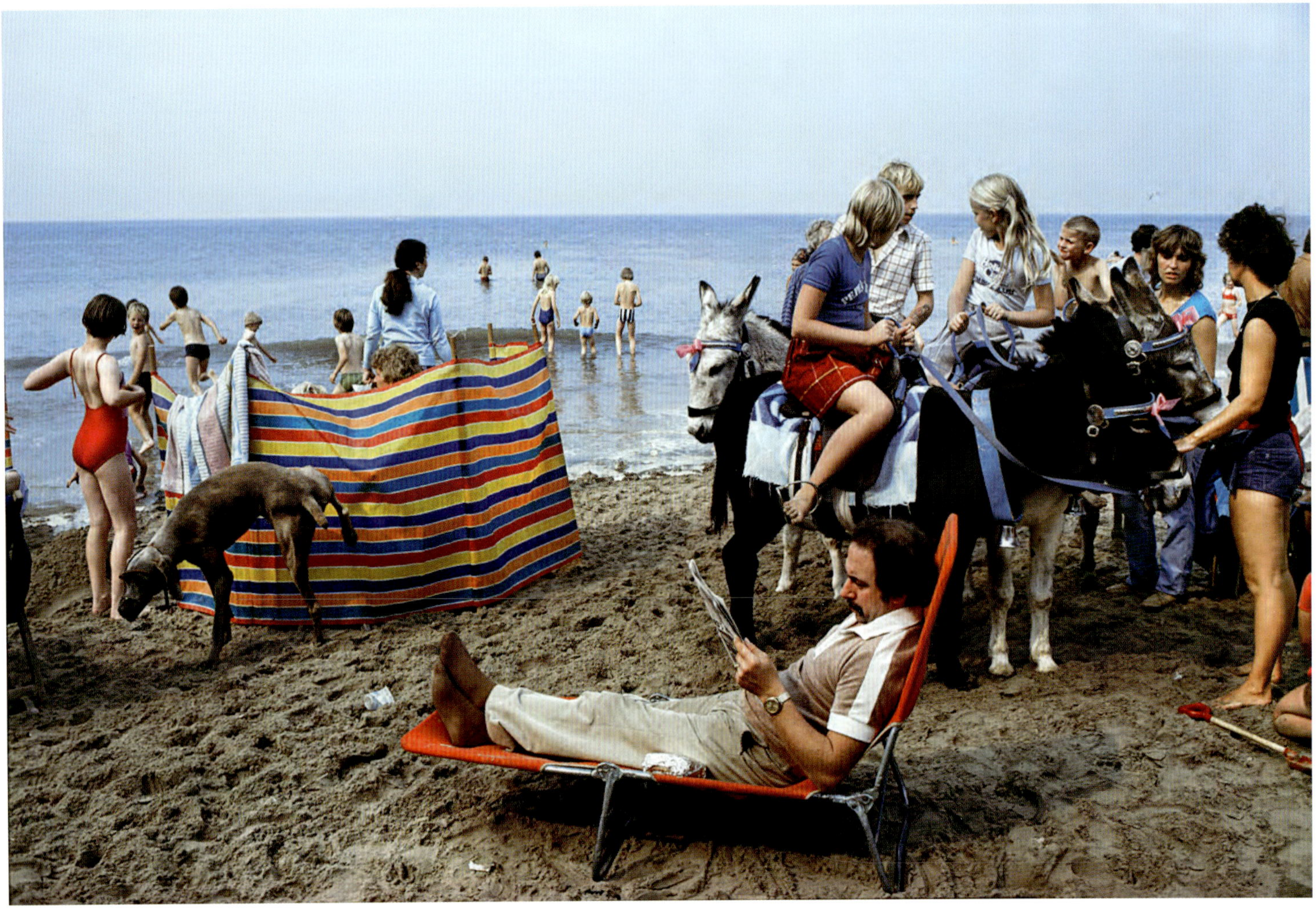

Blackpool beach, 1989.

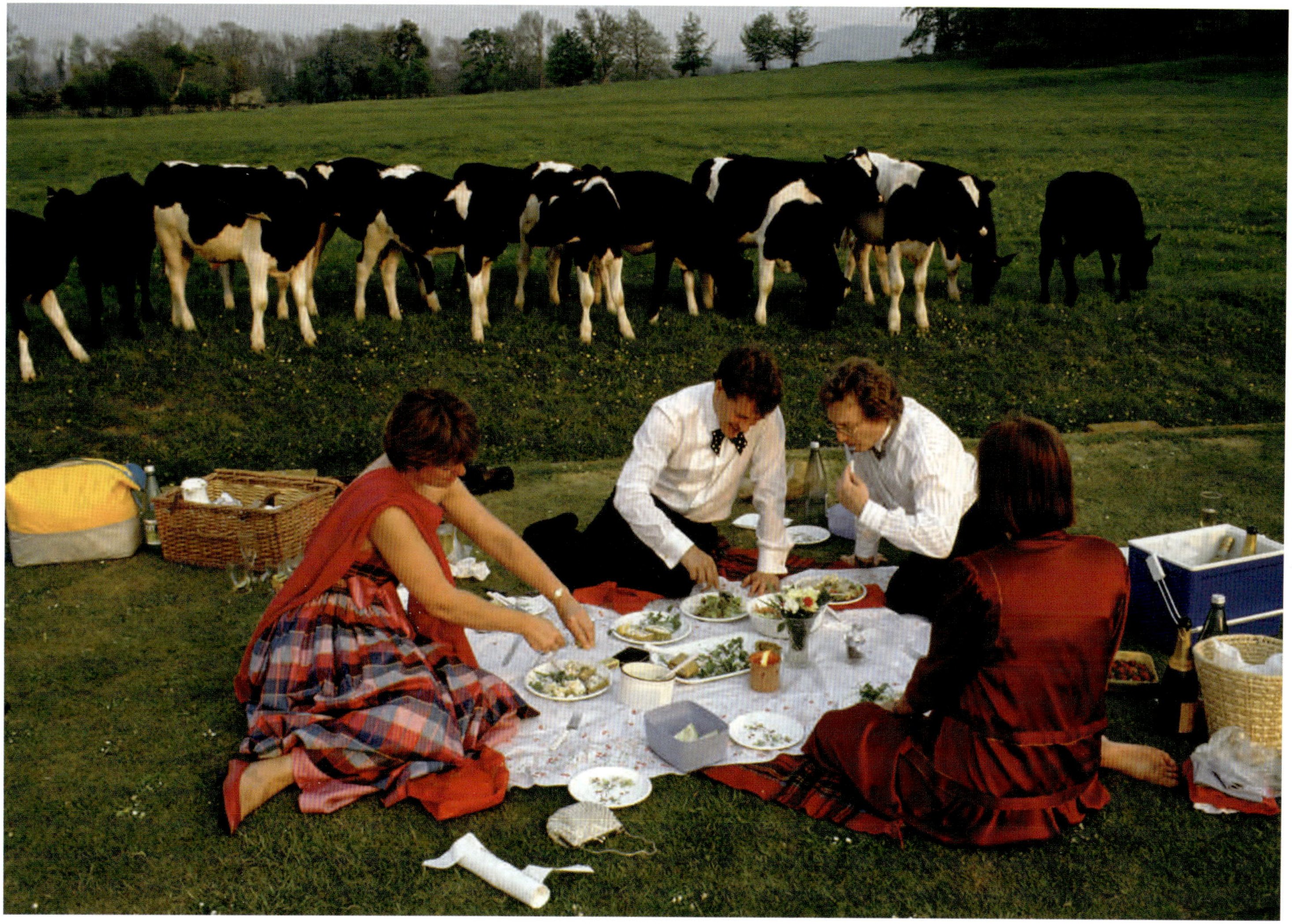

Picnic at the Glyndebourne Opera, 1988.

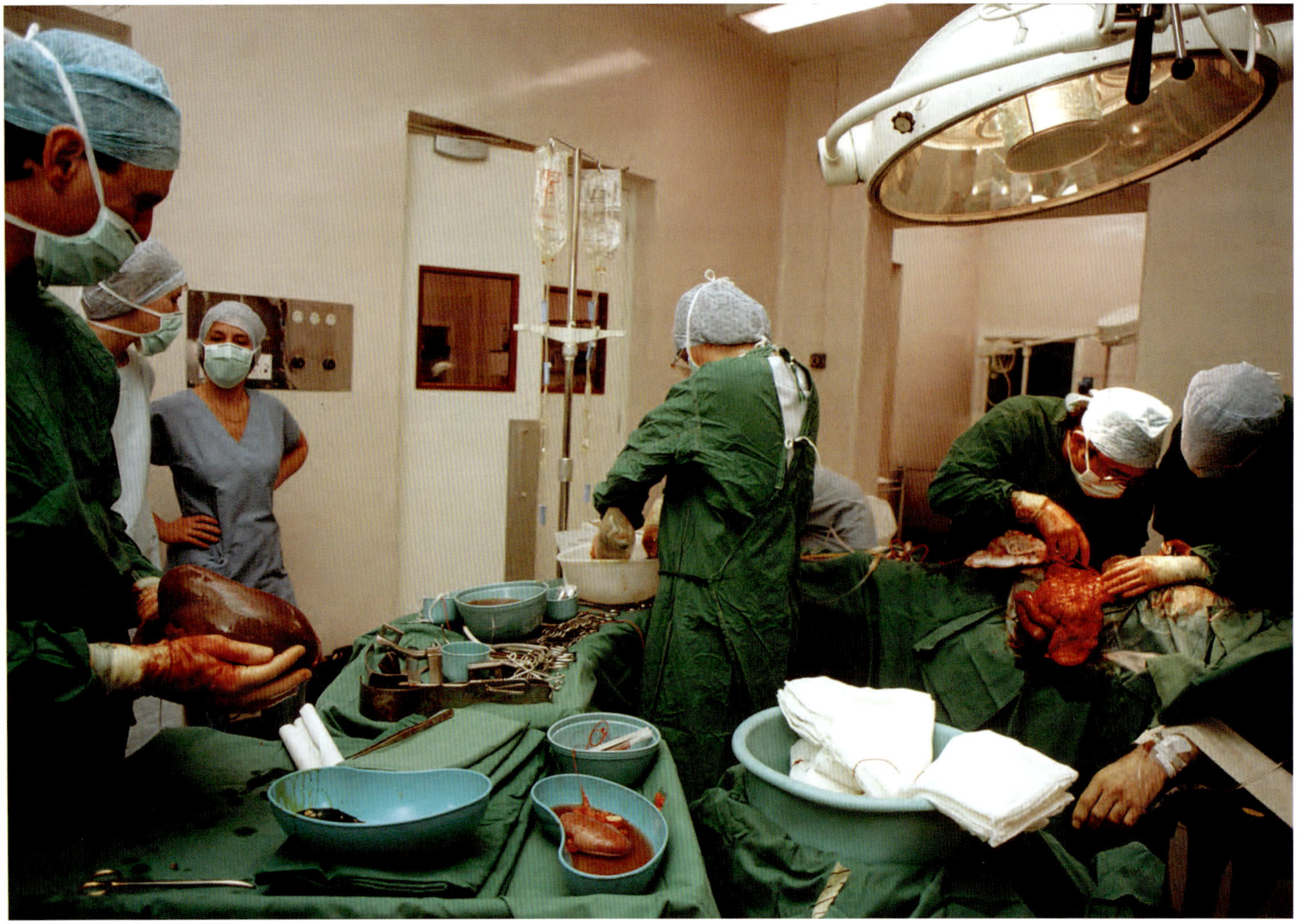

London. Liver transplant operation in Guy's Hospital, 1987.

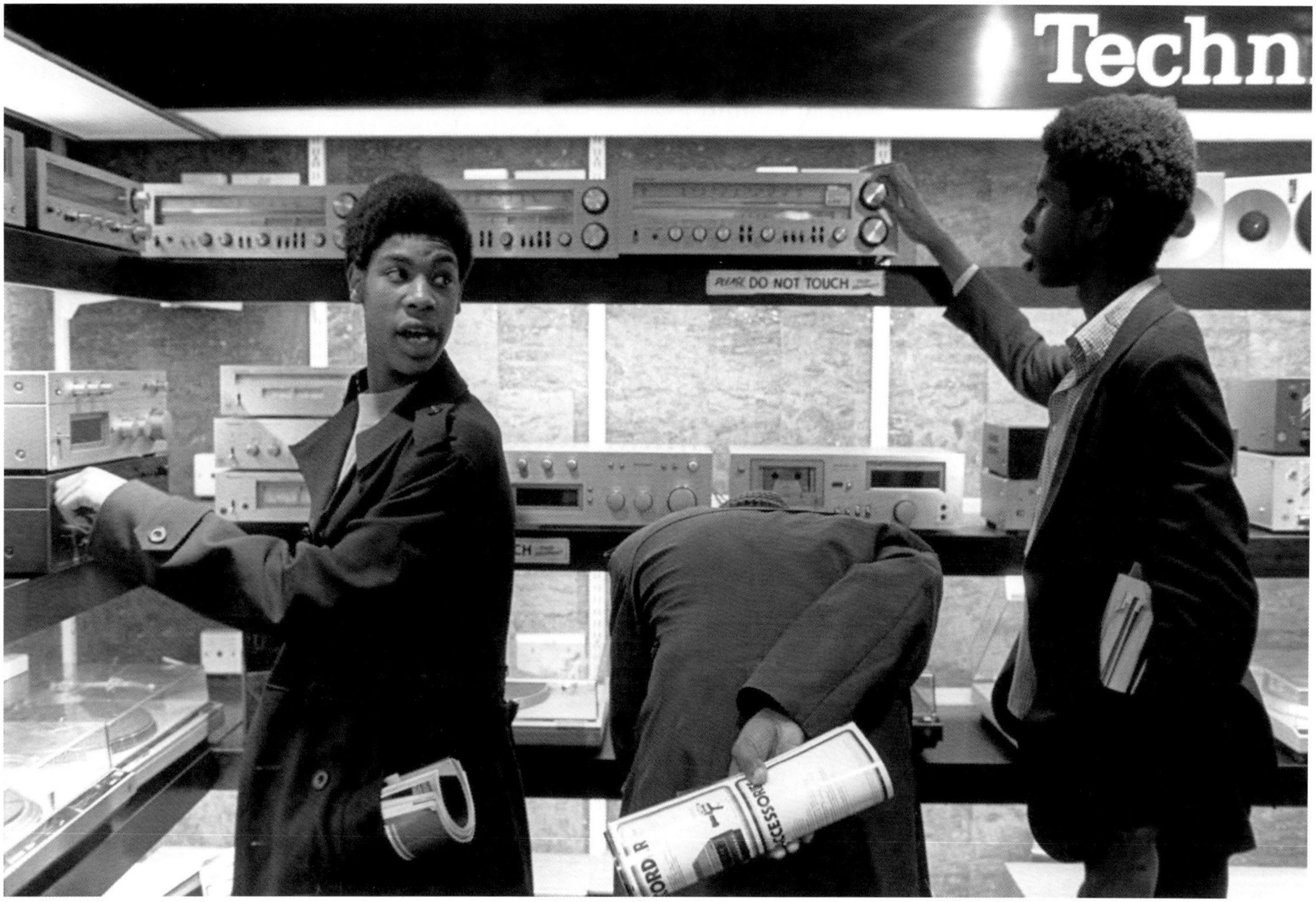

Stereo store in Tottenham Court Road, London, 1980.

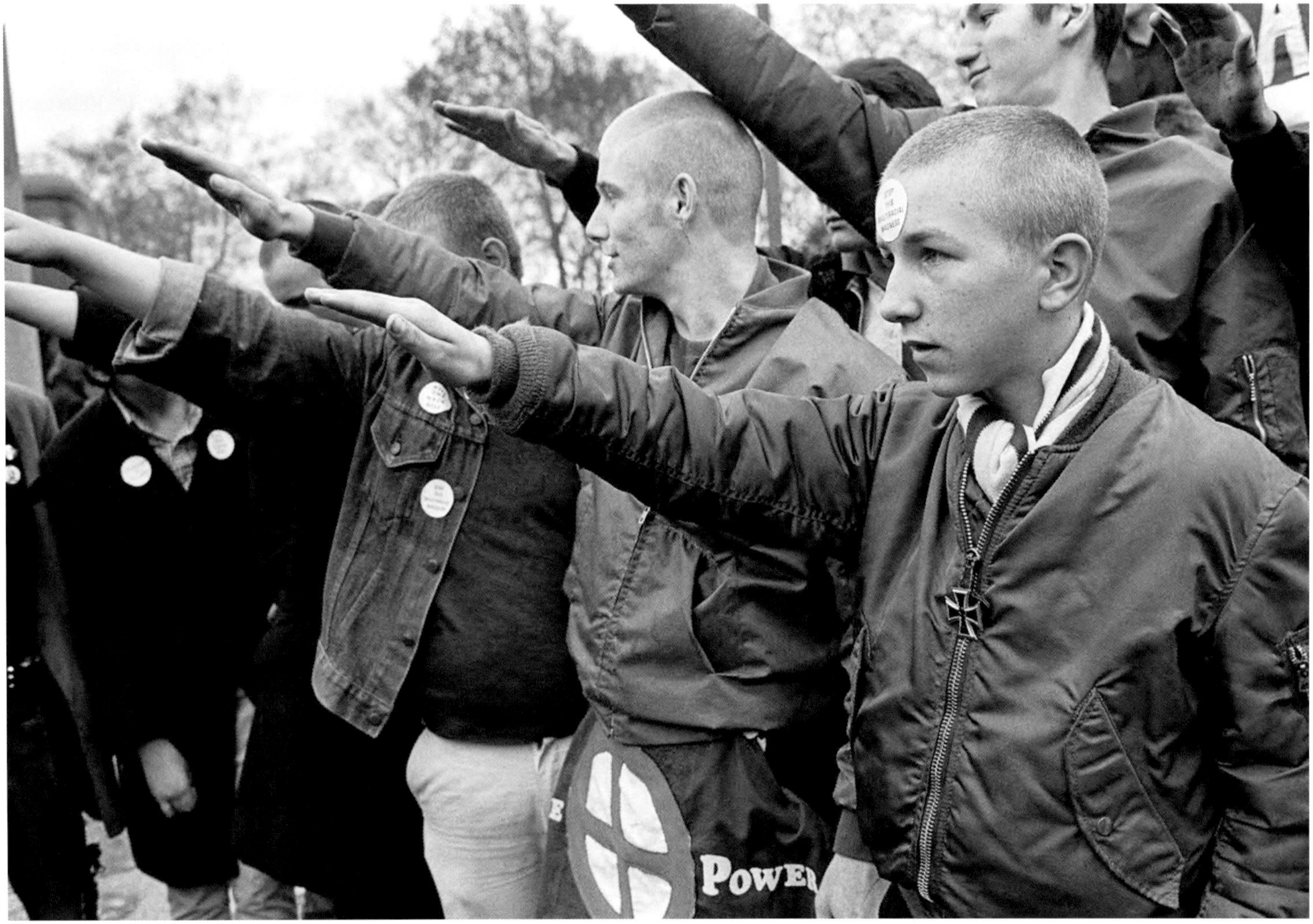

Racists give Nazi salute in London, 1980.

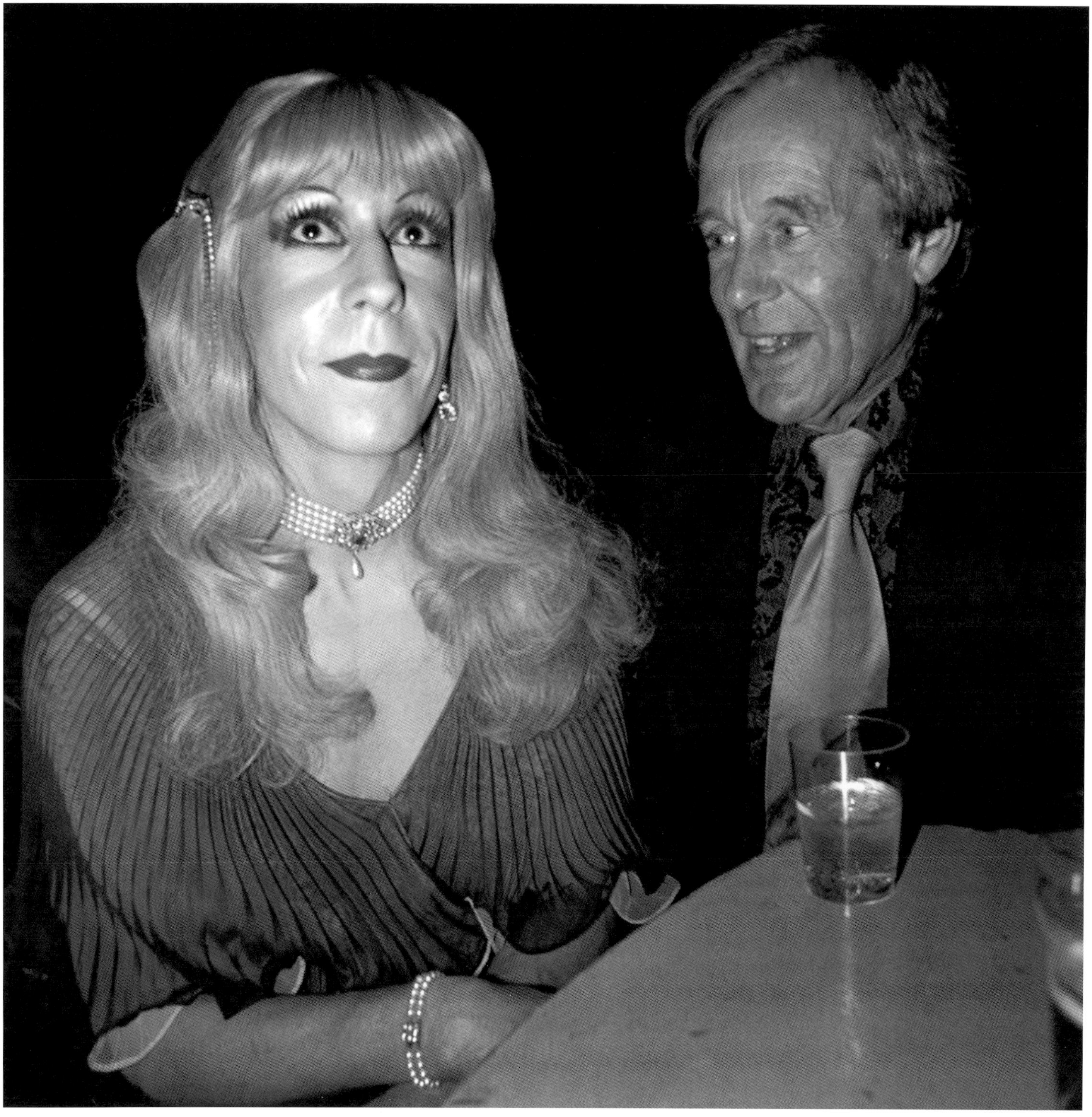

London. Drag Ball, 1982.

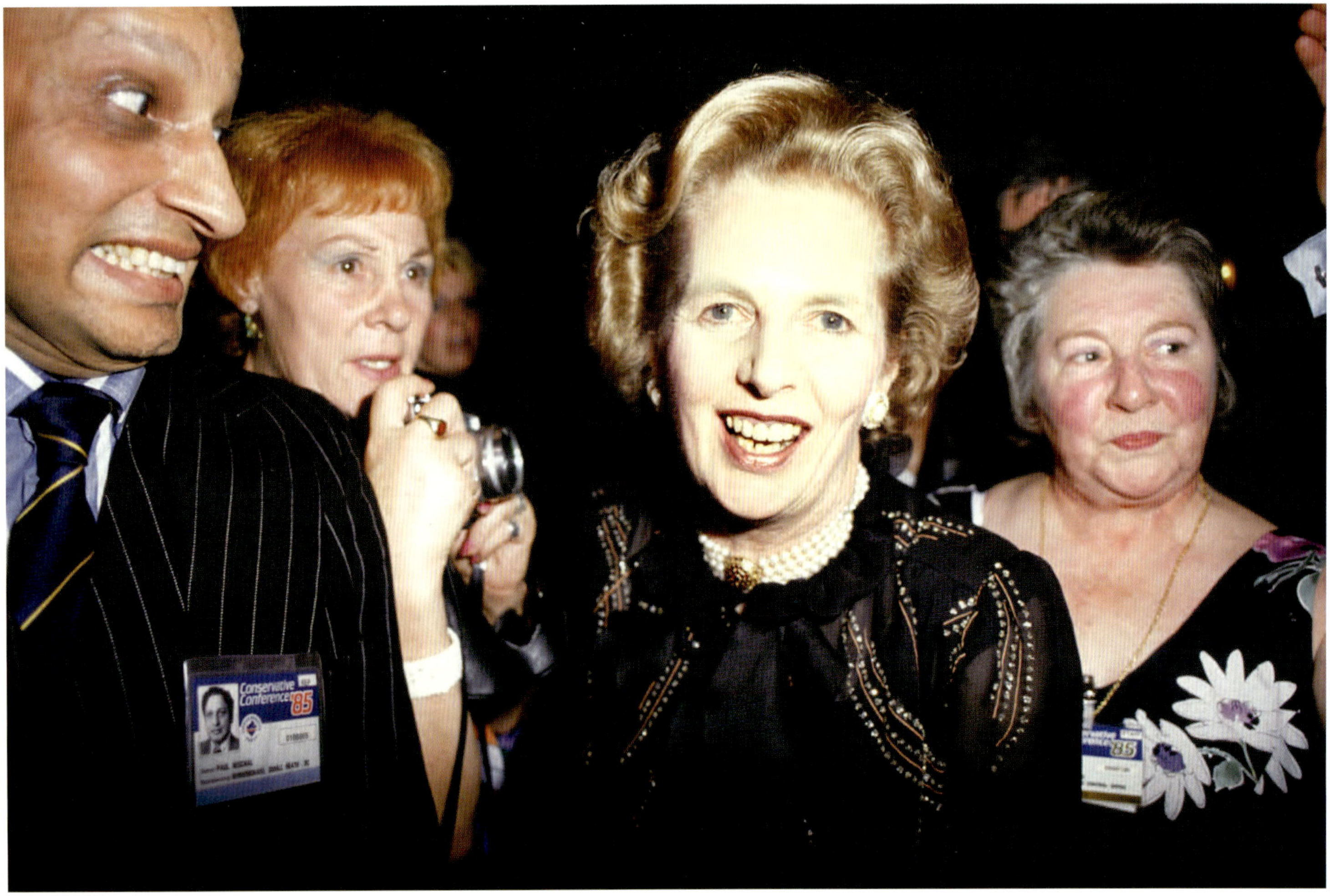

Prime Minister Margaret Thatcher during the Conservative Party Conference in Blackpool, 1985.

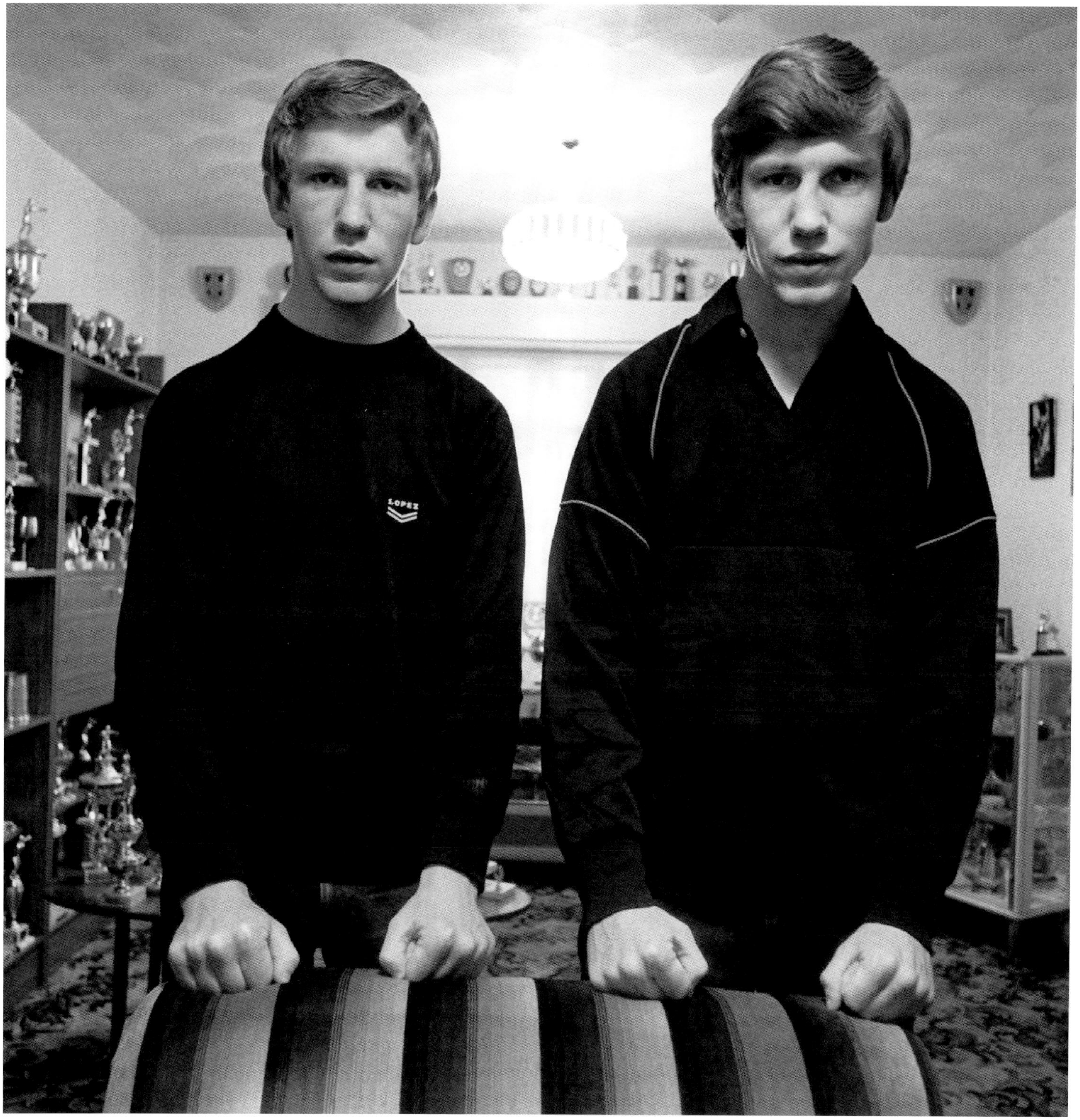

Boxing brothers in Hartlepool, 1982.

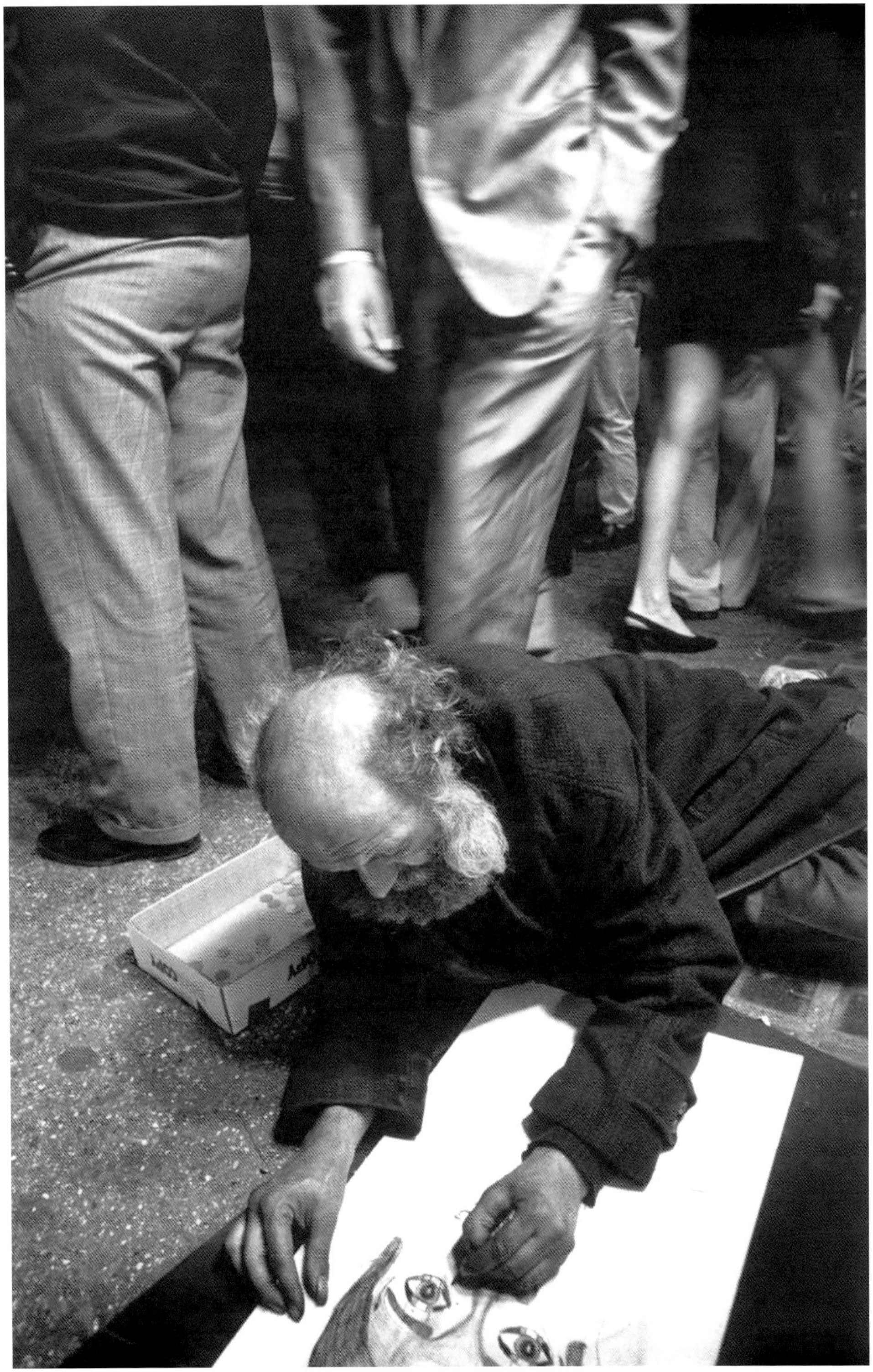

London. Bernard the Busker drawing in Leicester Square, 1989.

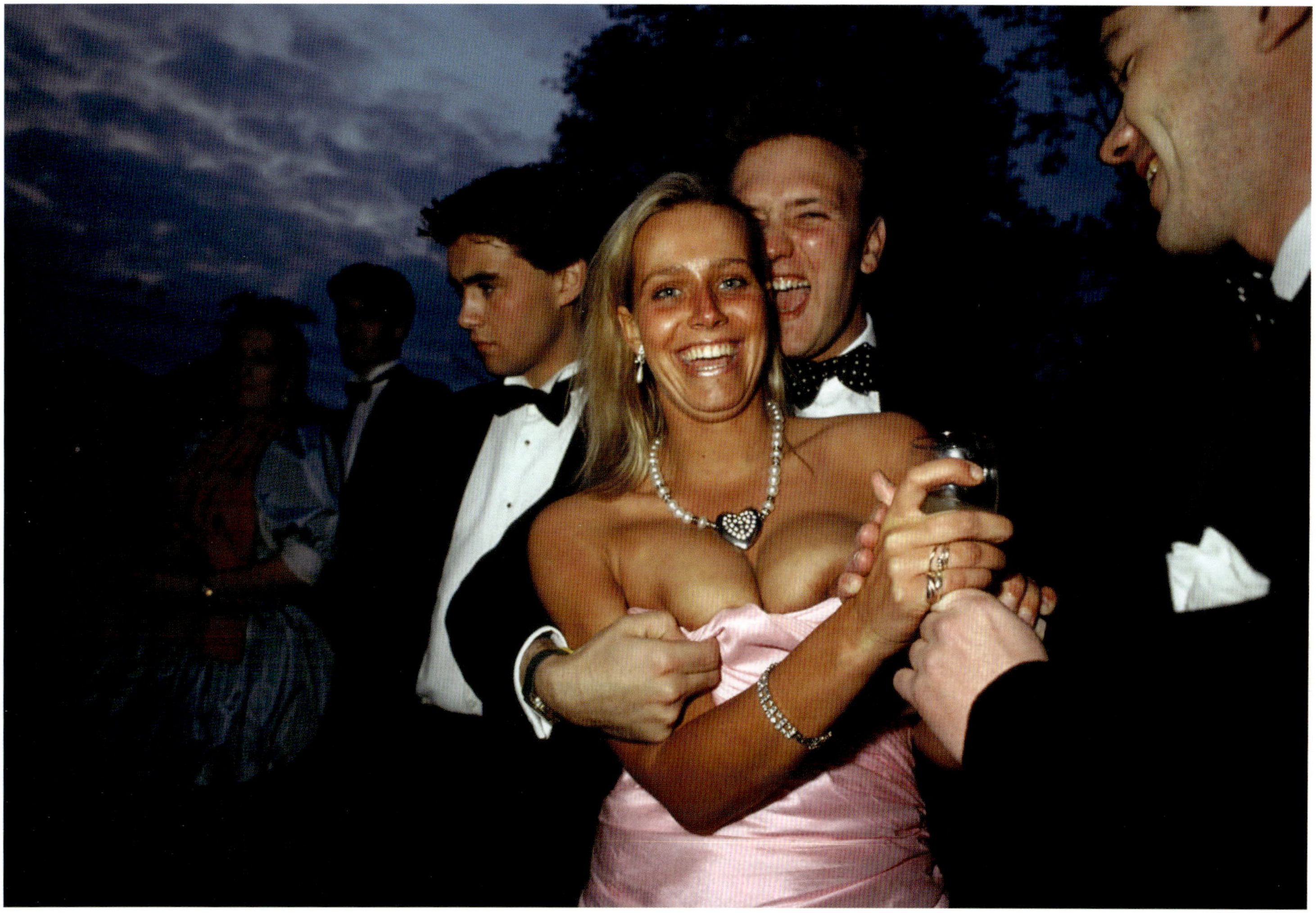

London. Juliana's Summer Party, 1989.

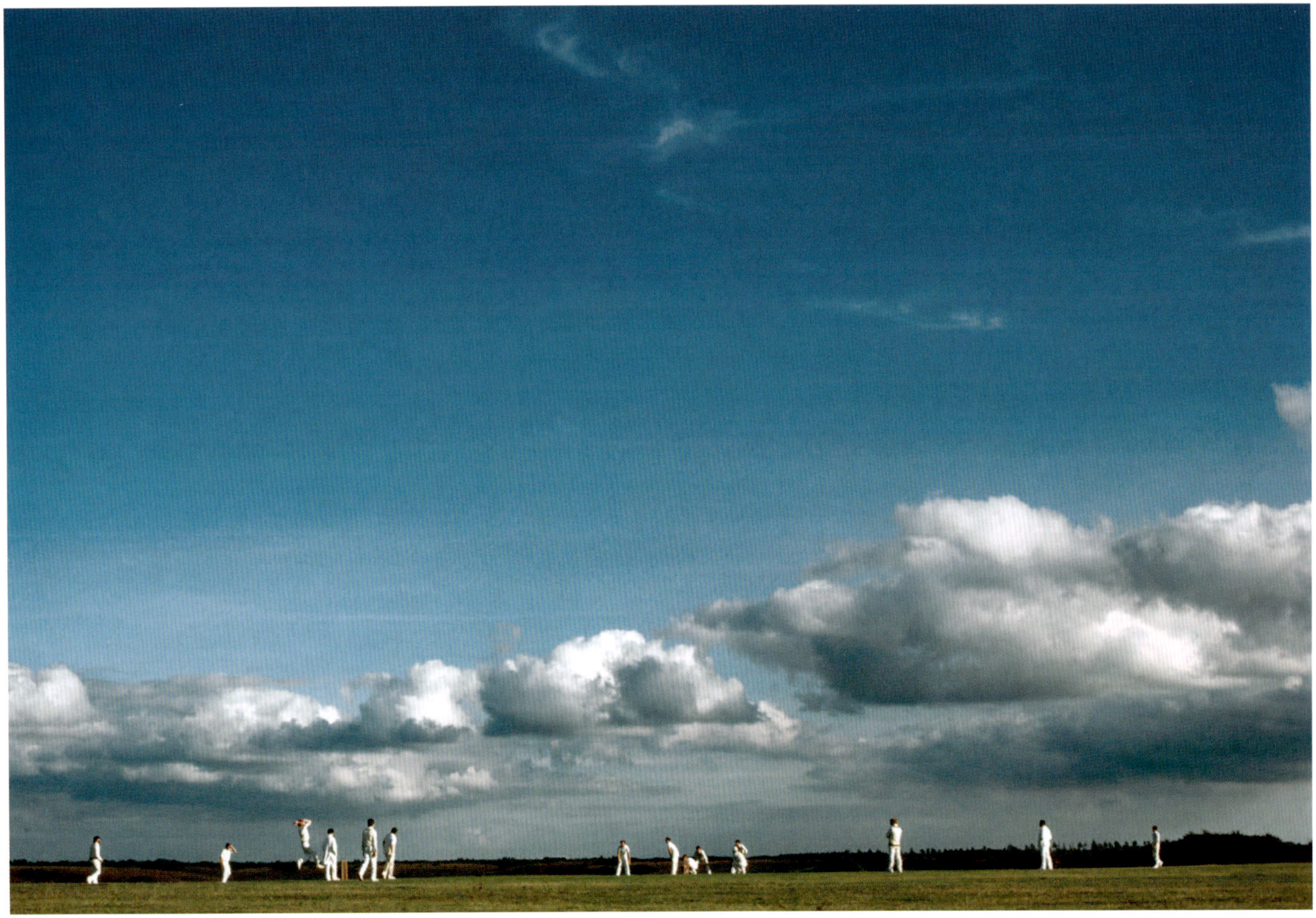

Hampshire cricket match, 1989.

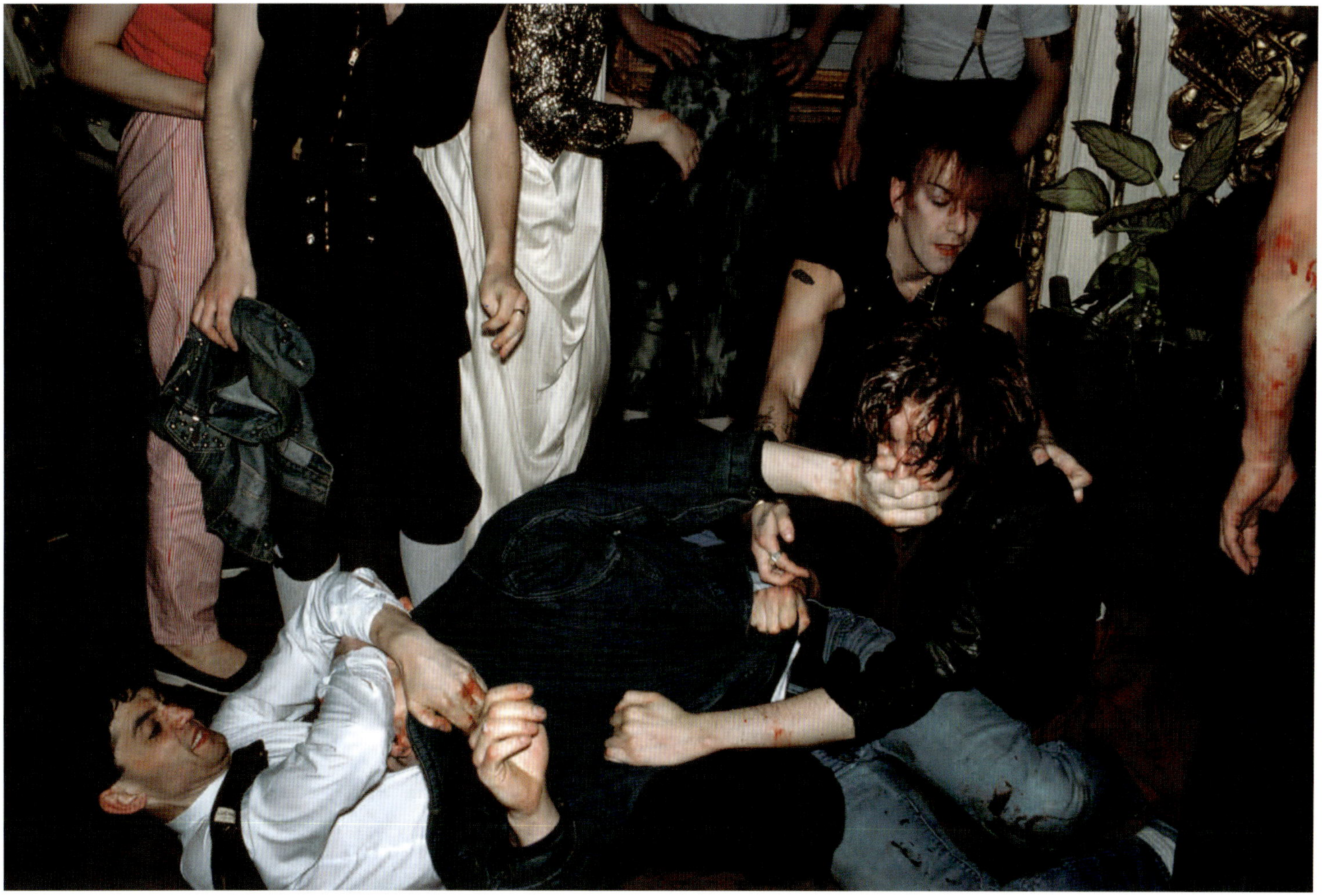

London. A fight in Camden Palace night club, 1989.

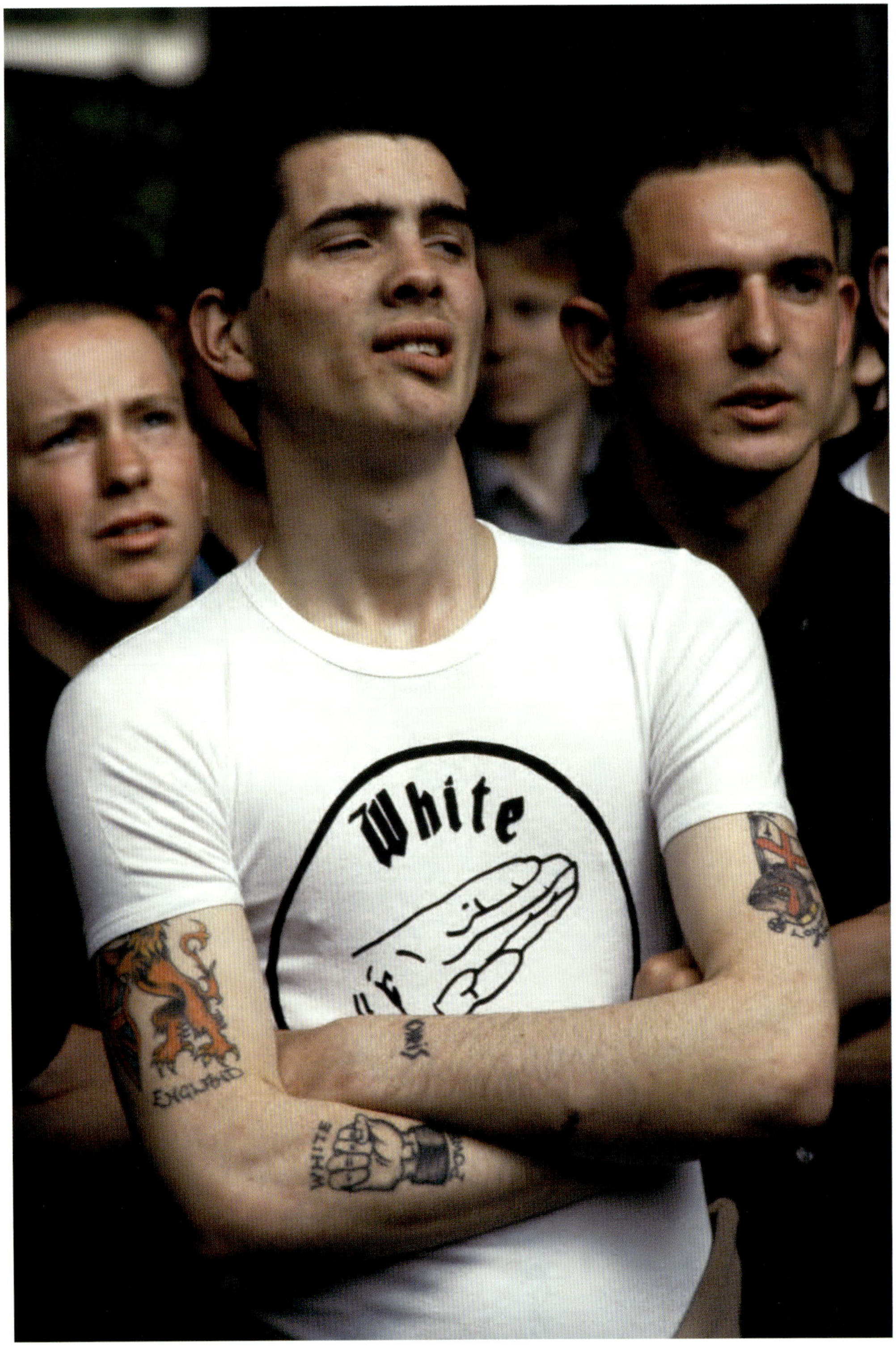

London. National Front movement demonstration, 1989.

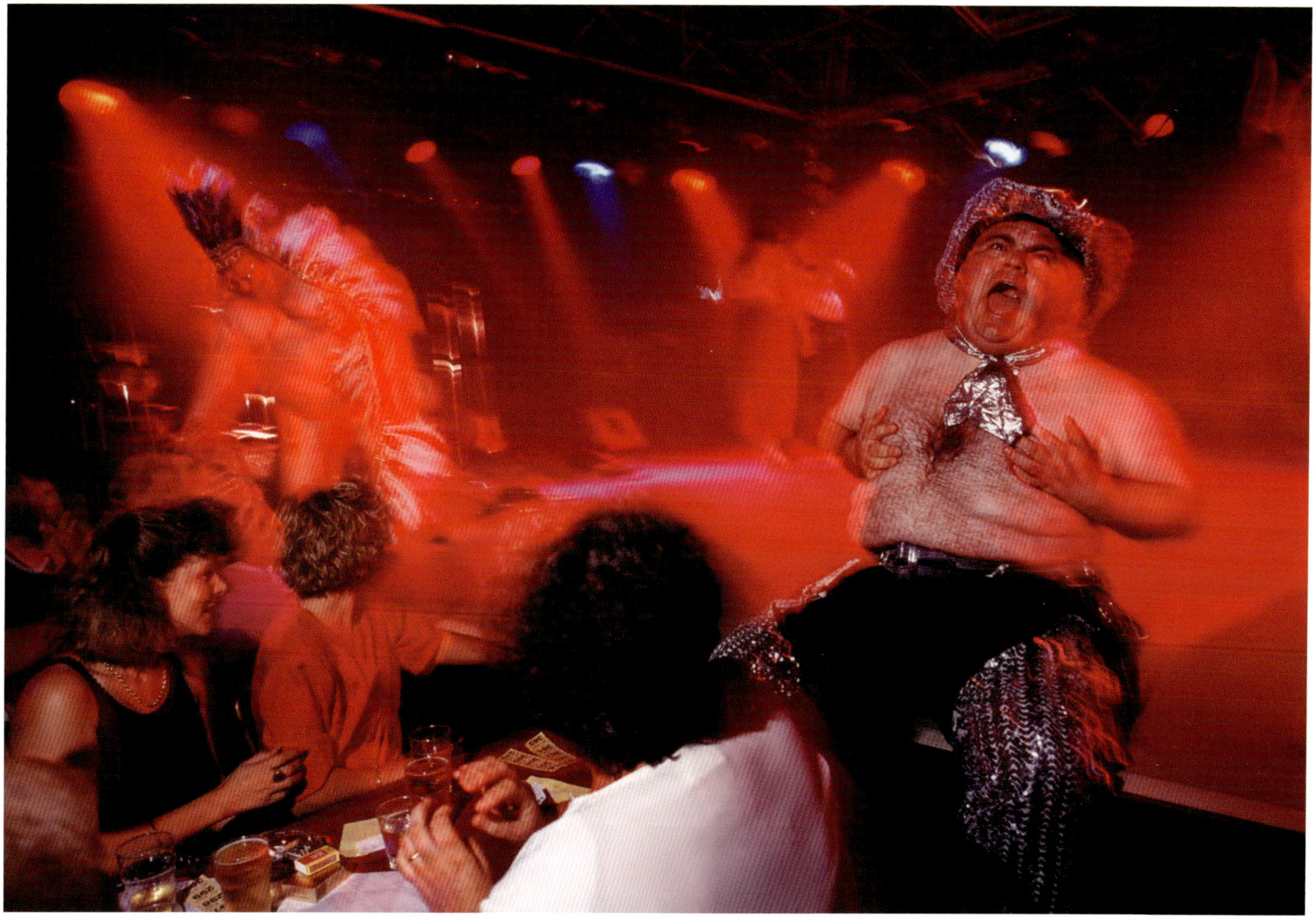

Blobendales perform at hen party in Essex, 1995.

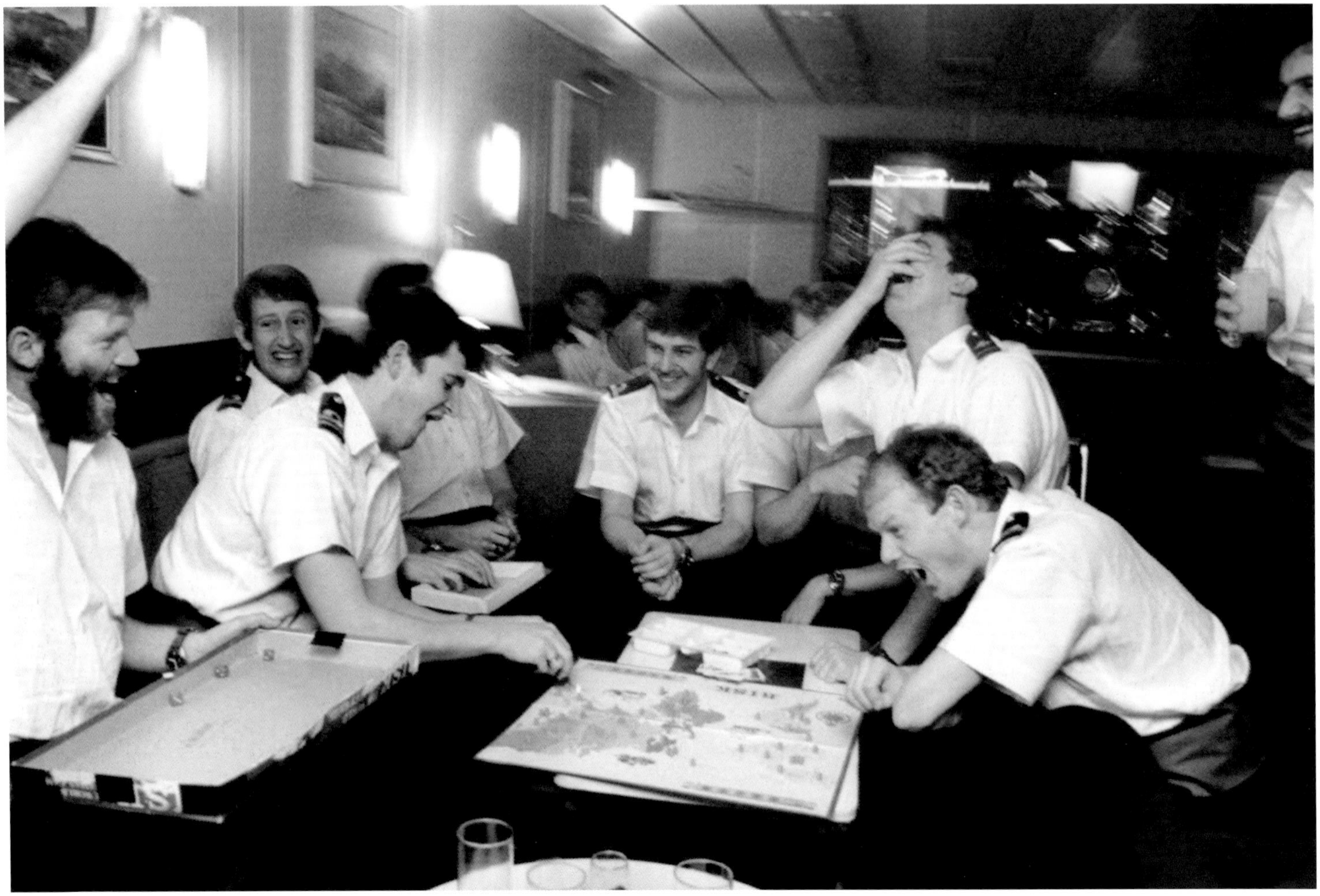

Officers relaxing on the aircraft carrier *HMS Invincible*, 1982.

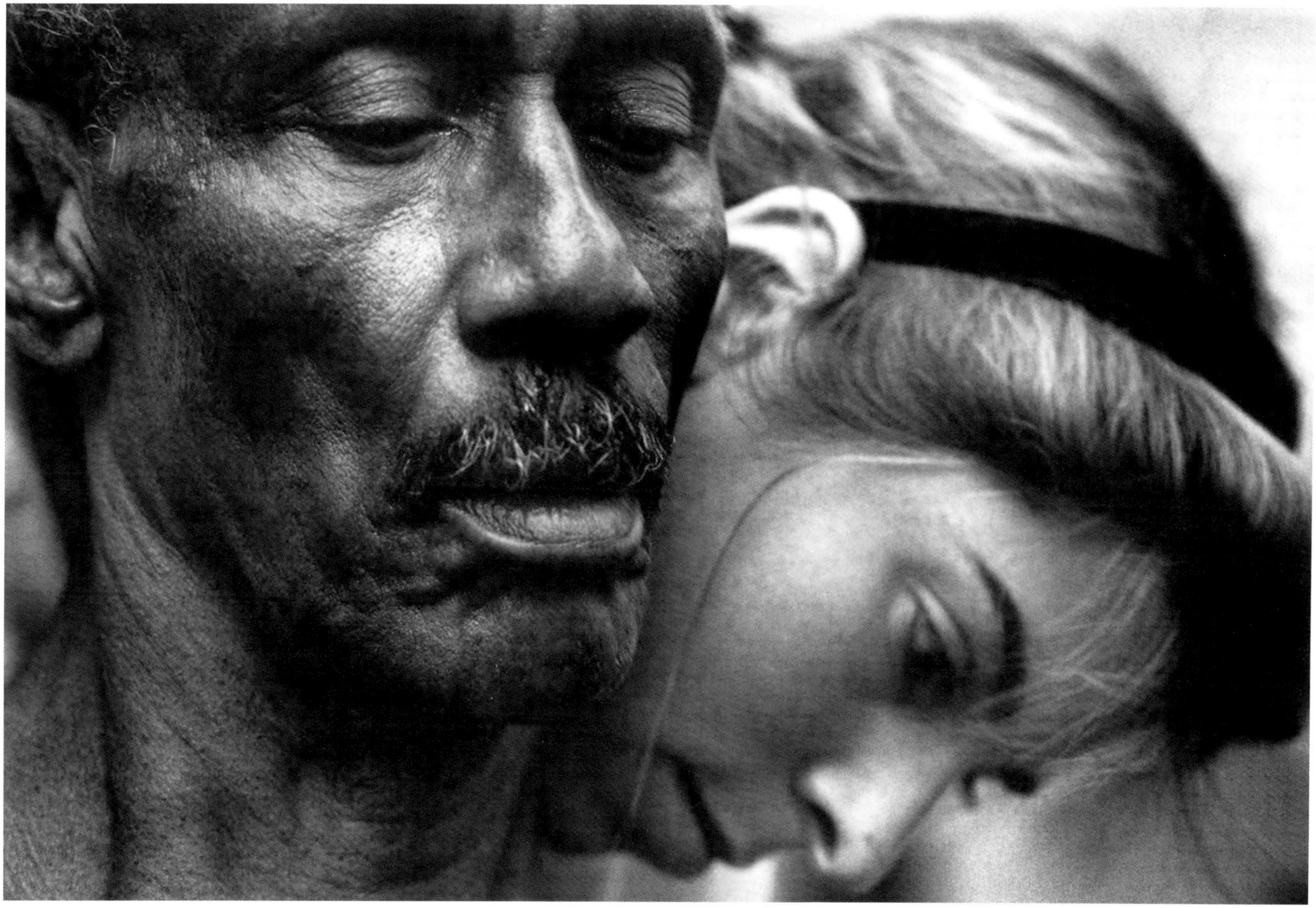

London. St Thomas's Hospital, Physiotherapist works with a patient, 1990.

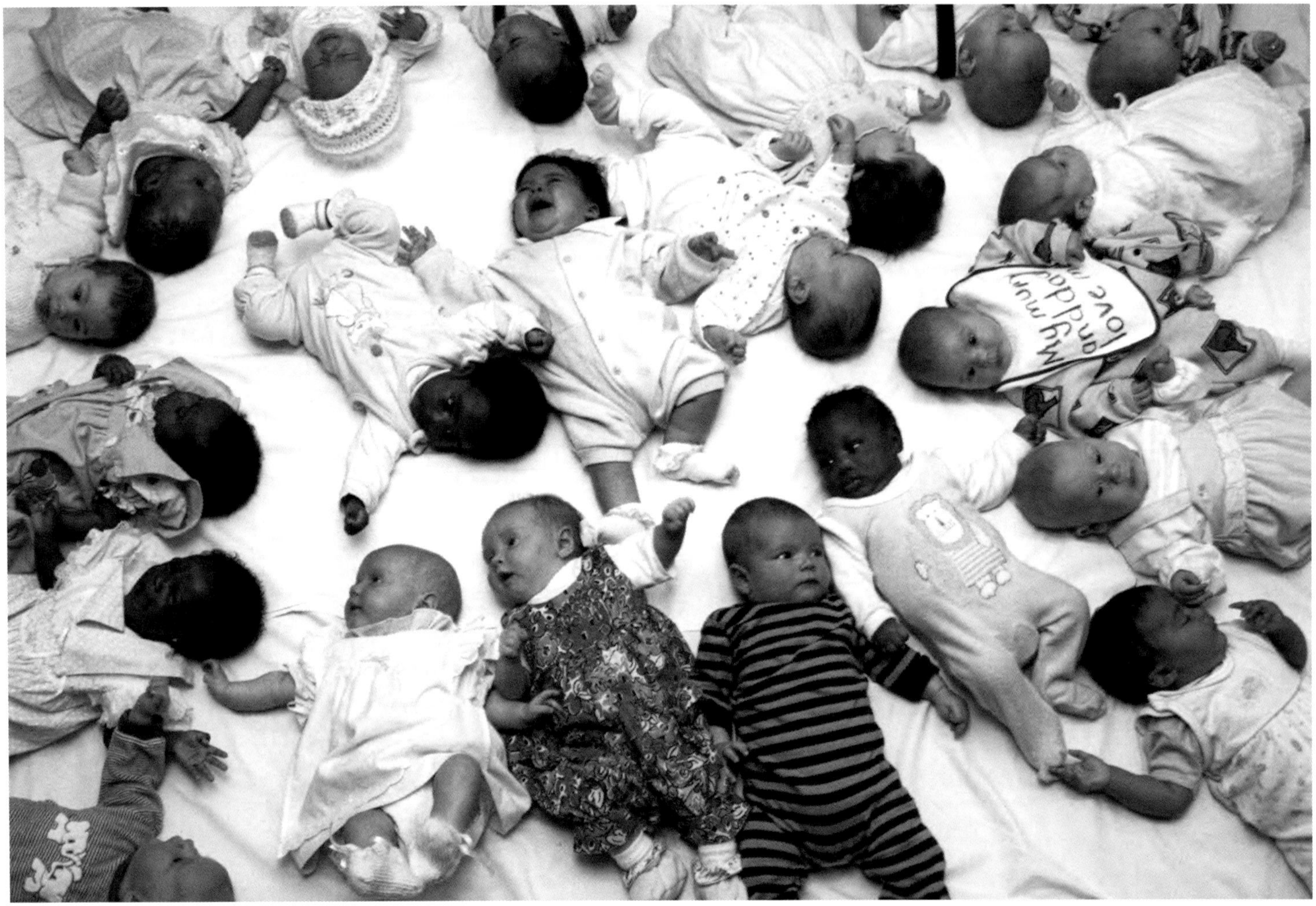

London. St. Thomas's Hospital. Babies at reunion of those mothers who gave birth in 1990.

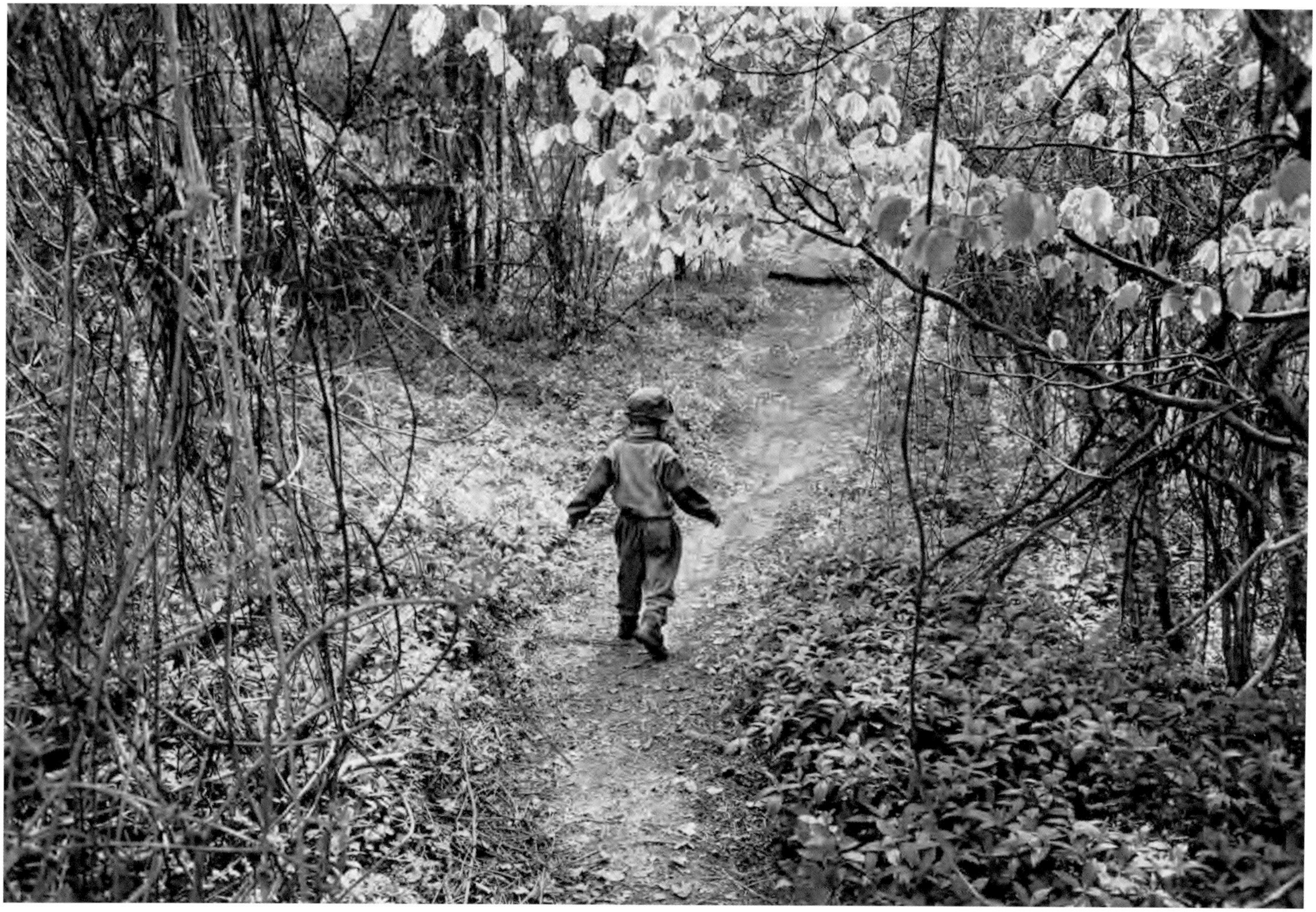

Cameron in the woods.

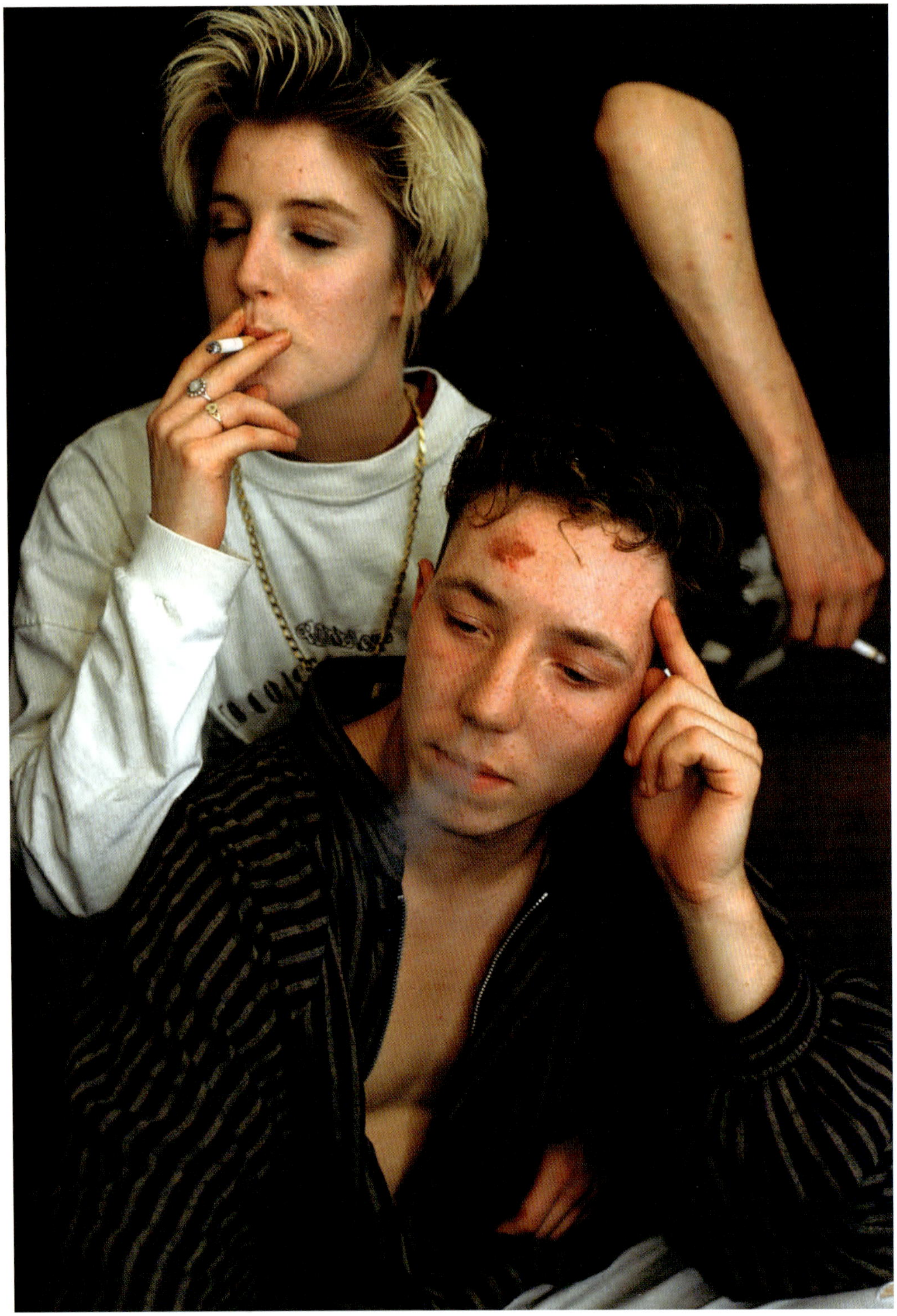

London. Homeless youths in a day centre, 1991.

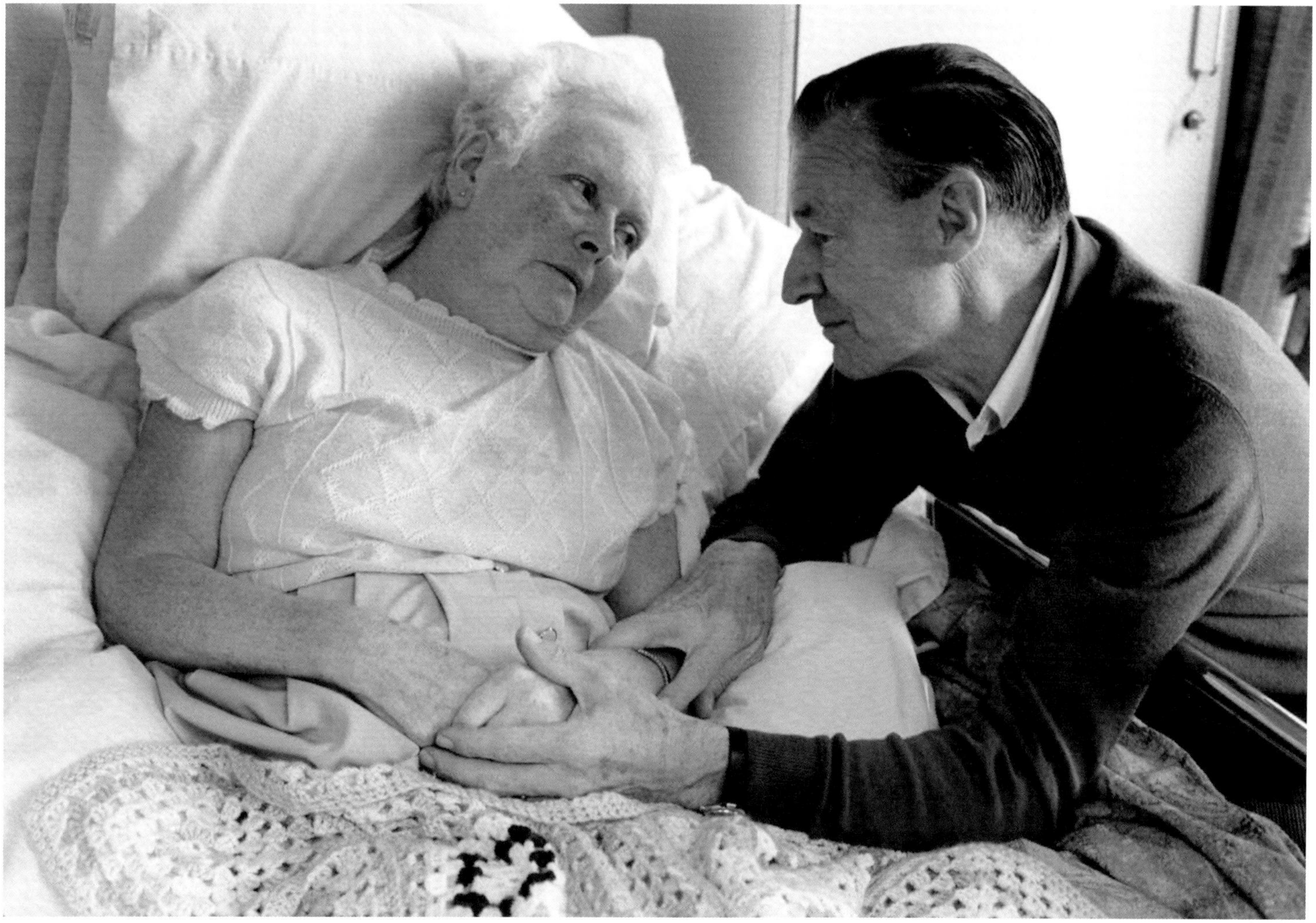

Couple in a hospice for terminally ill, 1992.

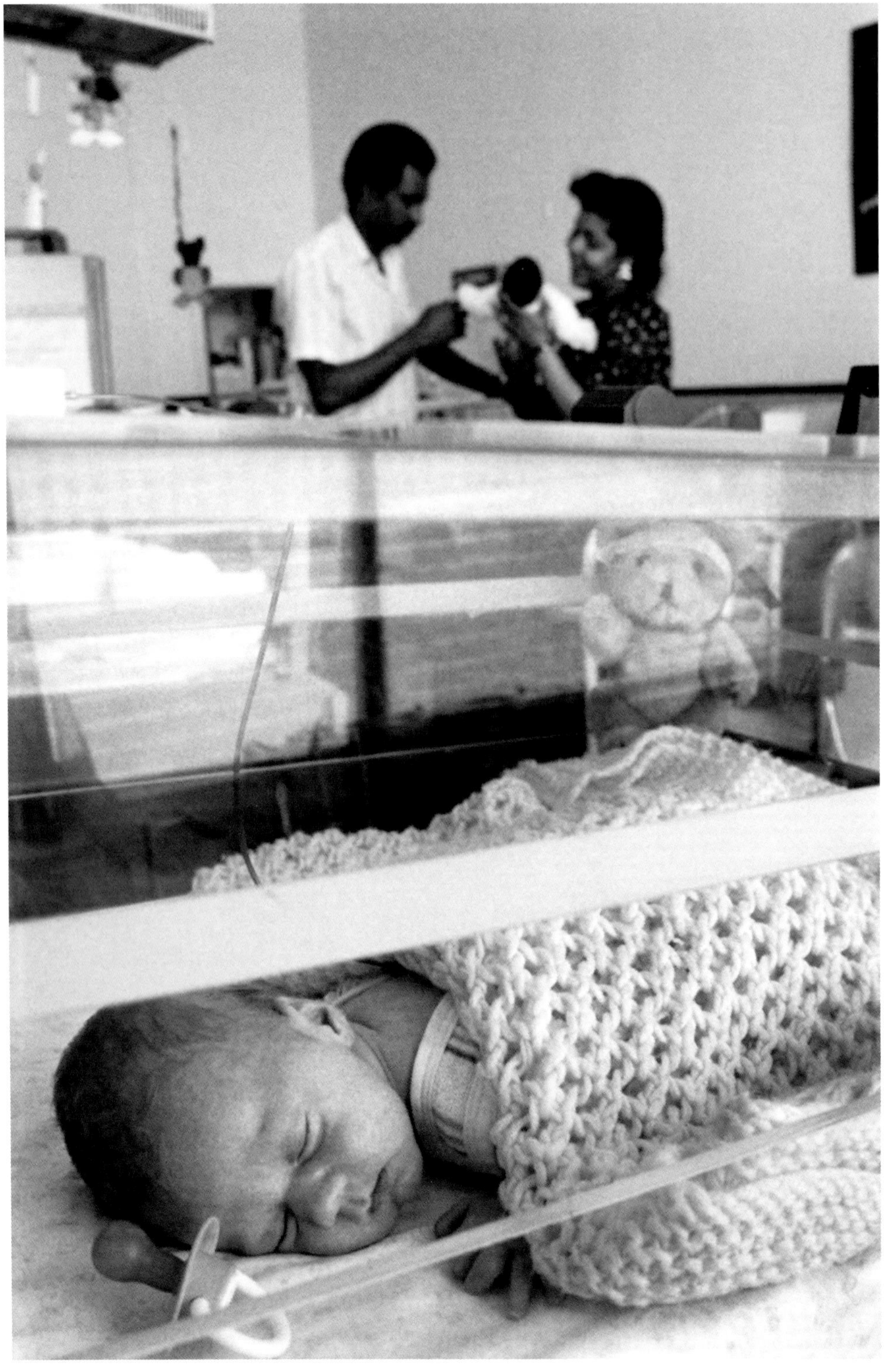

London. St Thomas's Hospital. Child in incubator in premature unit, 1990.

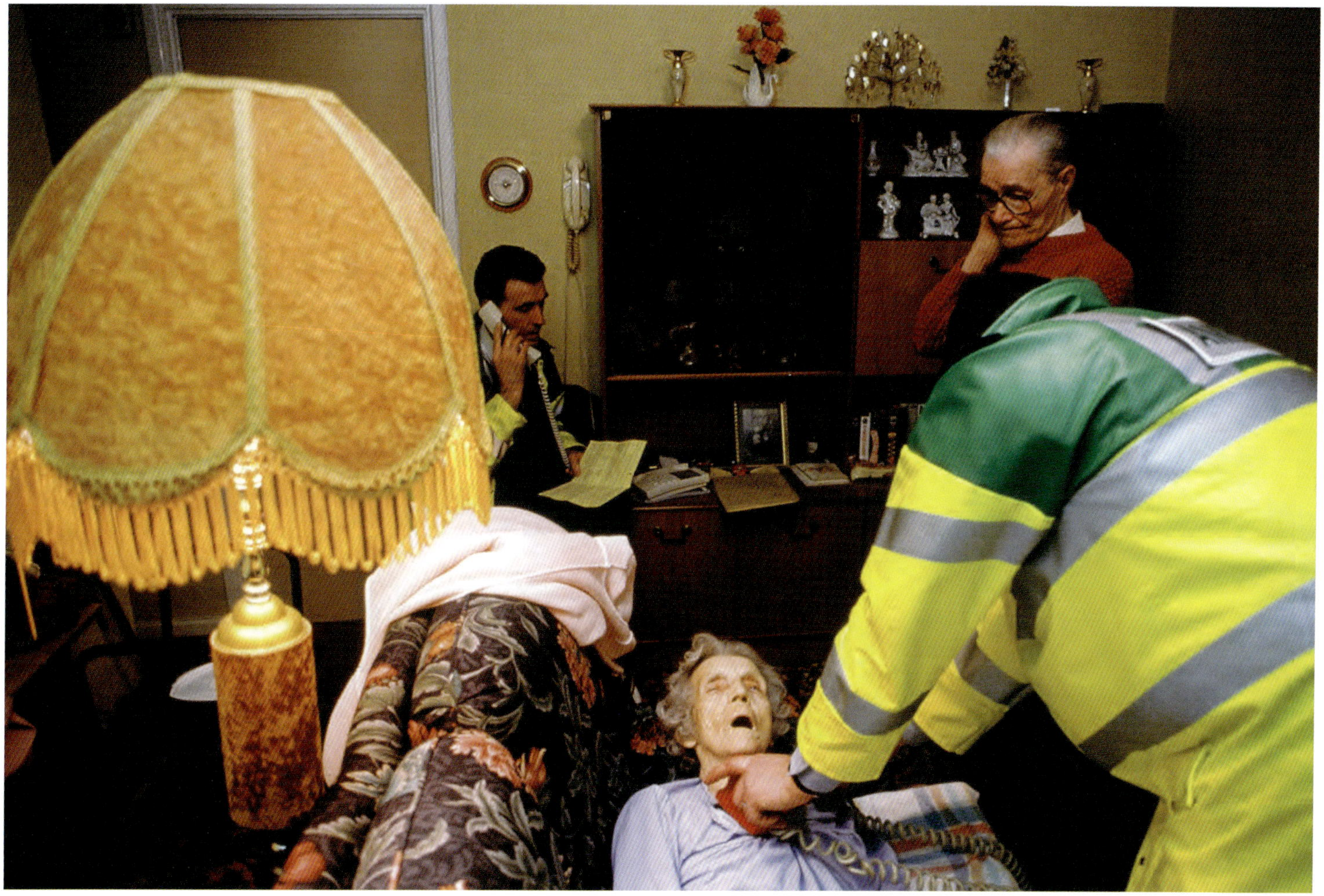

Manchester. Ambulance Service. Unsuccessful attempt to revive an old lady while her husband looks on, 1994.

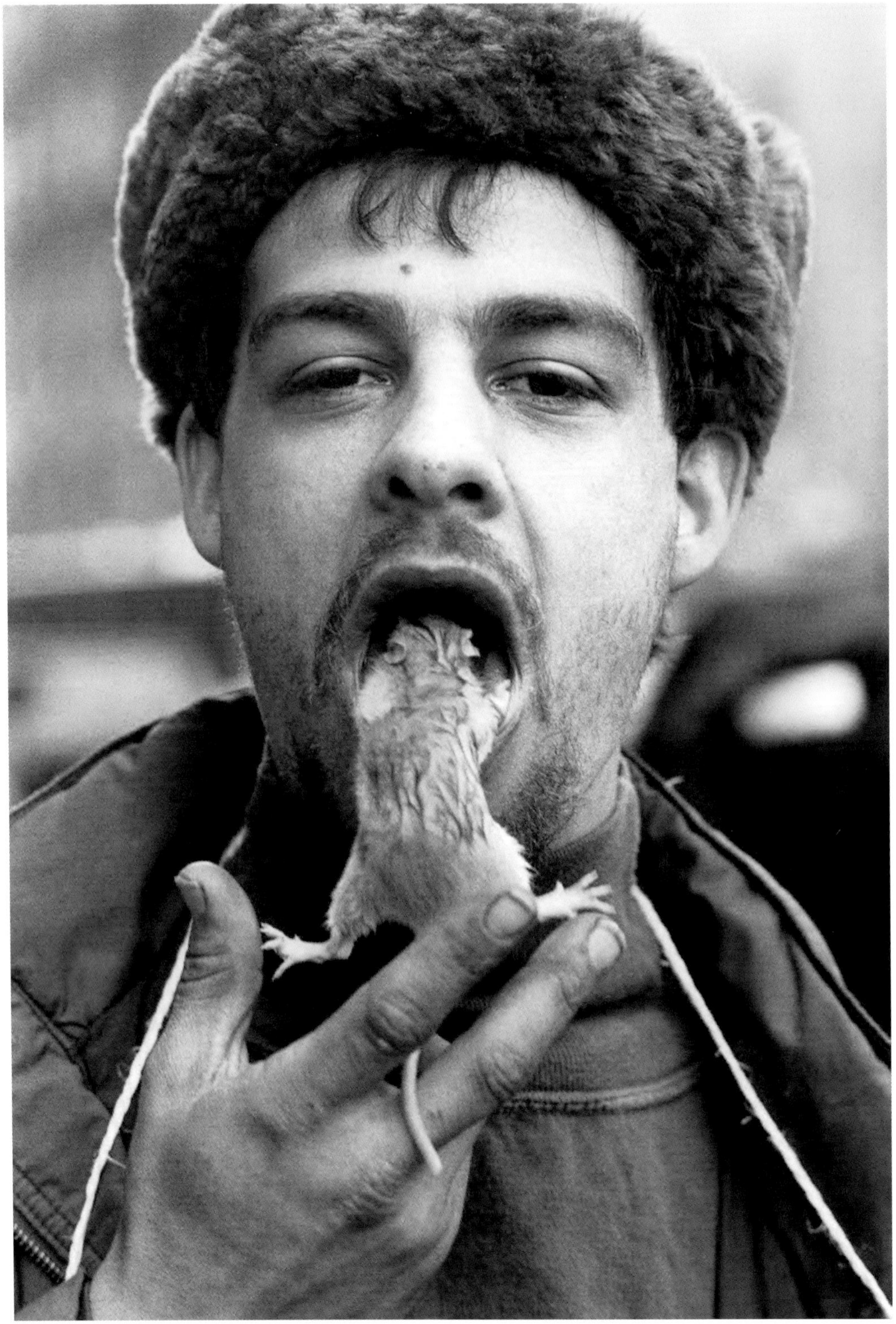

London. Young squatter with his pet gerbil, 1994.

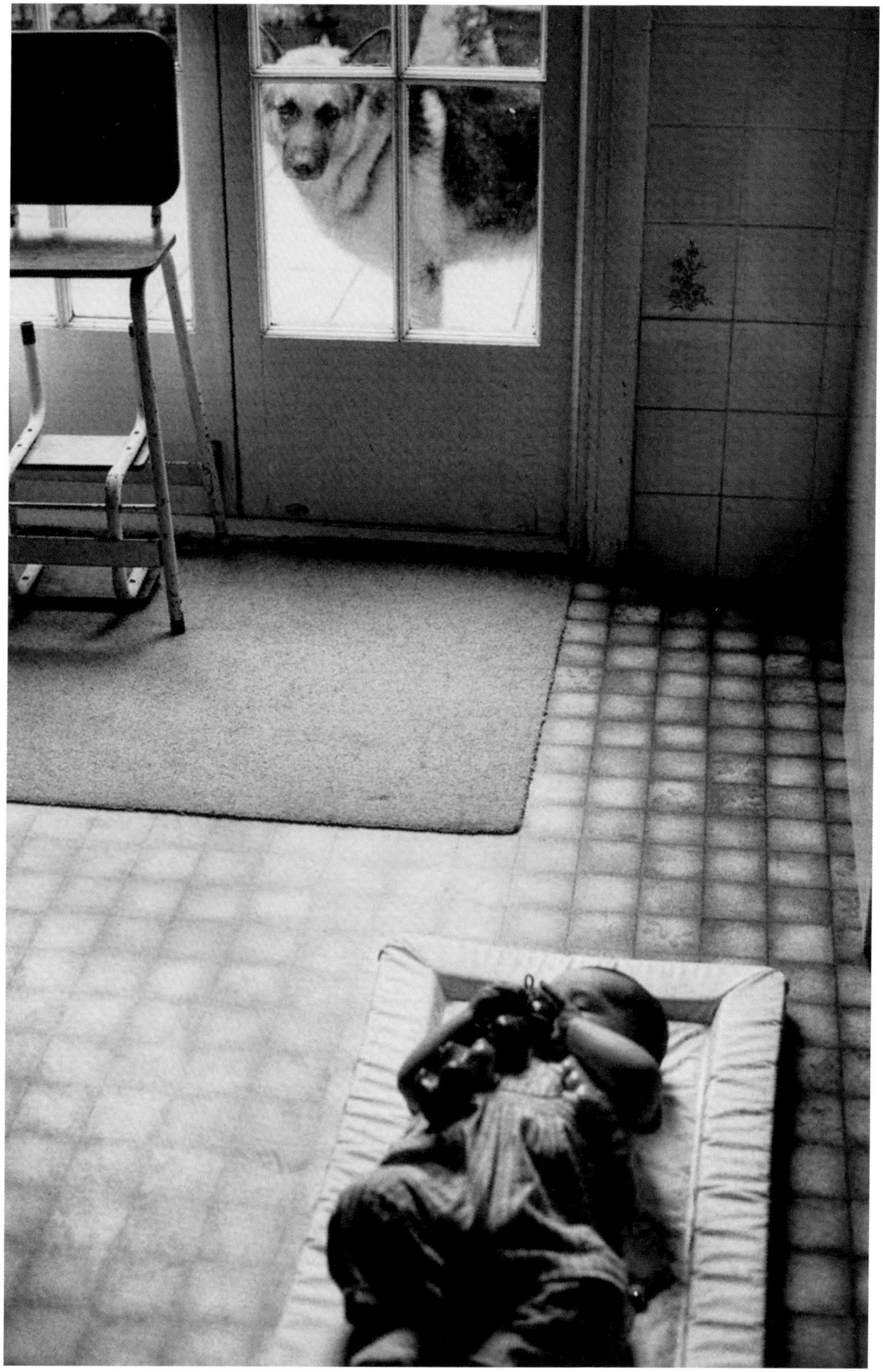

Child in a home in South London, 1991.

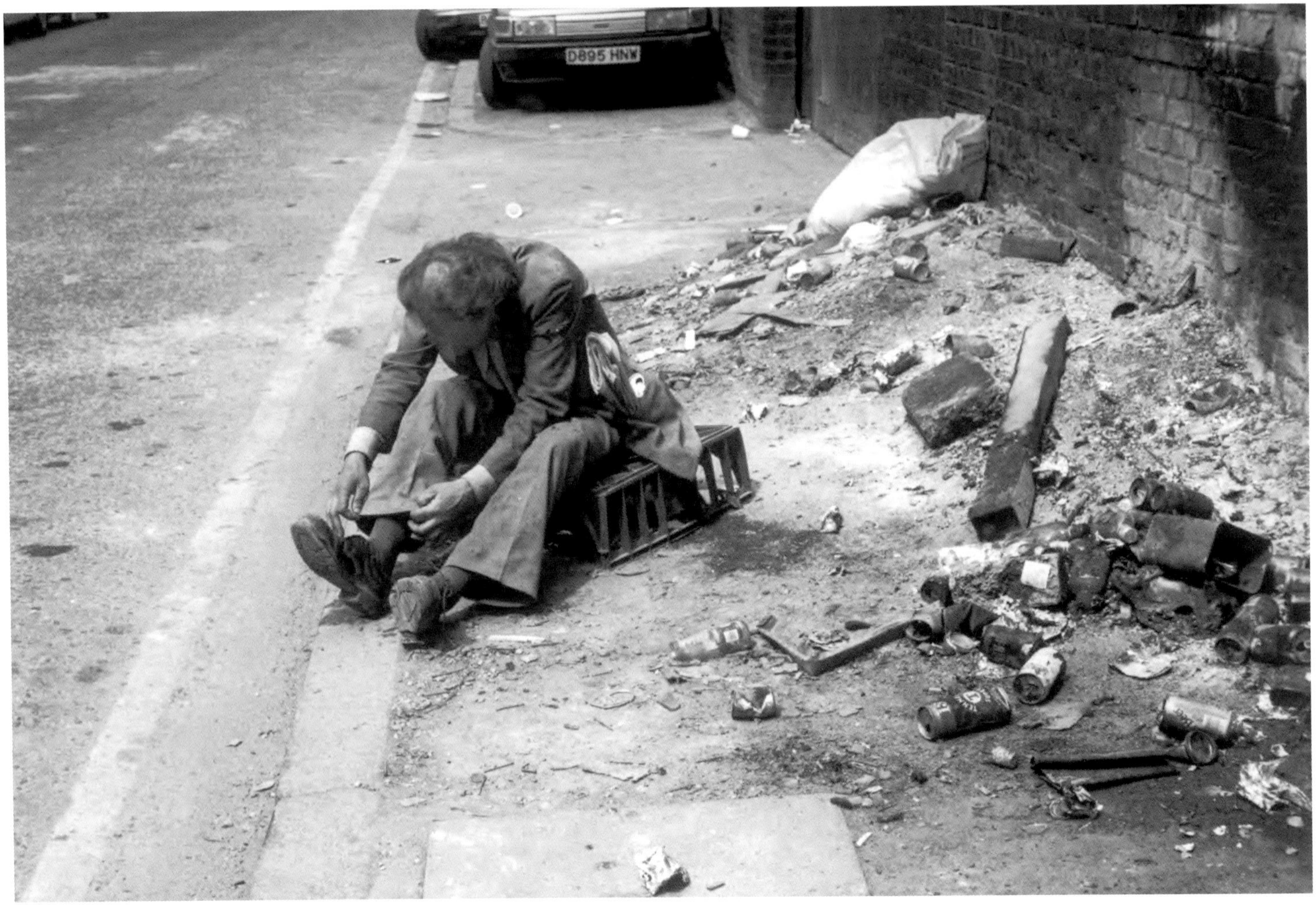

London homeless man, 1993.

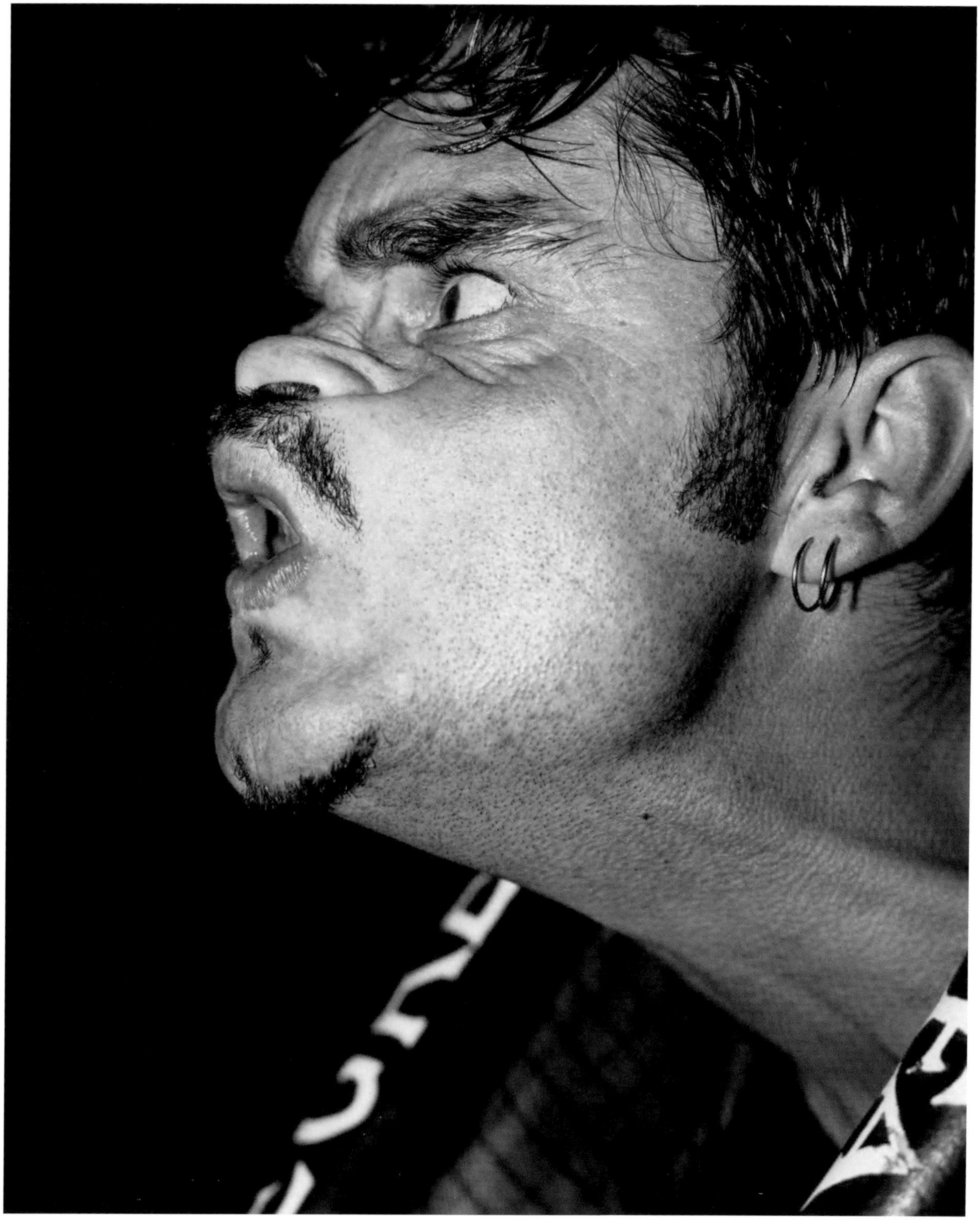

Gurning World Championships in Egremont, Cumbria, 1998.

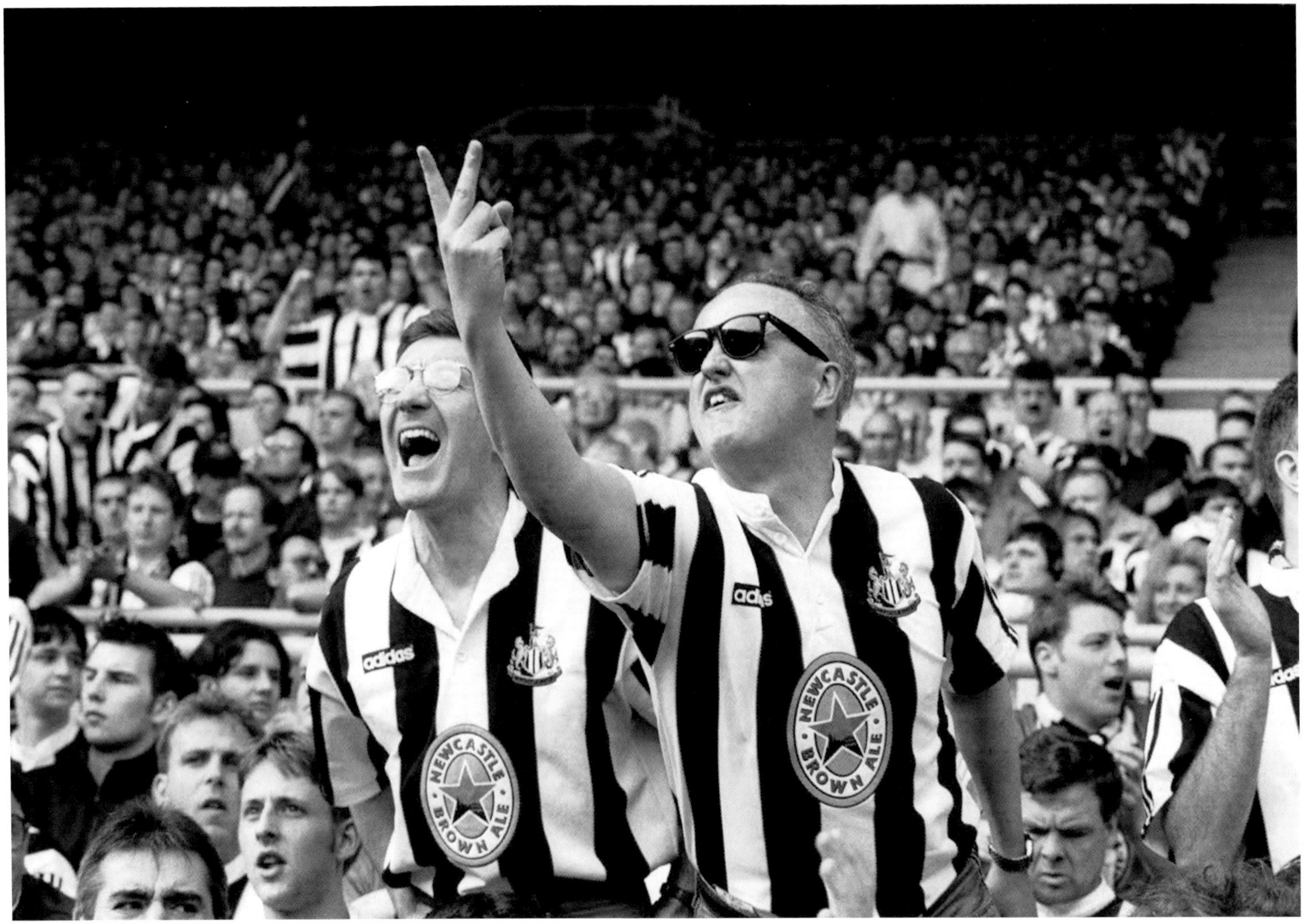

Newcastle fans abuse the referee, 1996.

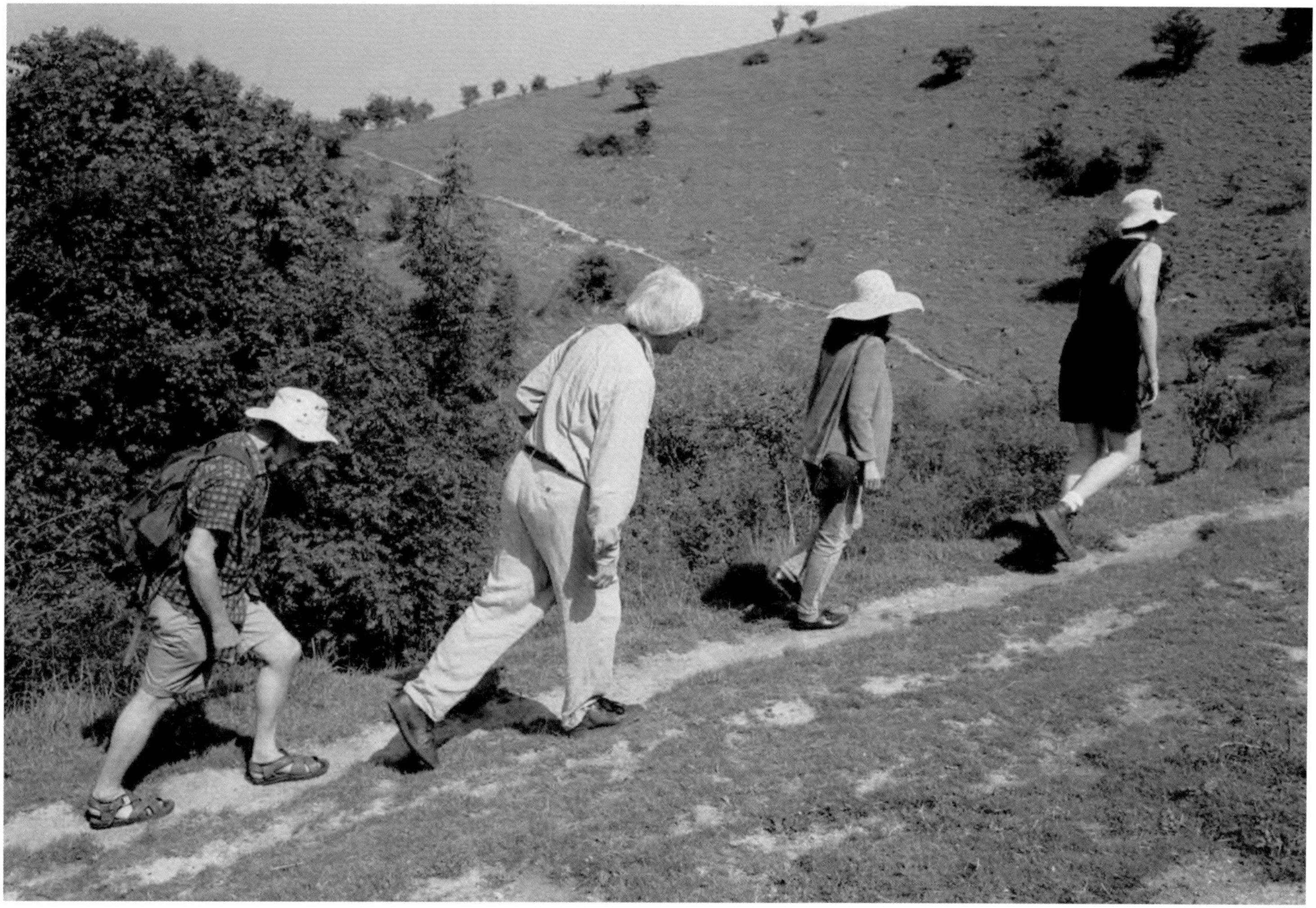

Walking in Sussex, 1997.

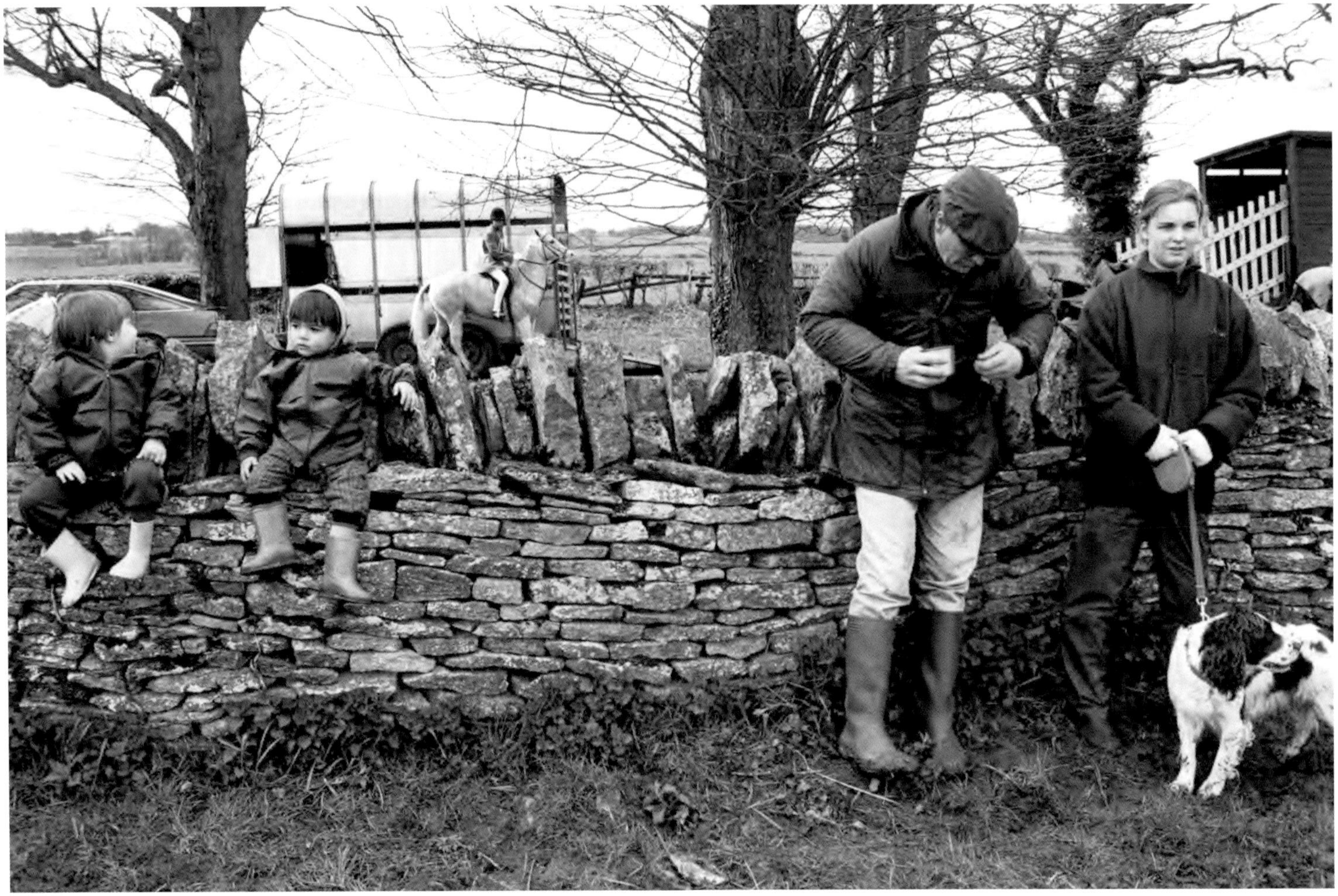

Cedric and Cameron at a pony show, 1994.

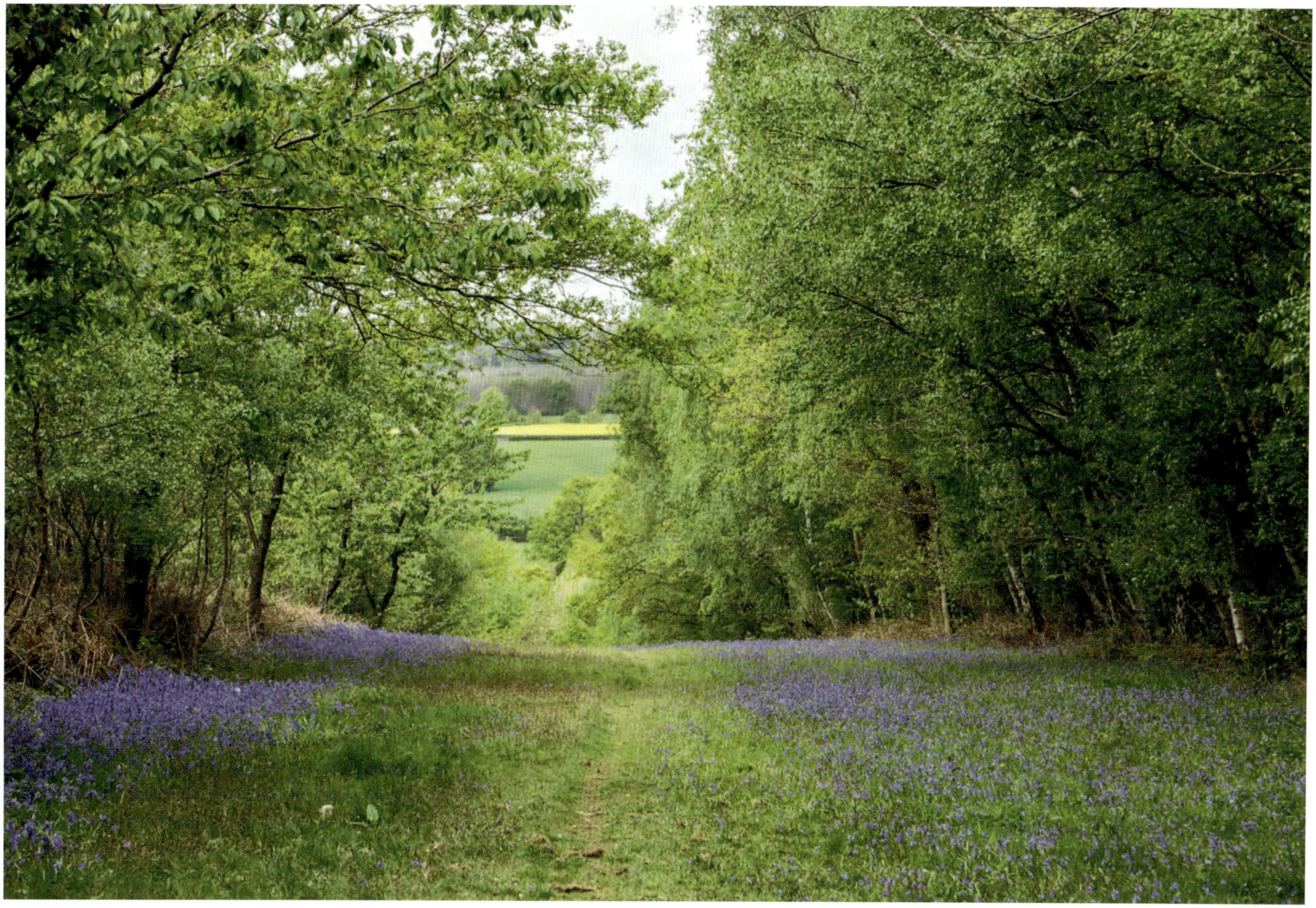
Bluebell landscape.

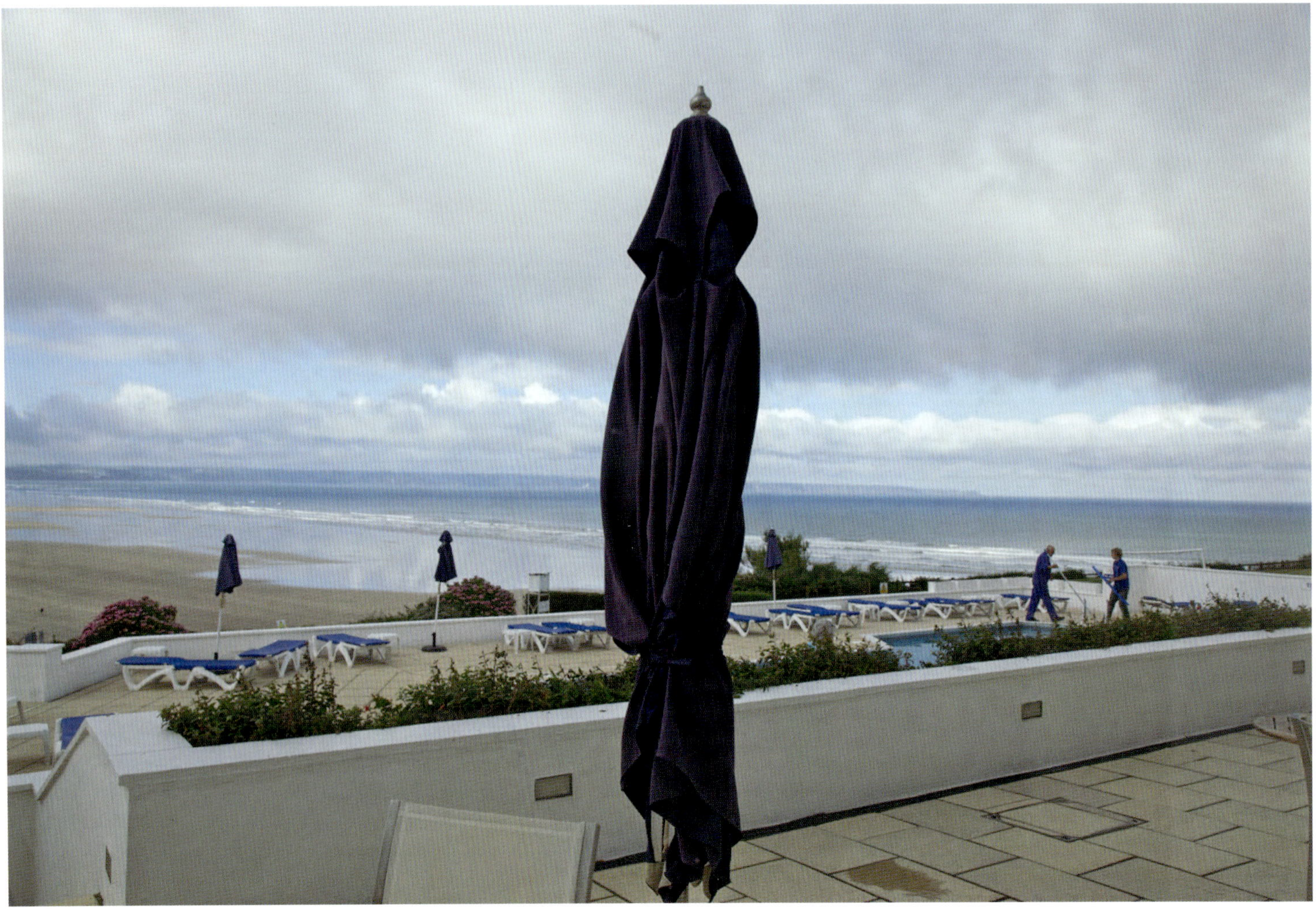

Ghosts on the coast.

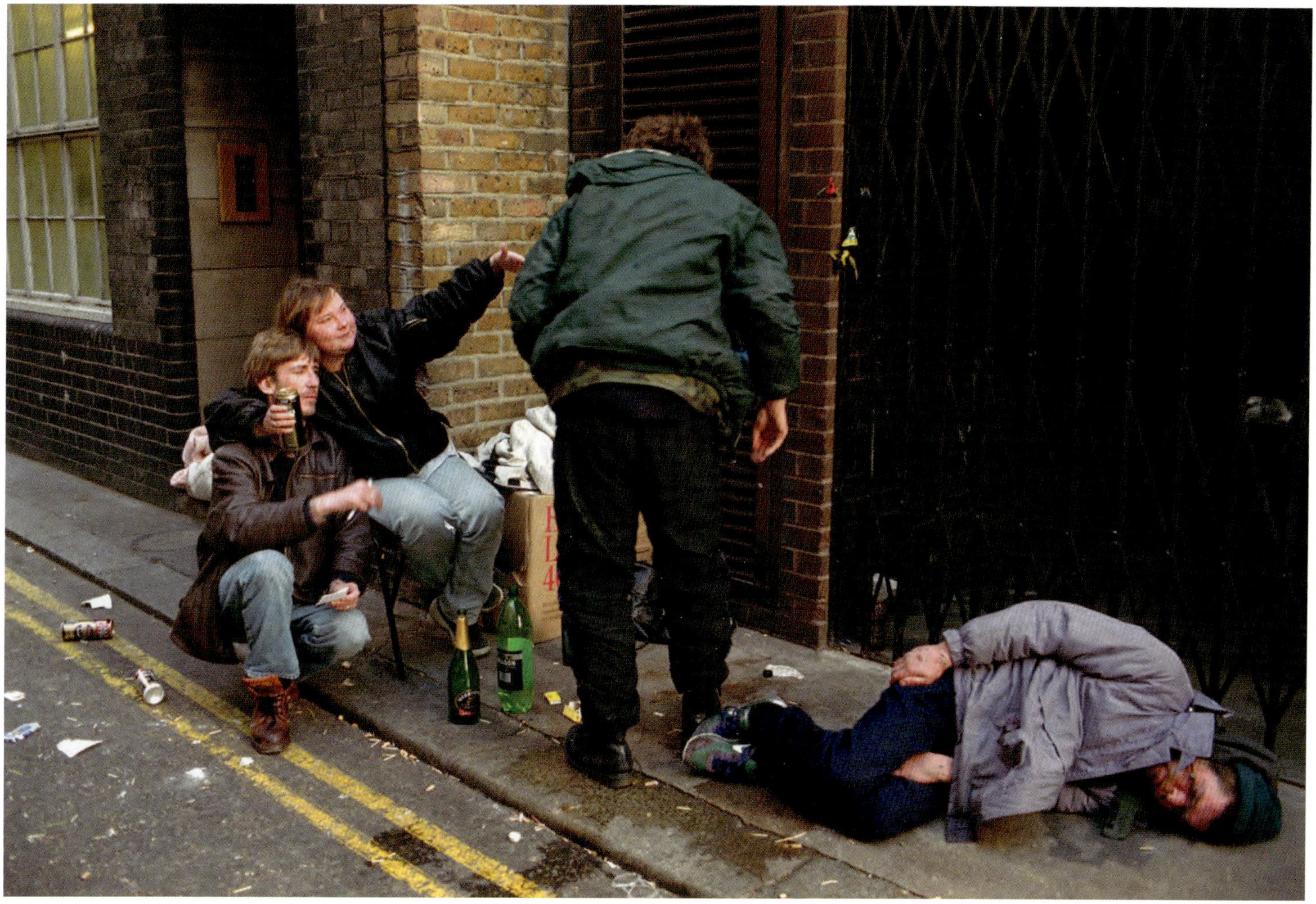

Homeless in London. Group behind Holborn station, 1999.

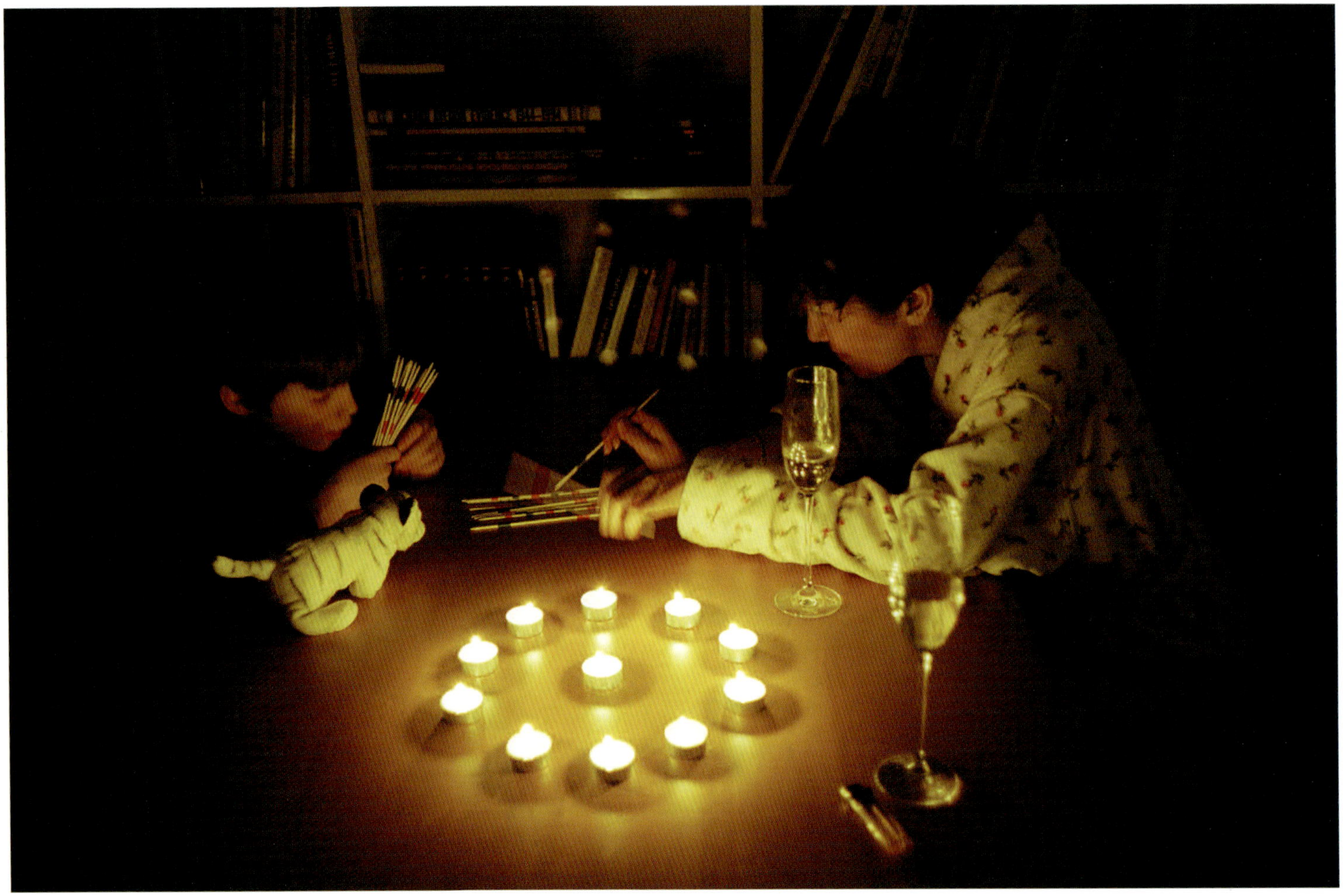

Miyako and Cedric play pickSticks on New Year's Eve, 2000.

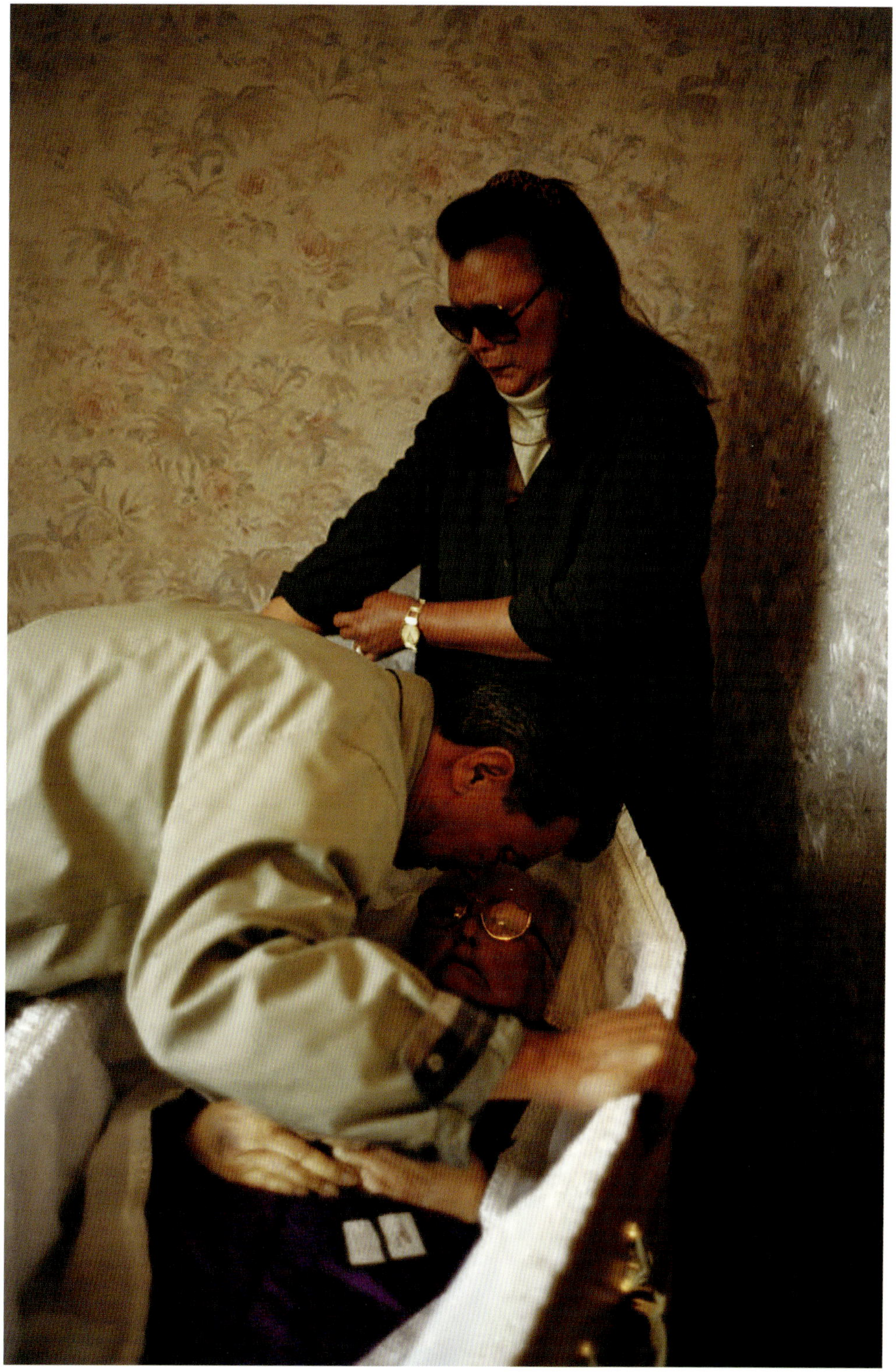

My brother Thein and sister Seyna at our mother's funeral in Northampton, 2001.

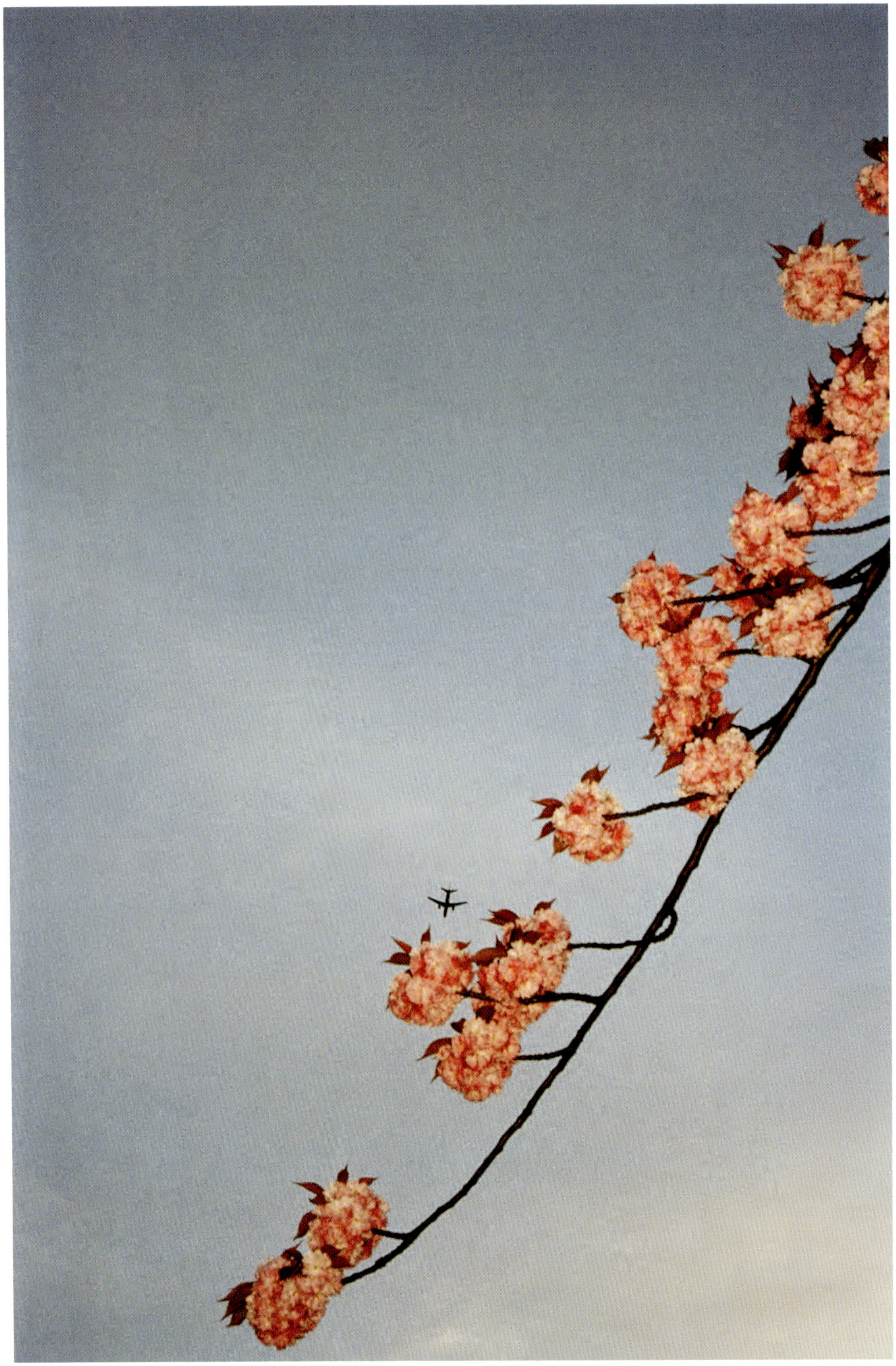
London. Cherry tree with plane, 2001.

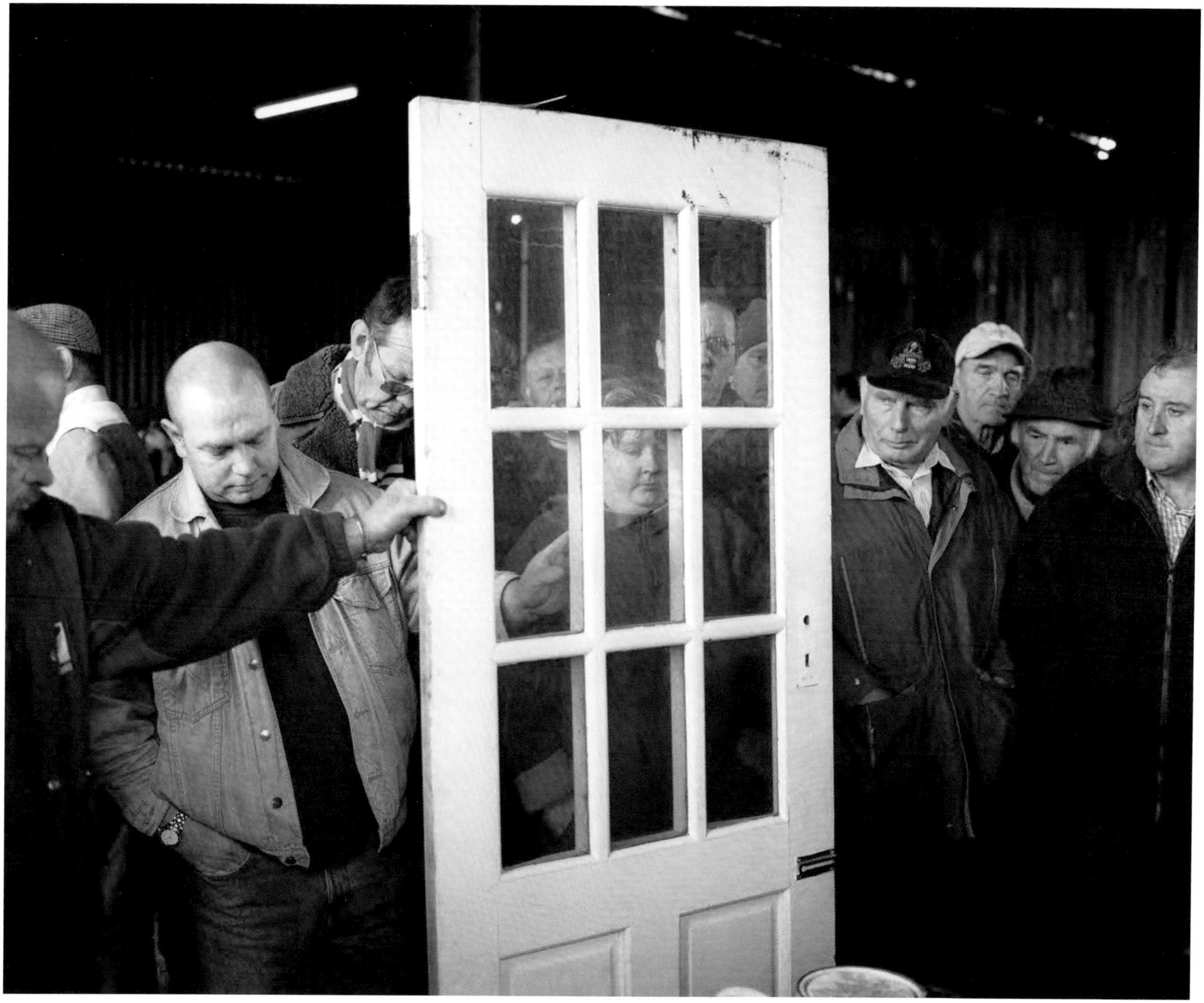

Inspecting a door at Haswell Plough Mart in Durham, 2005.

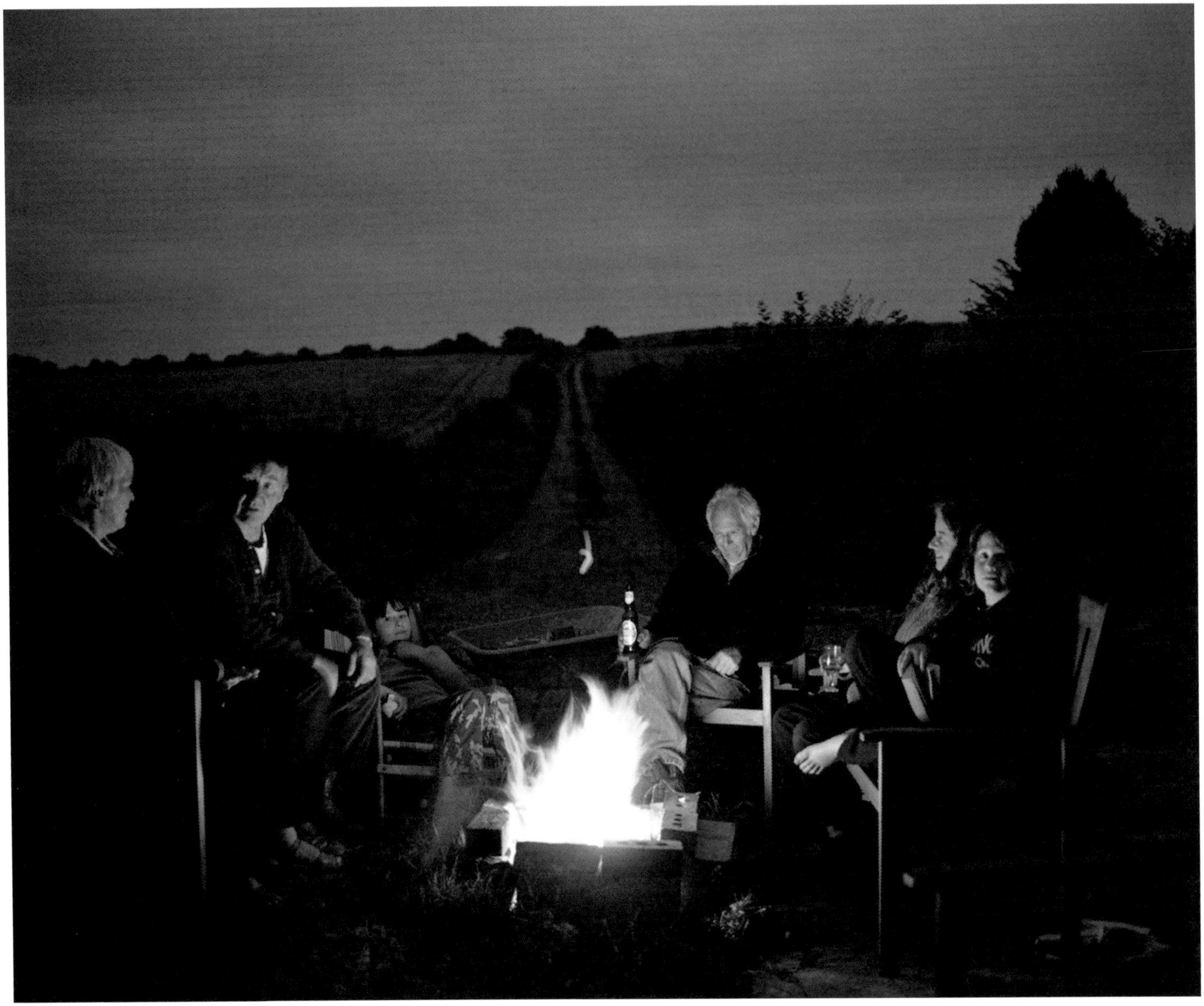

Murray Martin, family and friends have a barbeque at home in Easington, 2003.

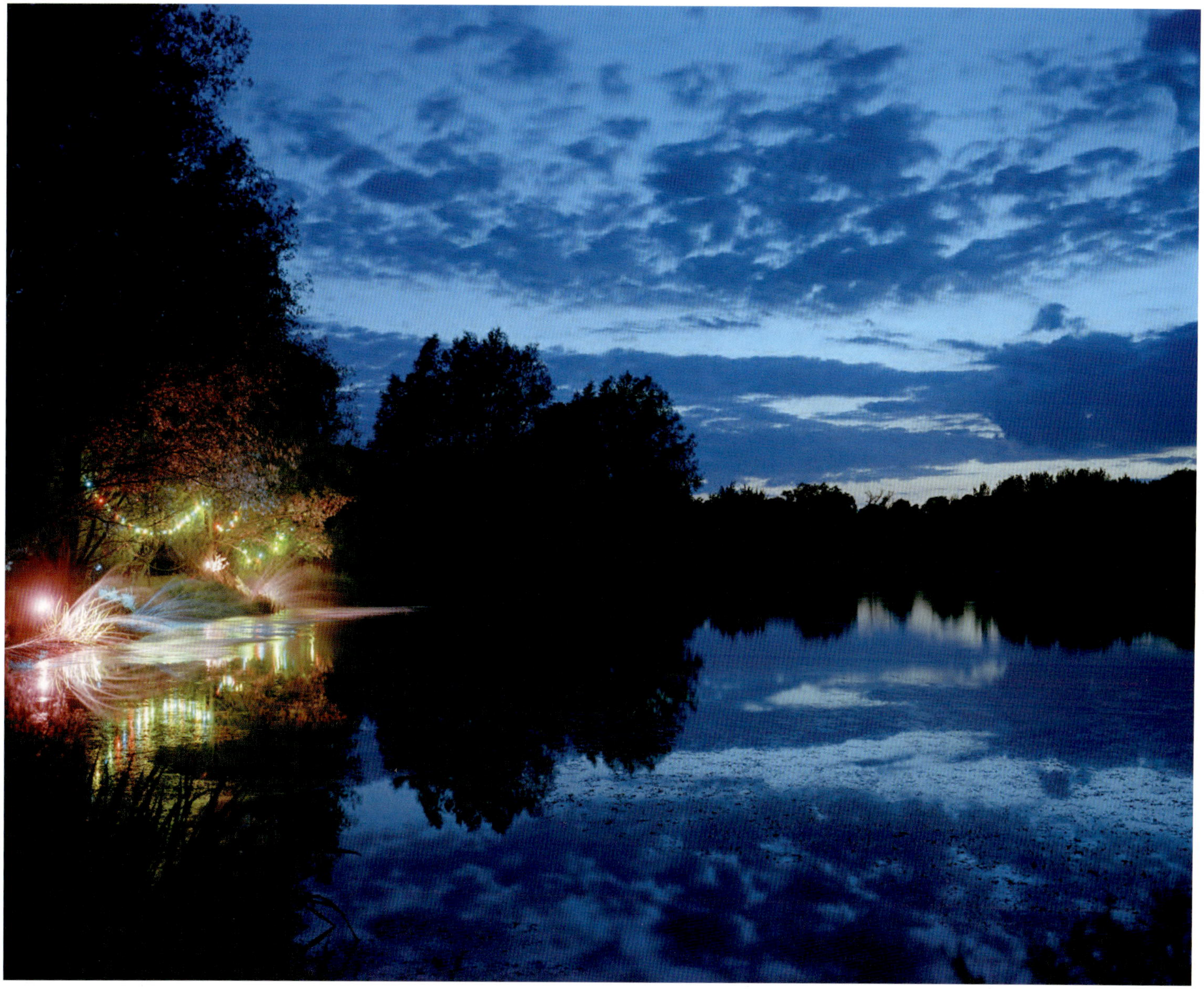

Summer Party lights, 2003.

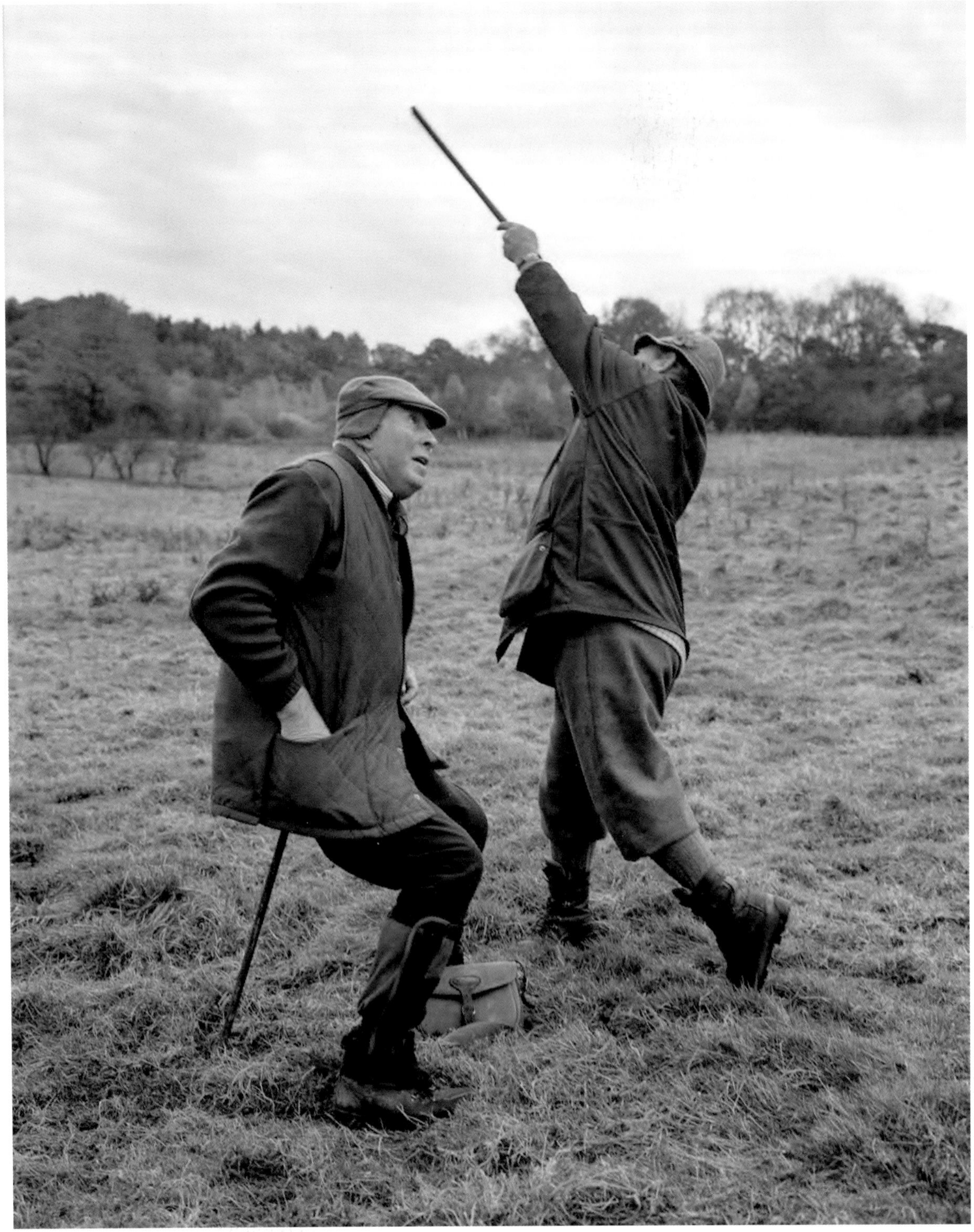

County Durham. Pheasant shoot, 2003.

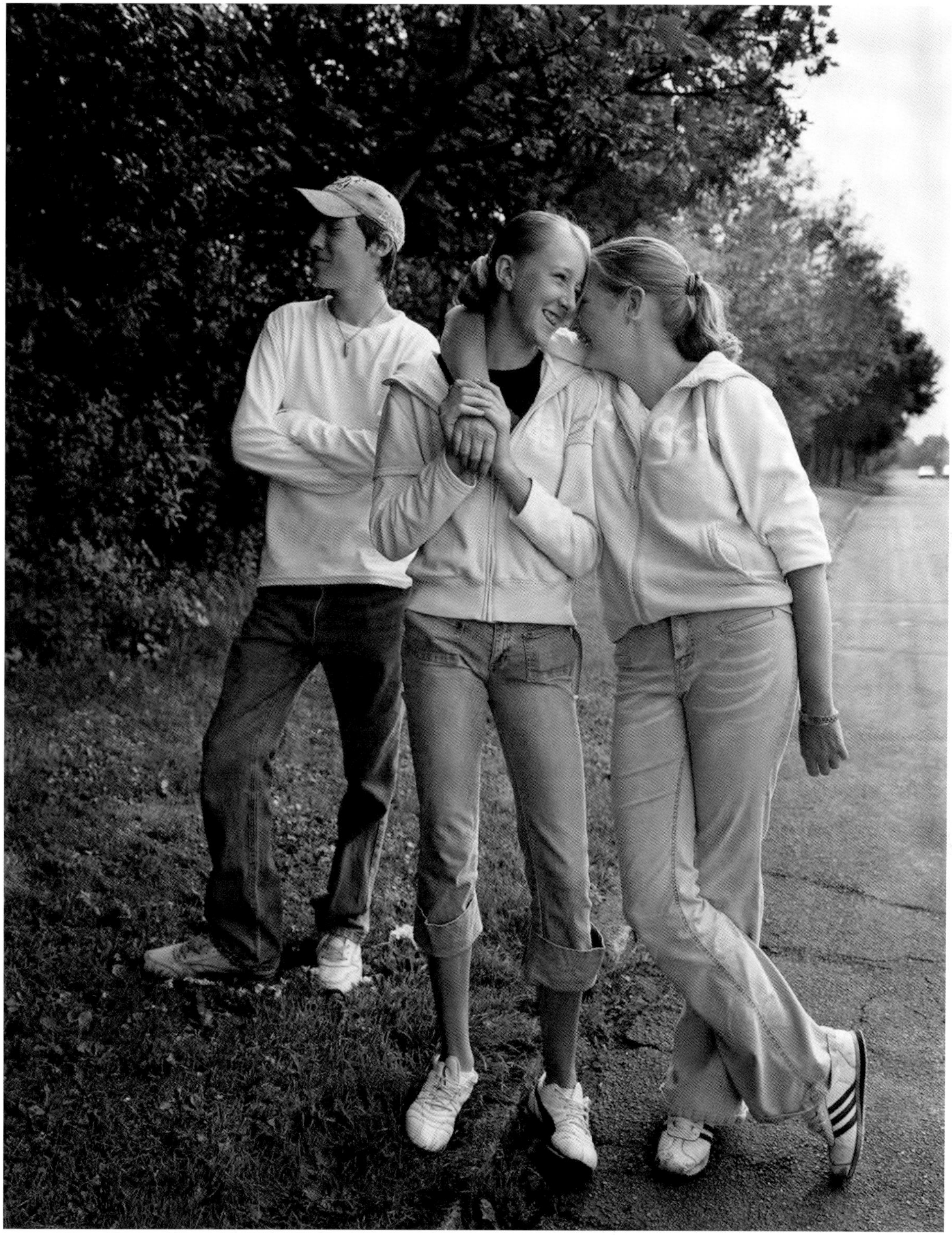

Hanging out in Horden in Durham, 2004.

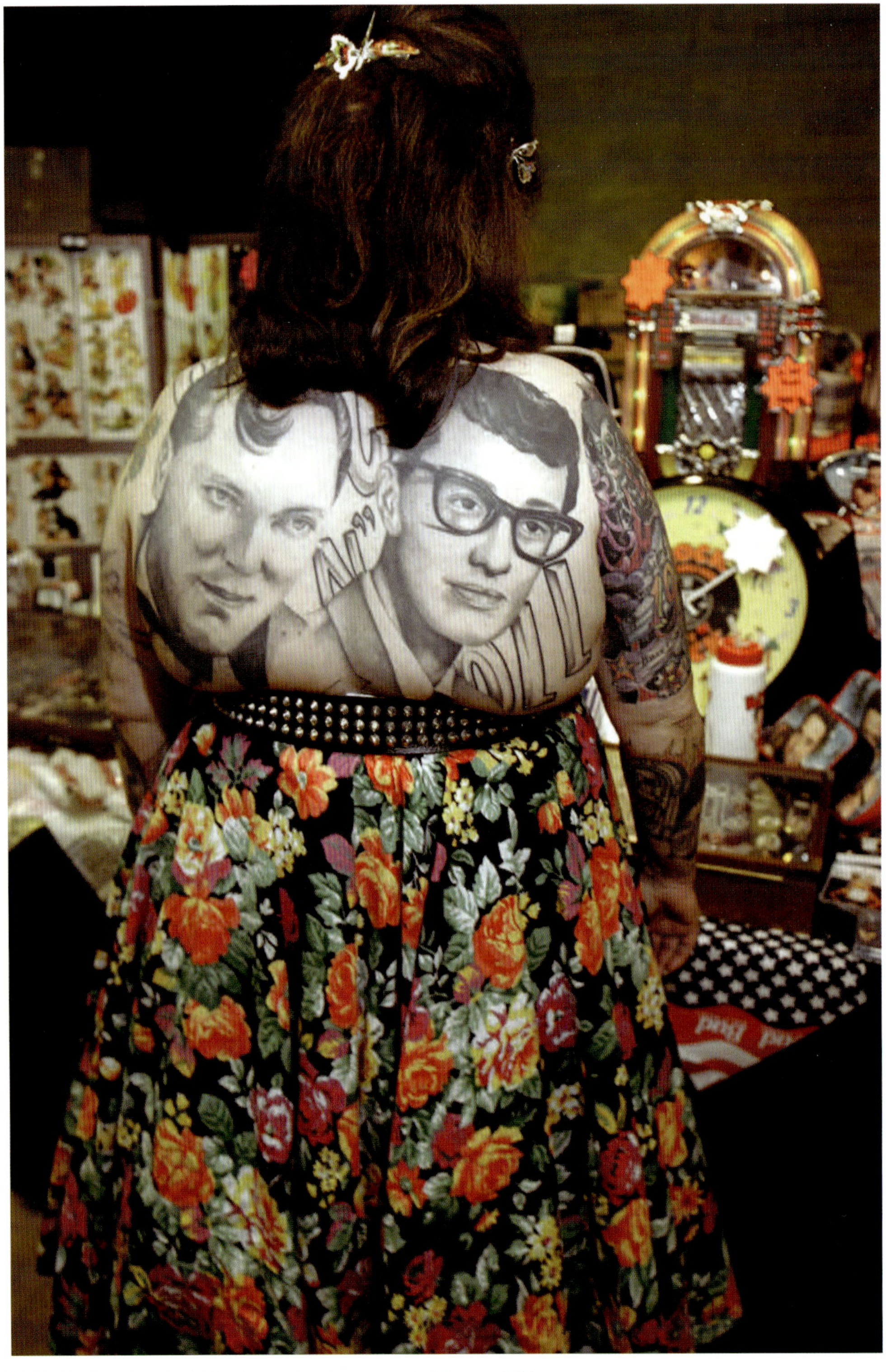

Teddy Boy Weekender in Reading – Peggy Warner with Tattoos, 2002.

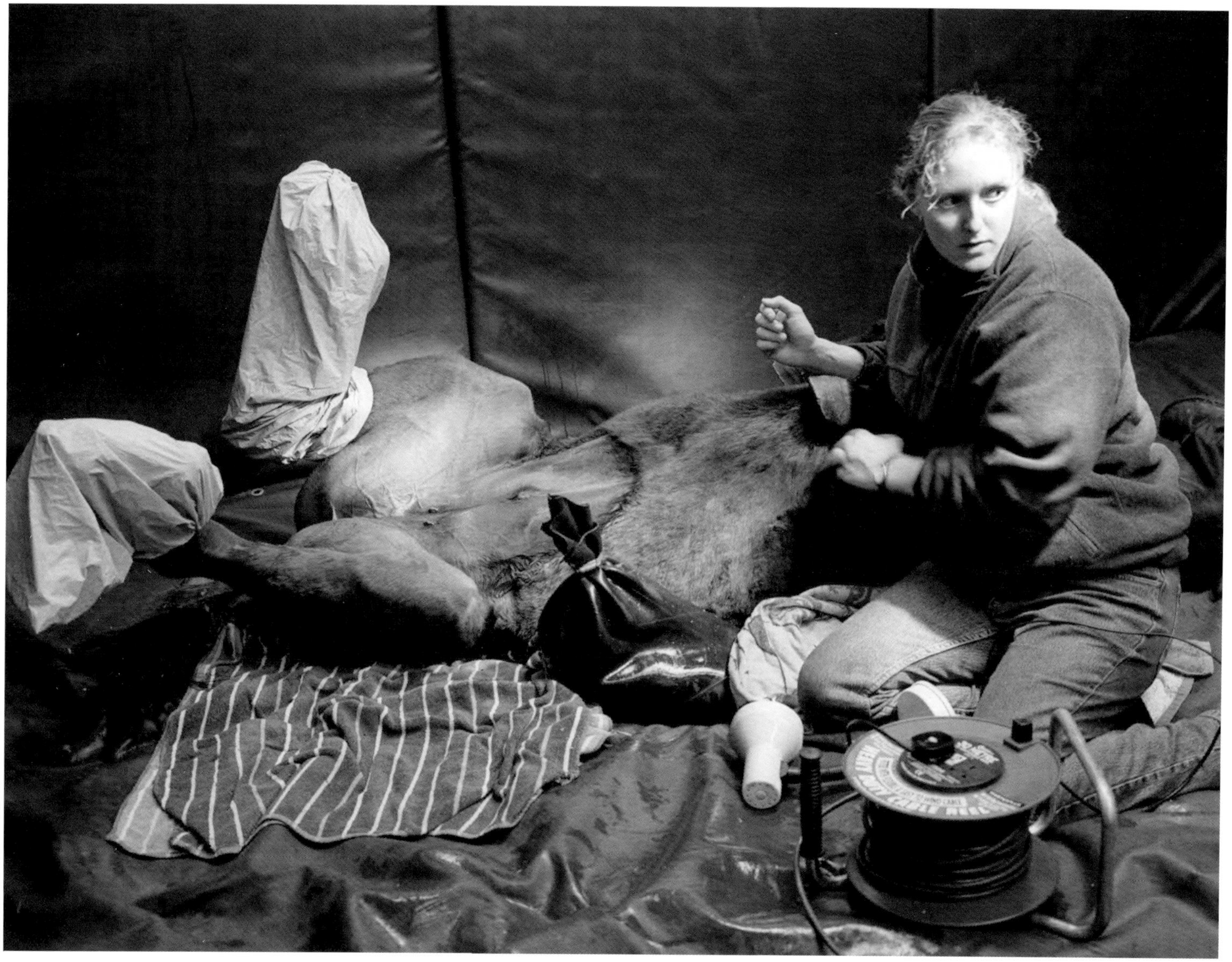

Operating on a horse for a hernia. County Durham, 2005.

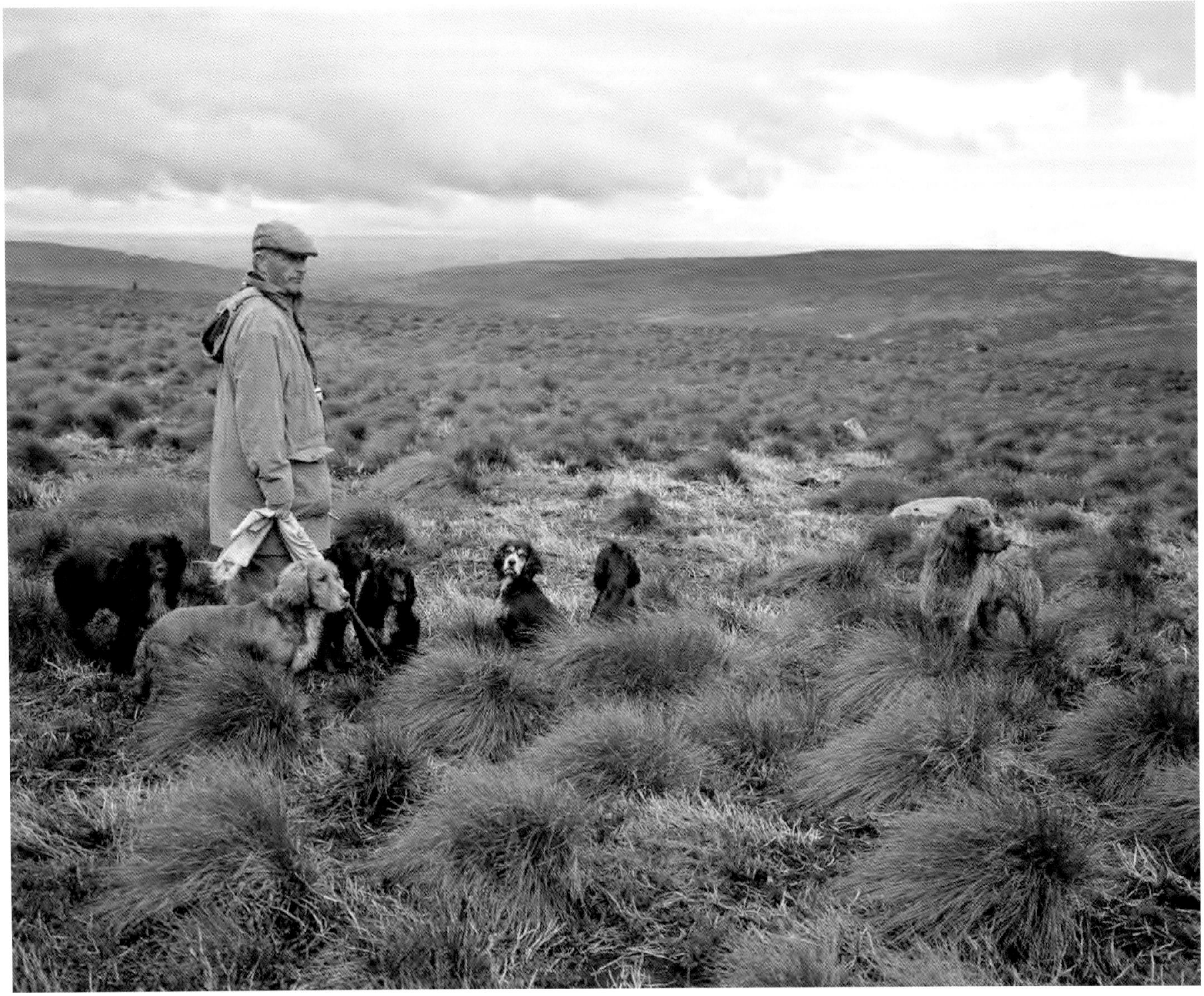

County Durham. Lindsay Waddell, Head Gamekeeper on the Raby Estate, during a grouse shoot, 2003.

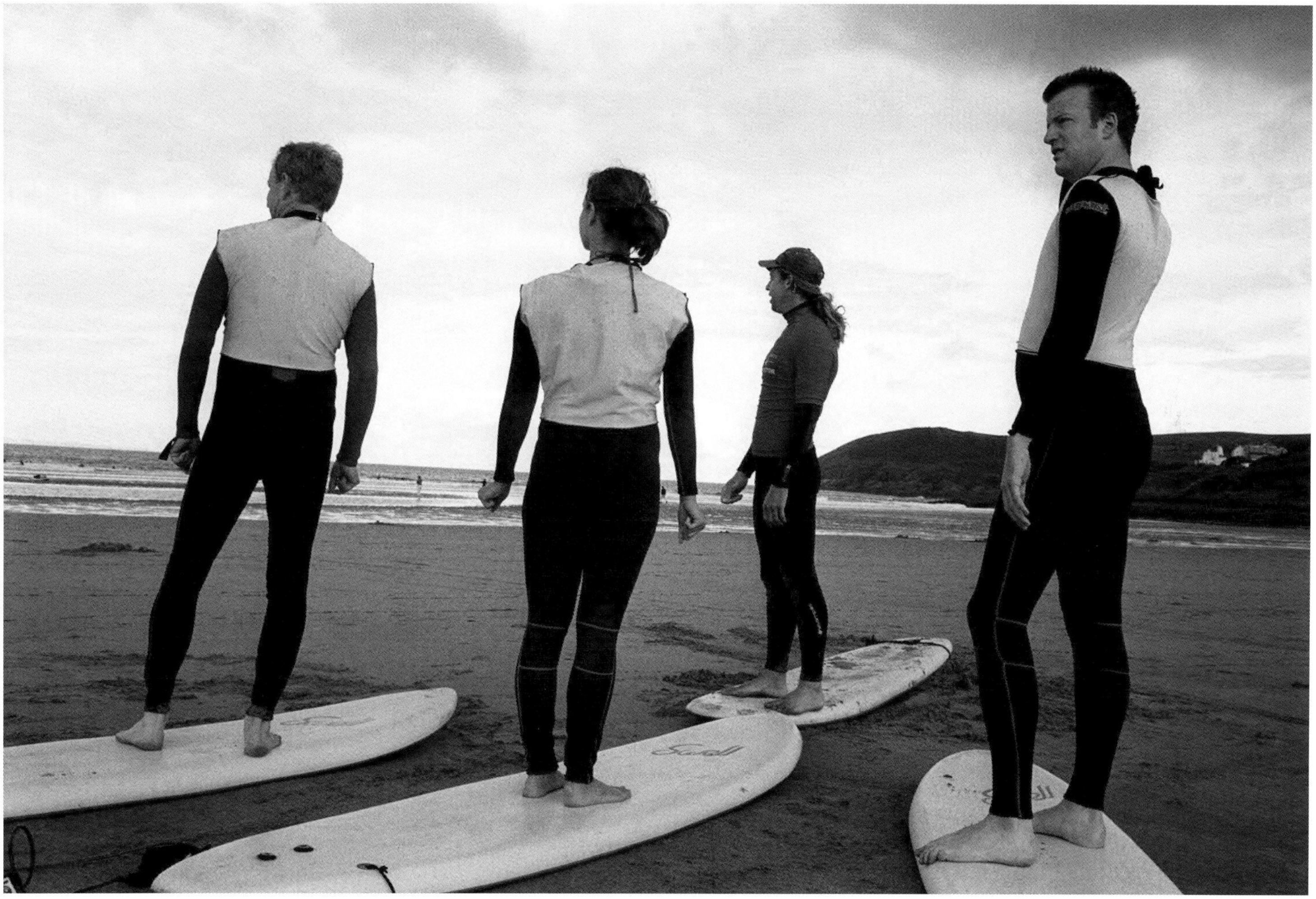

Devon. Surfers on Woolacombe beach, 2004.

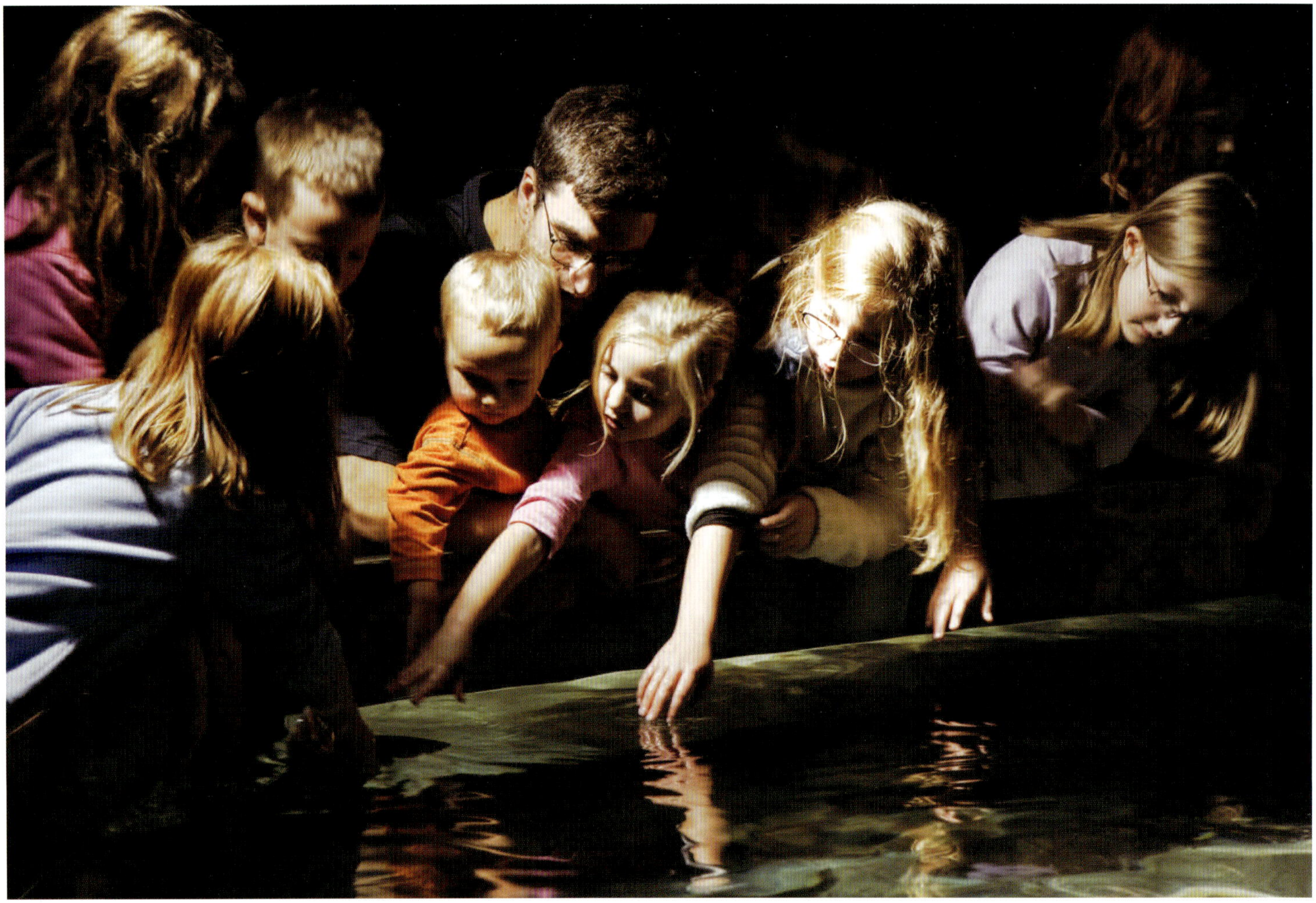

London Aquarium, 2005.

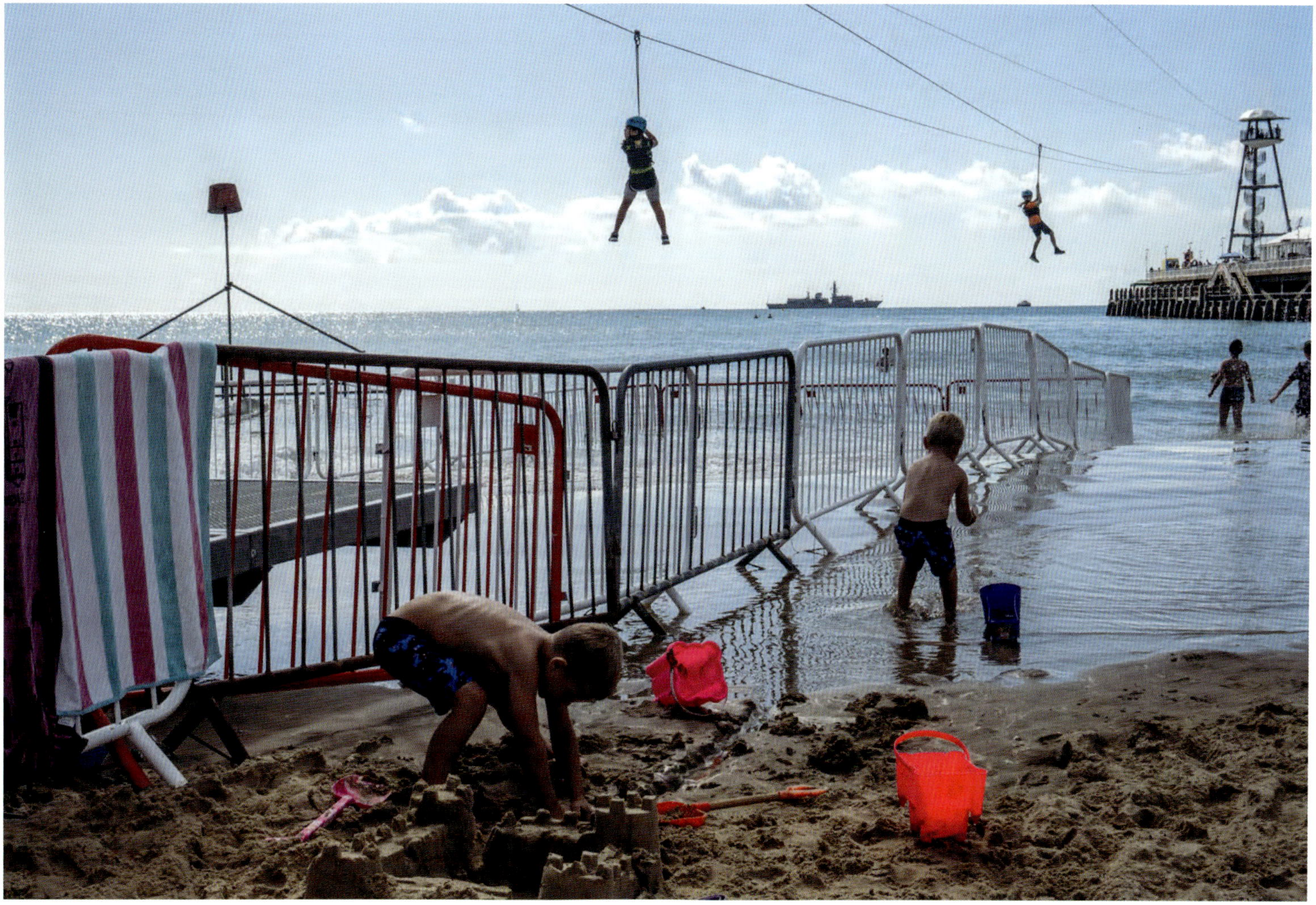

A day at the beach.

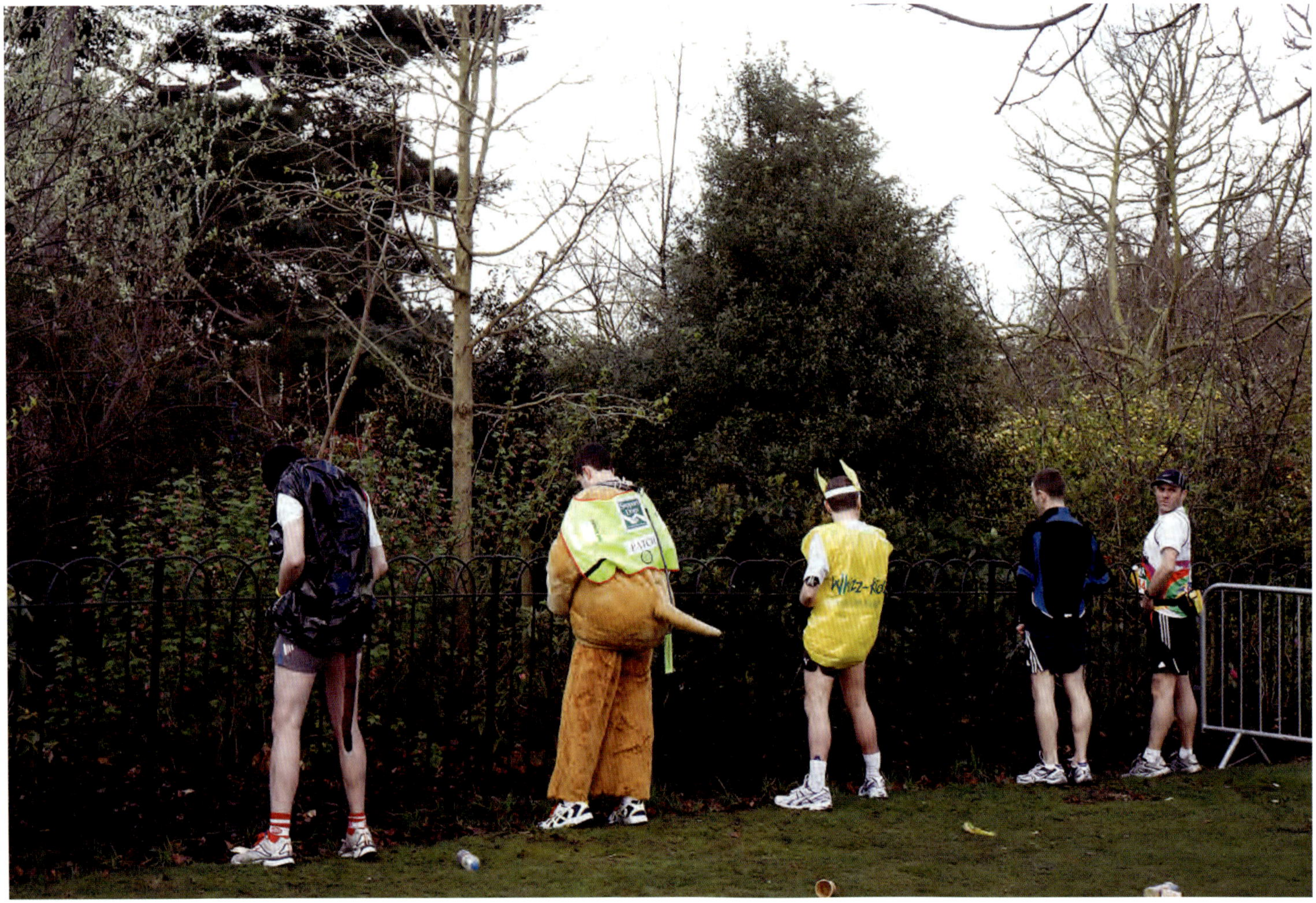

London. Greenwich Park, starting point red. Toilet just before start, 2008.

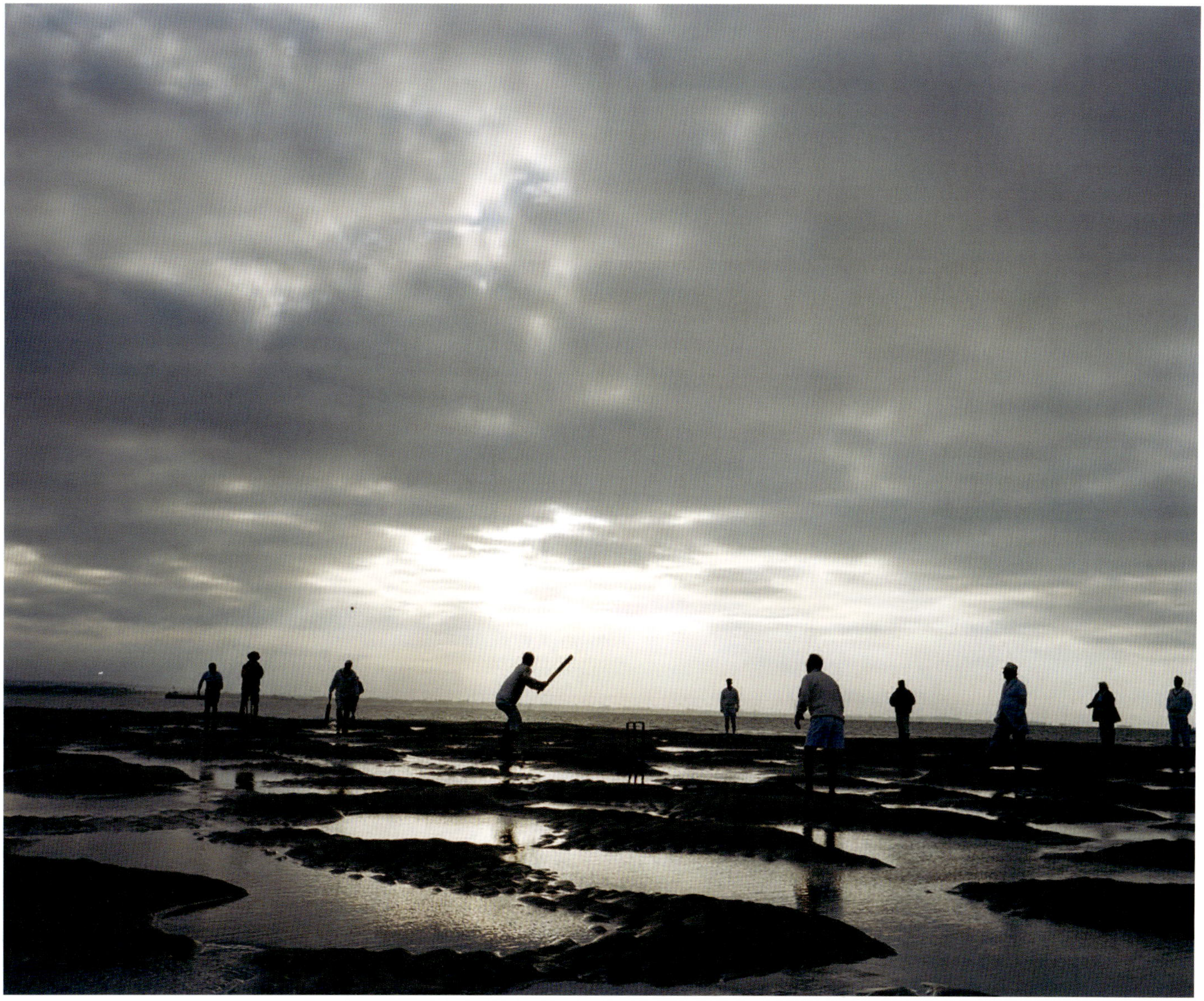

Cricket match played at low tide on exposed Bramble sandbank in the Solent, 2006.

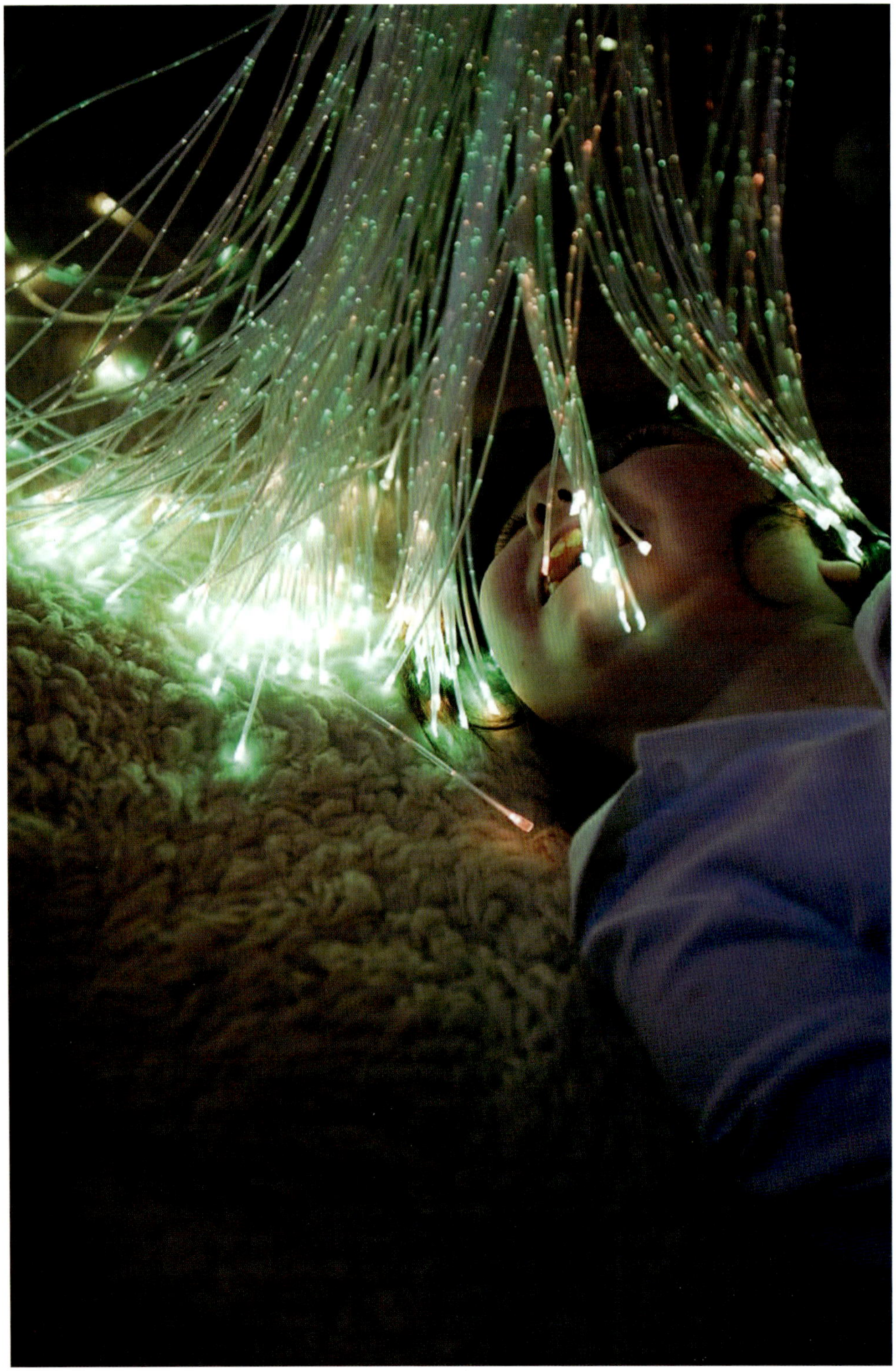
Amy who suffers from acute Cerebal Palsy with fairylights which help to stimulate her attention, Plymouth, 2009.

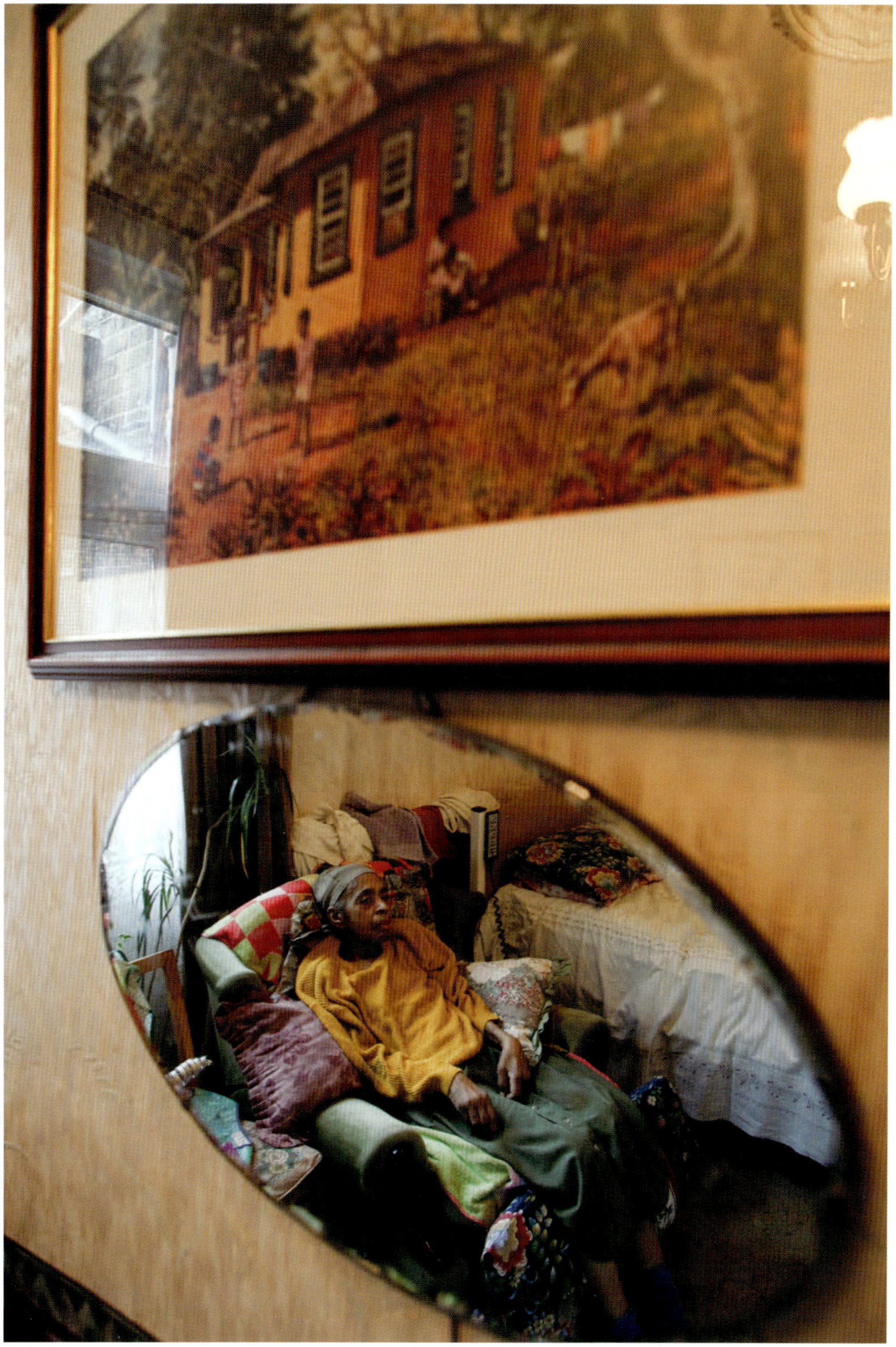

Dorothy at home in South London, 2009.

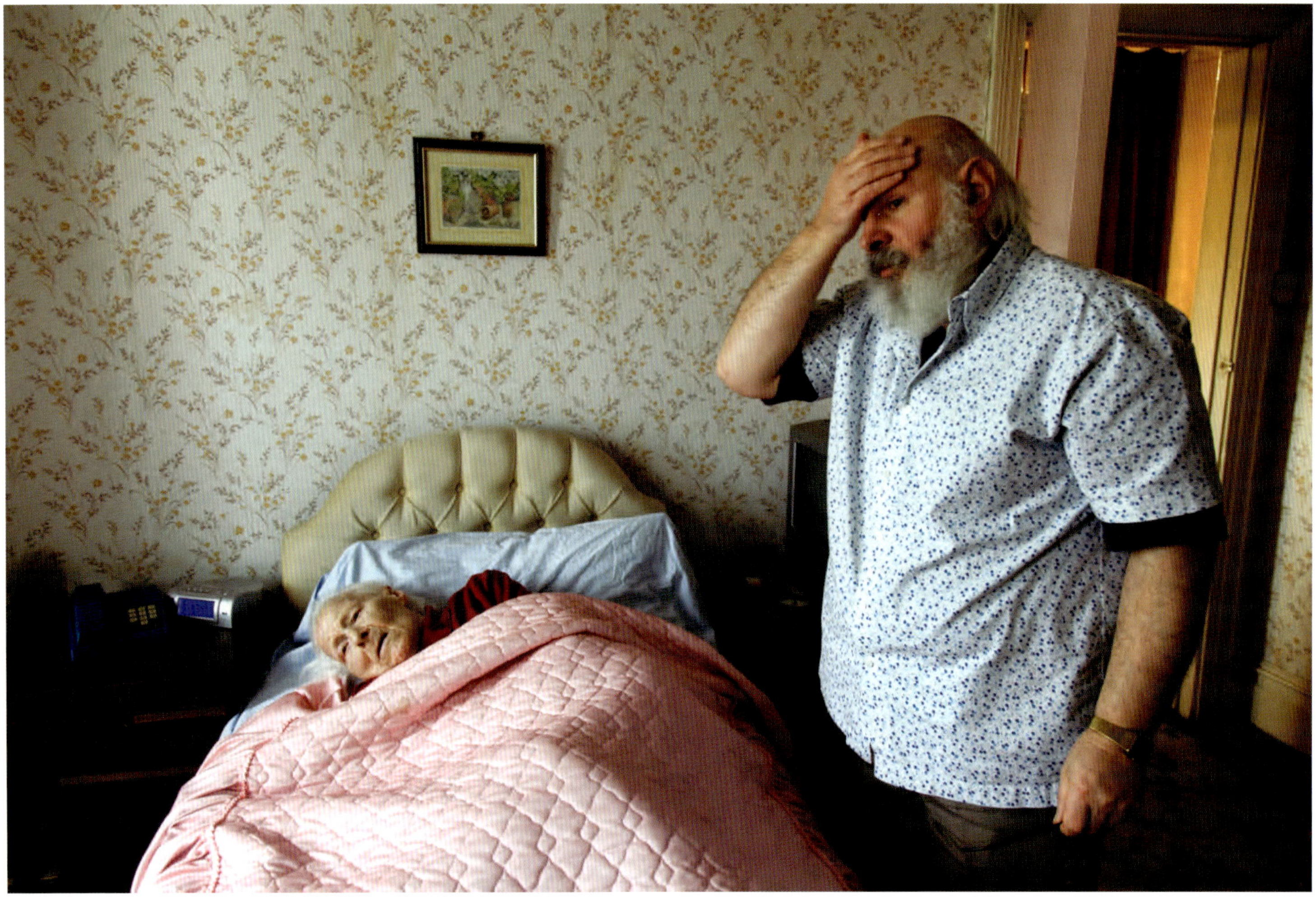

London. Ray Prike looks after his mother Doris (96) who has dementia, 2009.

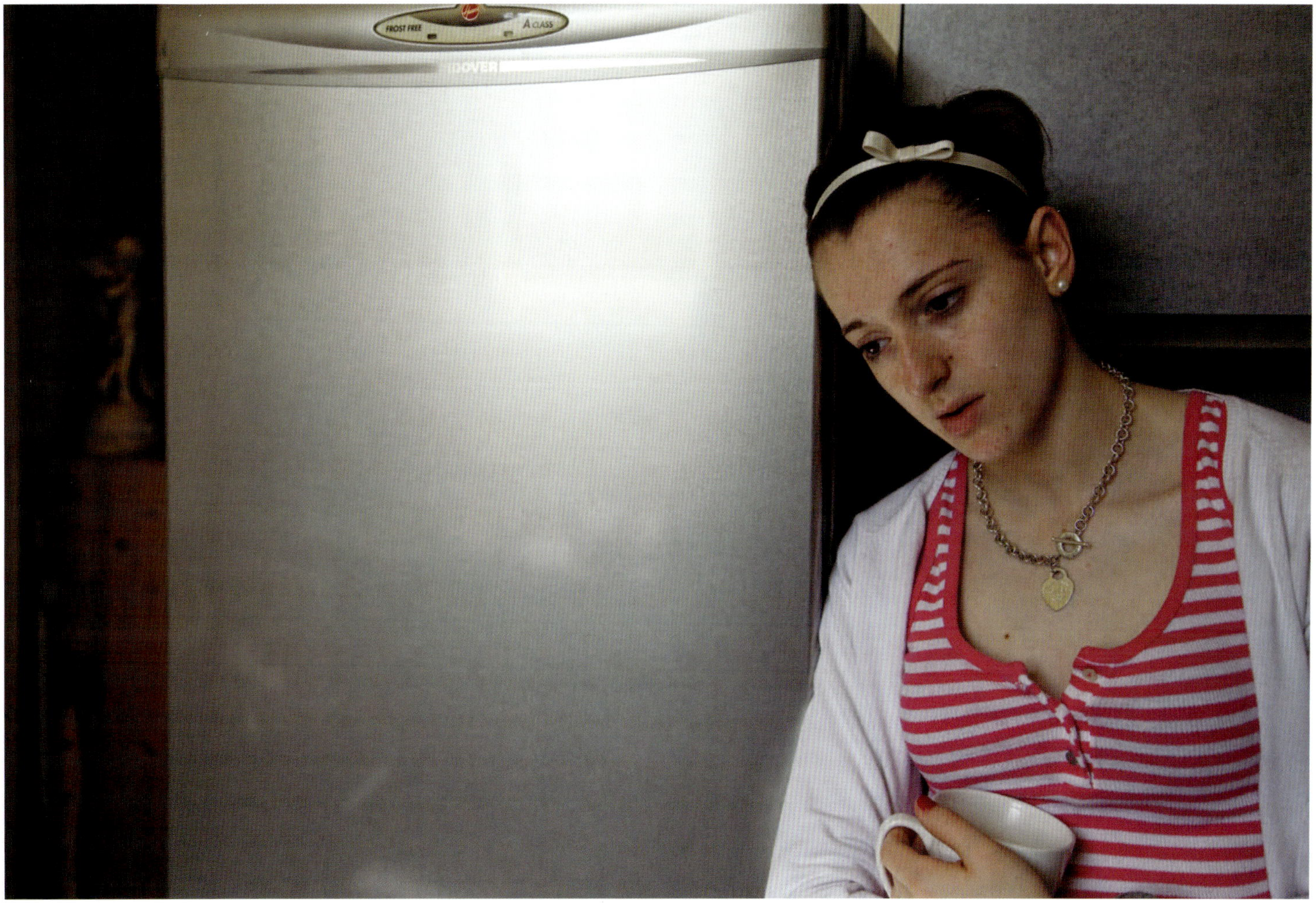

Bromley. Kelly who is 15 and helps look after her ill mother, 2009.

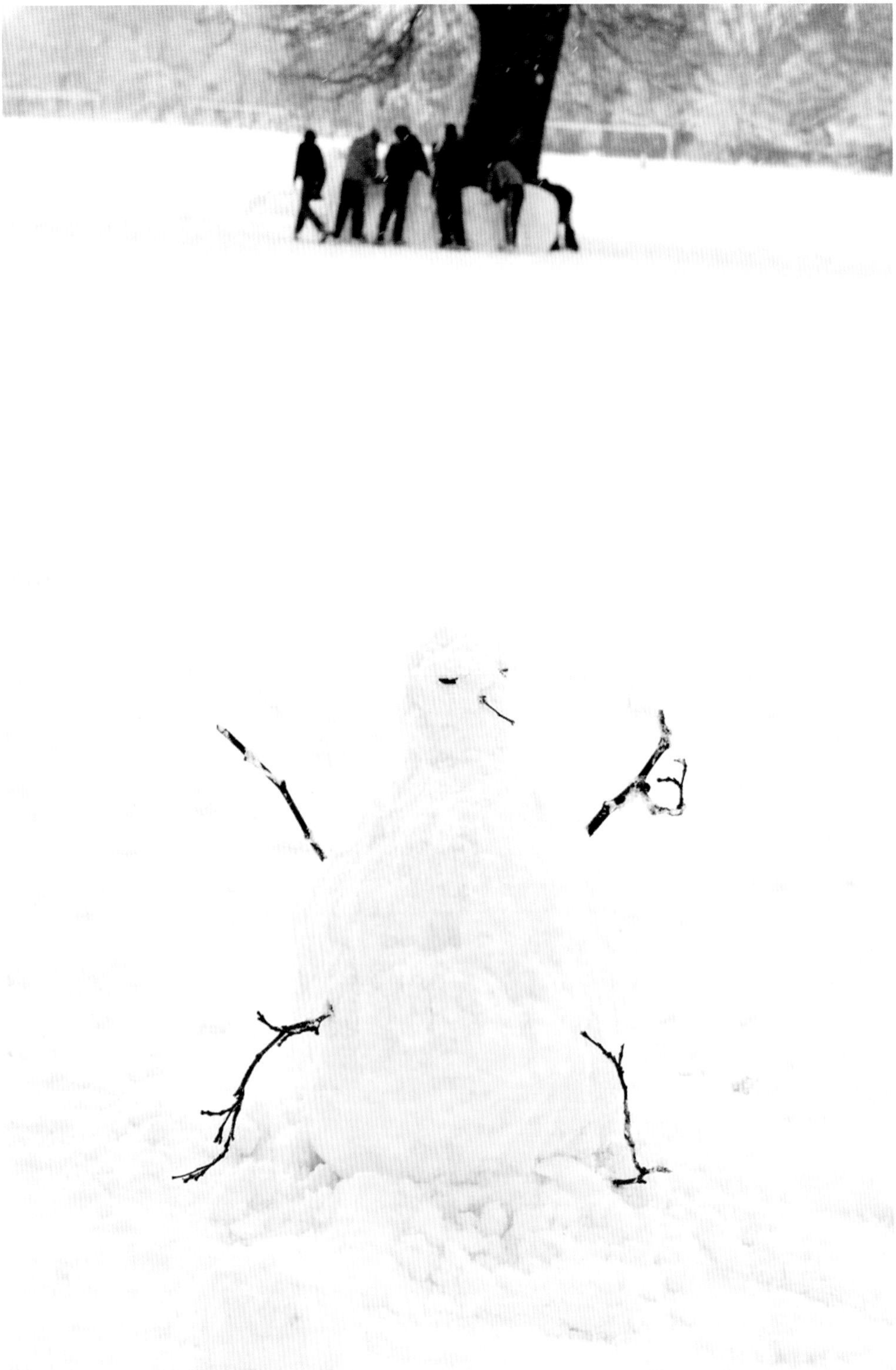

London. View from my window of snow in East Dulwich, 2007.

Thanks

Its always difficult to write one's thanks as a vast number of people are involved and its impossible to thank them all.

Top of the list has to be my wife Miyako Yamada who has supported me throughout the process of making the book and given me much needed advice. My publisher Andrew Peden Smith who had faith in me to do this book, and has let me get on with making it my own. The Magnum team in the London office have helped in various ways, and in particular Paul Hayward and Tom Groves in the production department. Sonalle Maroo has assisted me well.

Various friends have provided advice, support and criticism at different times, most notably Mark Edwards, Alex Webb, Rebecca Norris, Jocelyn Bain-Hogg, Simon Wheatley, Mark Sealy, Jonathan Ellery, Laura Noble, Michael Deimar, Steve Macleod and of course David Elliott for writing a well measured introduction.

Notes for Introduction

[1] Chris Steele-Perkins in "Father Teds," *Observer*, London, 26 January, 2003.

[2] See Jeremy Paxman, *The English. A Portrait of a People*, London, Michael Joseph, 1998; Roger Scruton, England: An Elegy, London, Chatto & Windus, 2000; Kate Fox, *Watching the English. The Hidden Rules of English Behaviour*, London, Hodder & Stoughton, 2004.

[3] See Nick Hubble, *Mass Observation and Everyday Life*, Basinstoke, Palgrave Macmillan, 2006; Bill Brandt, *The English at Home*, London, Batsford, 1936.

[4] Bert Hardy, *Down the Bay. Picture Post, Humanist Photography and Imagery of the 1950s*, Cardiff, Butetown History and Arts Centre, 2003.The Glyndebourne spread in colour on pp.75 and 76 seems to be a direct reference to Ray-Jones's 1967 image of the same subject. See Tony Ray-Jones *A Day Off. An English Journal*, London, Thames & Hudson, 1974.

[5] Photographs taken in Bangladesh were shown in his first solo exhibition *The Face of Bengal*, London, Camerawork Gallery, 1974.

[6] Strong echoes of Mass Observation here. With Nicholas Battye and Paul Trevor, as the Exit Photography Group, this project was published as *Survival Programmes in Britain's Inner Cities*, Milton Keynes, Open University Press, 1982.

[7] In 2003, looking back at his work on The Teds in the 1970s, Chris Steele-Perkins wrote: "They form a strange kind of community, but it had been that strange community which first fascinated me all those years ago. They have held onto something that was important to them. Kept faith. Those markers that once quickened our youth can still drive our dotage" *Observer, op. cit.* For images of his actual family, see pages ii, 8, 68, 78, 79, 83, 84.

[8] Chris Steele-Perkins interviewed by Bruce Chalifour, *After Image*, London, May–June, 2004.

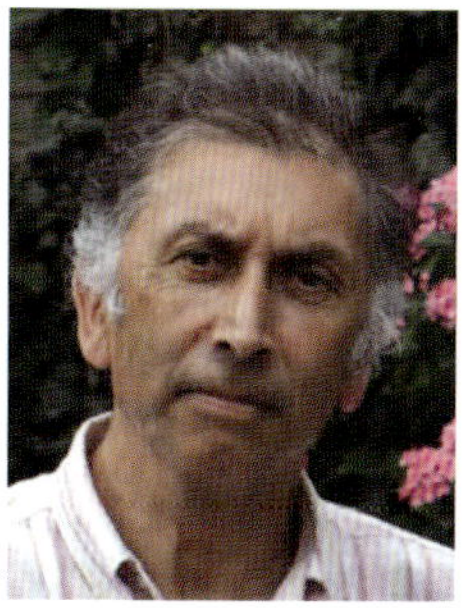

ABOUT THE AUTHOR

Chris Steele-Perkins, an internationally acclaimed and award-winning Magnum photographer has produced some of the most iconic images of British society in the last half-century, exploring homelessness, poverty, establishment and privilege as well as compassion and hope as described by Magnum 'with artful sensitivity'.

Born in Burma in 1947 he moved to England when he was two years old. His career has seen him travel widely, making significant bodies of work in his country of birth Myanmar as well as Japan, Africa and Afghanistan, all which has received critical acclaim. He calls his home country England, which remains a constant source of inspiration.

After marrying his wife, Miyako Yamada, he embarked on a long-term photographic exploration of Japan, publishing *Fuji* in 2000. A highly personal diary of 2001, *Echoes*, was published in 2003, and the second of his Japanese books, *Tokyo Love Hello*, in March 2007. His other books include *The Teds*, (1979), *Beirut: The Frontline Story* (1983), *The Pleasure Principle* (1989), *Afghanistan* (2000), *Northern Exposures* (2007), *Fading Light* (2012), *A Place in the Country* (2014), *The New Londoners* (2019) and *The Troubles* (2020).

In 2009, he published a very personal collection of work from over 40 years of photographing England – *England, My England*, with a new edition published in 2023.

Chris has worked on commission for many high-profile publications including *The Sunday Times* magazine and *The Guardian*.

He has won a number of prestigious awards to include:

'The Tom Hopkinson Prize' for British Photojournalism (1988)
'The Oscar Barnack Prize' (1988)
'The Robert Capa Gold Medal' (1989)
'Cooperative Society Award' & 'One World Award',
for the film 'Dying for Publicity' (1994)
'La Nacion Premier Photojournalism Award' (1994)
World Press Award, 'Daily Life' (2000)
Sasakawa Foundation Grant (2004, 2011)
Royal Photographic Society Terrence Donovan Award (2008)
Arts Council GB Award (2010)
Honorary Fellowship of The Royal Photographic Society